The
GOD
of the
WAY

The
GOD
of the
WAY

**A JOURNEY INTO THE
STORIES, PEOPLE, AND FAITH
THAT CHANGED THE WORLD FOREVER**

Kathie Lee Gifford
& Rabbi Jason Sobel

W PUBLISHING GROUP

AN IMPRINT OF THOMAS NELSON

The God of the Way

© 2022 Kathie Lee Gifford and Rabbi Jason Sobel

Published in Nashville, Tennessee, by W Publishing, an imprint of Thomas Nelson.

Unless otherwise noted, Scripture quotations are taken from the Holy Scriptures, Tree of Life (TLV) Translation of the Bible. Copyright © 2015 by The Messianic Jewish Family Bible Society.

Scripture quotations marked AMP are taken from the Amplified® Bible (AMP). Copyright © 2015 by The Lockman Foundation. Used by permission. www.Lockman.org

Scripture quotations marked BSB are taken from the Holy Bible, Berean Study Bible, BSB. Copyright © 2016, 2018 by Bible Hub. Used by permission. All rights reserved worldwide.

Scripture quotations marked ESV are taken from the ESV® Bible (The Holy Bible, English Standard Version®). Copyright © 2001 by Crossway, a publishing ministry of Good News Publishers. Used by permission. All rights reserved.

Scripture quotations marked ISV are taken from the Holy Bible: International Standard Version® Release 2.0. Copyright © 1996–2013 by the ISV Foundation. Used by permission of Davidson Press, LLC. All rights reserved internationally.

Scripture quotations marked JPS are taken from The JPS Tanakh: The New Translation of the Holy Scriptures According to the Traditional Hebrew Text. Copyright © 1985 by the Jewish Publication Society. Used by permission. All rights reserved.

Scripture quotations marked KJV are taken from the King James Version. Public domain.

Scripture quotations marked MSG are taken from THE MESSAGE. Copyright © 1993, 2002, 2018 by Eugene H. Peterson. Used by permission of NavPress. All rights reserved. Represented by Tyndale House Publishers, a Division of Tyndale House Ministries.

Scripture quotations marked NASB are taken from the New American Standard Bible® (NASB). Copyright © 1960, 1962, 1963, 1968, 1971, 1972, 1973, 1975, 1977, 1995 by The Lockman Foundation. Used by permission. www.Lockman.org

Scripture quotations marked NIV are taken from the Holy Bible, New International Version®, NIV®. Copyright © 1973, 1978, 1984, 2011 by Biblica, Inc.® Used by permission of Zondervan. All rights reserved worldwide. www.zondervan.com. The "NIV" and "New International Version" are trademarks registered in the United States Patent and Trademark Office by Biblica, Inc.®

Scripture quotations marked NKJV are taken from the New King James Version®. Copyright © 1982 by Thomas Nelson. Used by permission. All rights reserved.

Scripture quotations marked NLT are taken from the Holy Bible, New Living Translation. Copyright © 1996, 2004, 2015 by Tyndale House Foundation. Used by permission of Tyndale House Ministries, Carol Stream, Illinois 60188. All rights reserved.

Scripture quotations marked YLT are taken from Young's Literal Translation. Public domain.

Thomas Nelson titles may be purchased in bulk for educational, business, fund-raising, or sales promotional use. For information, please email SpecialMarkets@ThomasNelson.com.

ISBN 978-0-7852-9043-8 (HC)
ISBN 978-0-7852-9068-1 (TP)
ISBN 978-0-7852-9069-8 (eBook)
ISBN 978-0-7852-9070-4 (audiobook)

Library of Congress Control Number: 2021953080

Printed in the United States of America

23 24 25 26 27 LBC 5 4 3 2 1

I am humbly and profoundly aware that I am one of the billions of people who have been blessed to hear the redeeming message of Jesus' love and salvation and have been called to follow in His divine footsteps. I dedicate this book to all my brothers and sisters of the faith, and I pray that we, together as one body in Him, will continue to believe with our whole souls that Yeshua is the way, the truth, and the life.
—Kathie Lee

To the Lord, whose grace has been more than sufficient at all times and in every season!

To my wonderful wife, Miriam, whose love and support have been a tremendous source of strength and encouragement. To my boys, Avi and Judah; you are treasures who possess great talent to influence the world. And to my parents, who have been like wind beneath my wings.
—Rabbi Jason

CONTENTS

CONTENTS

PART FOUR: THE GOD OF THE OTHER SIDE

INTRODUCTION

This book exists because of a song I cowrote in October 2017 with Nicole C. Mullen in Franklin, Tennessee.

I had never met Nicole before our writing session that day, and it's the only song we have written together since. But that song we titled "The God Who Sees" went on to inspire an extremely successful short film featuring Nicole that I directed in Israel in spring 2018.

At this writing it has been viewed 7.5 million times and still elicits extraordinary responses on YouTube.

The success of "The God Who Sees" has confirmed to me what I am supposed to do with the remaining years of my creative life: tell the amazing, epic, ancient stories in the Bible in a brand-new way, using narration and symphonic orchestrations of original songs. They are called oratorios in the music world, and I have written three new oratorios with brilliant co-composers, orchestrators, and artists.

Because of the COVID-19 pandemic, I was prohibited from filming the new oratorios in Israel, but I was able to work with my extraordinary creative/production team to secure locations in Utah and Texas. The final result is an hour-and-a-half-long film called *The Way*, which is scheduled to be released at the end of summer 2022.

It was always my intention to release a companion book to accompany the film for teaching purposes. I asked my collaborator on the book *The Rock, the Road, and the Rabbi*, Rabbi Jason Sobel, to bring his extensive knowledge and expertise on biblical studies to the project.

I'm grateful that Jason agreed to join me, and the result of our efforts is the book you now hold in your hands.

I pray that it will bless you and deepen your walk with the living God.

My heart's desire is that you will be able to take what you learn and apply it to your everyday life as you "live, and move, and have [your] being" in the One who created you and loves you with an everlasting love (Acts 17:28 KJV).

Blessed be His holy (*Kadosh*) name forever and ever!

SHALOM!

KATHIE LEE

Part One

THE GOD OF THE
HOW AND WHEN

Kathie

Several years ago I was in early production for a small film I'd hoped to make in Tennessee. At the time, I wanted a song that would capture the essence of our little film. I wrote the lyrics and sent them over to my friend and brilliant songwriter Brett James to set them to music. As usual Brett returned it within hours, totally ready to demo in a recording studio.

So I called one of my favorite people and performers, Jimmie Allen, to record it for us, and he came right over. Jimmie has since emerged as one of the most successful artists in country music and at the time of this writing is nominated for his first Grammy Award as Best New Artist.

He nailed the song. But just as so often happens, the film itself fell through, leaving us with a great song that had nowhere to go—that is, unless the Lord revealed He had a different plan. And He did.

After the success of "The God Who Sees" song, something extraordinary happened. I realized that I had only scratched the surface of exploring all the epic, inspiring, and miraculous stories in the Bible. It dawned on me that I had literally hundreds of songs just sitting around waiting for a home (we songwriters call them our "trunks").

The song Brett and I had written for the ill-fated movie was already titled "The God of the How and When," and it was perfectly adaptable for a brand-new oratorio by the same name.

I immediately set out to tell the stories of Abraham and Sarah, Moses, Joshua, and Mary, the mother of Jesus. They all had one thing in common: each story represented a promise from God. Some of those promises, however, took centuries before they were fulfilled, requiring a great deal of waiting from the one who had received the promise. And, as any believer can tell you, waiting on God is one of the hardest things to do. Trusting Him in the process is equally difficult, but it's in the *believing* that we truly please the God who made the promise.

In the case of Abraham and Sarah, the Bible tells us in Genesis 12:2 that God told Abram (his name at the time) that He would make him the father of a great nation. To do this, he of course would have to have an heir, though it seemed impossible because his wife, Sarai (her name at the time), had been barren for many years. In fact, Sarai actually laughed when she heard that she would become pregnant and bear a child.

Sure enough, though, decades after God's initial promise to them, their son, Isaac, was born when Abraham was one hundred years old and Sarah was ninety (Genesis 21)!

Of course, this was the beginning of the great nation of the Hebrews that took root with Isaac's twelve grandsons, their families, and their families' families. But after six hundred years of growing more populous than "the stars of the heavens" (Genesis 22:17 NASB), they were enslaved in Egypt. God made a promise to deliver them from Egypt and take them to a land of their own—the "promised" land.

But someone had to deliver them from the brutal and ruthless tyranny of Pharaoh, the powerful king of Egypt.

So God called an eighty-year-old shepherd from Midian who had fled Egypt decades before, instructing him to go back to the place of his birth and convince this all-powerful, evil leader to let God's people go. The fact that this elderly and, by his own admission, completely incapable man was successful in this mission is nothing short of miraculous.

The legendary story continued on after Moses died and his faithful follower Joshua was called to lead the Hebrew nation to the Promised Land. Again, God's promise took awhile to be fulfilled, but Joshua and the Hebrews eventually entered the "land flowing with milk and honey" more than forty years after leaving Egypt (Exodus 3:8 NASB).

Many centuries later an angel visited a young Hebrew virgin named Mary and told her she had found favor with God and would bear a child she would call Jesus, which means "God saves."

Back in the days of Abraham, God had promised the eventual father of Israel that his seed would be a blessing to all nations and that it would bring about the birth of the Eternal Deliverer, one who would be far greater than Moses (Genesis 22:18).

Then, for centuries afterward, the great prophets of Jehovah God prophesied that this Messiah would be born of a virgin (Isaiah 7:14), a miracle even more improbable than when God parted the Red Sea for Moses and the Hebrew people. Nevertheless, the angel told Mary she would be that virgin.

Nine months later the Savior of the world came into the physical world He had created with His Father in the beginning.

The God of the How and When is still building His Kingdom through the lives of the billions of followers of Jesus (Yeshua), the Savior of *all* humankind.

Blessed be His holy name.

one

ABRAHAM

Rabbi Jason

Being Jewish was extremely important to the Sobel household. Our family was a living legacy of Holocaust survivors. Most of my mom's relatives died during that unthinkable horror, and the old photographs lining the walls and shelves of our home served as a memorial. Growing up, when I looked at them I was reminded of their stories that I had heard again and again. Before my grandmother Gerta was able to escape Germany, she focused on getting her family out first. She gave her visa to her brother and his wife, who strapped their baby into a backpack and hiked safely across the Alps to freedom. My grandmother next tried getting a visa to her parents, but it was too late. After being loaded onto a train like cattle and shipped to a concentration camp, they were murdered in transit because of their faith. In large part because of these inspiring stories of sacrifice, being Jewish was always something deeply ingrained in the very fibers of my being. I grew up with a rich understanding of my identity as a Jew.

Part of that identity came from my intensive study of the Torah (the first five books of the Bible). For years, in addition to regular school, I attended Hebrew school two days a week and went to synagogue every Saturday. As a kid with competing interests like basketball and girls, my studies became a bit of a love-hate relationship. Somewhere along the journey, though, as I read the stories of the Jewish personalities, the characters came alive, leaping off the pages, affecting me deeply—David the king, Moses the emancipator, Ruth the loyal woman of God, and Abraham the man of incredible faith.

Believing the Promise

Abraham is one of the most influential figures in the Bible. In Genesis 11, at the start of his journey, Abraham was known as Abram. Though Abram was a native of Ur of Chaldea, located in what is now southern Iraq, God called him and his family to migrate approximately six hundred miles to Haran, today's southeastern Turkey.

Imagine picking up all your belongings with your family and leaving behind a life of comfort and safety in a thriving metropolis and heading for the unknown. That's exactly what Abram and his family did, traveling through rocky terrain fraught with danger, in a slowly moving caravan with sheep, donkeys, camels, and other livestock.

After his father's death, Abram received a second call from God involving a promise that would later have enormous implications for the Jewish people (Genesis 12:1–2). In another bold step of faith, Abram left Haran with his nephew Lot "not knowing where he was going" (Hebrews 11:8). Instead of trying to figure out where and how, he chose to trust God's guidance as he moved his caravan farther into the unknown. Then, while setting up camp one day by the great oak of Moreh at Shechem, some four hundred miles beyond Haran (Genesis 12:6), Abram received the great promise from God.

> "I will make you a great nation,
> And I will bless you,
> And make your name great;
> And so you shall be a blessing;
> And I will bless those who bless you,
> And the one who curses you I will curse.
> And in you all the families of the earth will be blessed. . . .
> To your descendants I will give this land." So [Abram] built
> > an altar there to the LORD who had appeared to him.
> > (Genesis 12:2–3, 7 NASB)

God appeared to Abram, speaking comforting covenantal words and promises. This is the first such appearance of these kinds of words mentioned in the Torah. Since Scripture is clear that no man can see God and live (Exodus 33:20), most scholars conclude the visitation was likely an angelic vision or human form. Regardless, God chose Abram to receive physical and spiritual blessings. On the physical side, Abram would become the father of the Jewish people through a son, Isaac. Out of this line, Messiah would be born. On the spiritual side, Abram had a unique relationship with his Creator. The two fellowshipped together under the stars and perhaps in the cool of the mornings, walking and talking. Listening with his spiritual ears, Abram recognized something greater than himself was going on and therefore obeyed God without question. Did he sometimes mess up? Of course he did—such as when he did not tell Pharaoh that Sarai was his wife, out of fear he would be killed (Genesis 12:10–20). Yet God quickly forgave this man He had called to be the father of a great nation. God continued telling Abram to expect to have heirs even though, by this time, he and Sarai were well past their childbearing years. What God was doing did not always make sense to Abram's natural mind, but his faith did not waver because he trusted and rested in God's faithfulness and timing.

God's timing in our lives is one of those things that often trips us up. We sometimes wonder what He is doing and question if He is even listening. We ask God for something, and seemingly nothing happens. We want Aunt Martha healed, but she remains sick or even dies. We want that promotion, but someone else gets it. Instead of getting the answer we want, we often get silence. We struggle like Job. "I cry out to you, God, but you do not answer; I stand up, but you merely look at me" (Job 30:20 NIV). But in the end, faith recognizes that God is wiser than we are and that He is outside of time. He sees the whole picture and is doing something bigger than we can imagine. As we acknowledge Him, trust Him, and lean not on our own understanding, He lights the path for us to follow (Proverbs 3:5–6). Abram recognized this and trusted God's faithfulness. As hard as it is at times, so should we. Another writer put it this way:

> Let us learn this lesson—God never forgets, he cannot forget! He sees the end from the beginning; he is in the eternal now. He is from everlasting to everlasting. He is not in the flux of time; he is outside it. He does not see things as we do. He seems to forget but he does not.[1]

Like many people, my life has had its ups and downs. Looking back, I can now appreciate those lingering seasons of wrestling and waiting, but I'm not going to try to sound all super spiritual and say it's easy. Wrestling and waiting are tough! And years of wrestling and waiting will wear a person down. Deep down in the core of my being, I had an intuitive sense of destiny for ministry. I knew God had a plan for me and that He always provided, yet my endurance was wearing thin. I was weary, and nothing seemed to be happening. At times the silence was indeed loud. *How much longer, Lord? How long?*

Struggling to find out what I was to do for the Lord, I even contemplated giving up my dreams of ministry and returning to law school, since every good Jewish boy (and his mother) knows that he should be either a doctor or a lawyer. While those certainly are noble occupations, for me it would not be God's best. Somewhere, beneath the chaos and the silence, I could hear His still, small voice wooing me, telling me not to pursue other things—that He had a calling on my life and I should stay focused and wait.

God asked Abram to wait. In Genesis 13:14–18, He expanded on His promise to Abram. He promised not only land but also to "make [his] seed like the dust of the earth so that if one could count the dust of the earth, then [his] seed could also be counted" (Genesis 13:16).

Years later the idea of one heir, let alone children "like the dust of the earth," seemed impossible to Abram and Sarai. Every time they saw their aged faces reflected in still waters or polished bronze, the couple was reminded that they were well beyond childbearing years.

Fully aware of Abram and Sarai's fatigue from wrestling and waiting, God decided to give Abram a new vision. He took him out of his tent—out of his circumstances—and showed him something different. "Look up now, at the sky, and count the stars—if you are able to count them," God said to Abram. "So shall your seed be" (Genesis 15:5). This new perspective from God renewed Abram's faith (v. 6), and he believed the promise. This one verse is so critical to all of Scripture that, many years later, the apostle Paul, whom I like to call Rabbi Paul, established his definition of salvation on it (Romans 4; Galatians 5). Salvation does not come by the law or works; it comes through God's mercy and faith. God renewed Abram's faith. Abram realized God was in control and there was nothing he could do outside of believing God's promises.

God's promises are never in doubt. When we endanger God's promises, there will be consequences, but that doesn't stop God from moving forward with His purposes. We can still trust Him when our field of vision is narrow. Often our field of vision is limited to "my, me, and mine," but we need to expand it until we can see God using our lives in His design. Sometimes when things seem impossible, we need to walk "out of our tent" and let God cast a new vision for us.

After Abram received that new vision and promise from God, nothing appeared to change. The years continued to slip by, and no children came to him and Sarai—not a one. There was just silence. Sarai was still barren, and they weren't getting any younger. Weary of waiting, Abram and Sarai felt God had forgotten them and His promise. But then, in His perfect timing, God stepped in and did something wonderfully significant. He changed their names from Abram to Abraham, from Sarai to Sarah. He added the same letter to their names—the Hebrew letter *hei* (ה). In Jewish thought, the letter *hei* signifies the creative power and potential to conceive children or give birth to any promise of God. This single letter was a game changer! It was after God added the letter *hei* to their names that the miracle of conception occurred.

Adding the letter *hei* to both of their names is also symbolic of the letter of the divine breath (Genesis 2:4) and the letter of the divine promises (Psalm 33:6). As a woman in her nineties, Sarah's womb was dead, and then God breathed new life into her just as He breathed the breath of life into Adam. God's divine breath supernaturally flowed through Sarah, empowering her to give birth to the promised heir.

God still specializes in breathing life into dead situations. Just as He breathed into Sarah's womb, God wants to breathe into you and your potential, empowering you by His Spirit, so you can birth into reality the promises He has placed inside you. You have potential. You have His promises. Now let Him breathe on you and give you a new vision and path.

Abraham didn't know when. He didn't know how. But he believed and trusted. He understood deep in his heart that Adonai (the divine name of God often translated as LORD) was the God of the How and When. No doubt Abraham had to exercise patience before receiving the promise. Yes, God had spoken to him, but he also knew the silence and wrestling that comes with extended waiting. The Bible tells us that twenty-five years passed before his son was finally born (Genesis 12:4; 21:5). Almost three decades passed from the time God first called Abram in Haran to the time Isaac was born.[2] Abraham left Haran when he was seventy-five. When he was one hundred, God decided it was time to give him a son with Sarah. Abraham surely wandered the land, gazing up into the night sky and attempting to count the thousands upon thousands of visible stars as they sparkled. Perhaps as a shooting star blazed across the horizon, he pondered the impossibility of it all. In our modern world with billions of city lights, few get a chance to view the stars as Abraham did. The stars Abraham looked up at danced against a backdrop of pure blackness, making them shimmer like diamonds. Unable to count them, Abraham would see with his eyes of faith beyond the magnificent cosmic handiwork to the Creator. *How much longer, Lord? How long?*

Though Abraham showed impatience at times, he never wavered in his trust in God's promise. "Even when Abram did not see how God could fulfill His gracious promise to him regarding an heir, he trusted the Lord anyway. He looked beyond what he could see to what God could see."[3]

Testing the Promise

According to Jewish tradition, it was on the Feast of Trumpets (or what most know today as Rosh Hashanah) when God supernaturally breathed life into

Sarah's womb and Isaac was conceived.[4] The Feast of Trumpets is when Jewish people observe their new year. It's a celebration of new beginnings and blessings. Several other things are celebrated on that day—including the creation of the world, the day Joseph was released from prison and promoted to the palace, and the day Israel's servitude in Egypt stopped.

One of the primary Scripture readings on Rosh Hashanah is the binding of Isaac in Genesis 22. Why? Because the event is *that* critical. After all those years of Abraham waiting for his promised son, the Lord tested Abraham by commanding him to offer Isaac as a sacrifice on a mountain in the land of Moriah. What is so incredible to me is that Abraham didn't hesitate! Of course, Abraham had human feelings just like all of us, so I can't imagine that there were no internal struggles going on. I'll never forget the time my firstborn son was sick and had a seizure. Right in front of me, he turned blue and started foaming at the mouth. After calling 911, I dropped to my hands and knees and cried out for God to spare his life. Sacrificing my son as Abraham was commanded to do is inconceivable to me, yet he obeyed! He didn't ask God for an explanation. Abraham obediently set off with his son to do what God told him to do.

Even when Isaac noticed they had everything necessary to make a burnt offering except for the actual offering, Abraham reassured his son, "God will provide for Himself the lamb for a burnt offering" (vv. 7–8 NKJV). Once again, we find Abraham not evading his son's question but completely trusting God. He made a statement of faith. He didn't know *how*, and he didn't know *when*, but Abraham knew God would provide. He was prepared to offer up what must have been the dearest, most precious thing in his life for God.

Abraham bound Isaac on the altar and drew back to offer his beloved son to the Lord. At the last moment, though, before the knife plunged down, an angel called out and stayed his hand. Abraham looked up and saw a ram caught in the thicket by its horns. God, who is all knowing, had already provided a ram. God had seen Abraham's character and trust. After offering the ram in place of Isaac, Abraham named that place "ADONAI Yireh,—as it is said today, 'On the mountain, ADONAI will provide'" (v. 14).

Abraham's faith led him to accept what was beyond understanding. He obeyed without questioning; his faith was built on God's promises and provision. Author and rabbi Russell Resnik wrote,

> The call of faith is often—perhaps always—demanding. To respond, we must leave behind all that is comfortable and follow the Lord into unknown territory. And the journey of faith does not end with this initial call. We must walk by faith, not only at the beginning of the journey, but throughout. We will have to resist lots of chances of turning back.[5]

All of us have a choice to make. We can choose to follow God like Abraham did, to trust Him completely, believing His promises, or we can turn back. When my son had his seizure, I almost turned back. Instead, by God's grace, I was empowered to trust during the time of testing. God tested Abraham *ten* times[6] throughout Scripture's recordings of his life. Each time, Abraham chose to trust and obey. Likewise, it is important for us as believers in Yeshua to understand that encountering trials doesn't necessarily mean we have lost our way or our calling. It could mean we are exactly where we are supposed to be. The presence of pain, struggle, and waiting does not equate to the absence of God, though it often feels like it. Even amid unthinkable trials, we can still choose to be people of incredible faith, led by God the Father as Abraham was. We must all remember Hebrews 11:6, which says, "Without faith it is impossible to please Him, for he who comes to God must believe that He is, and that He is a rewarder of those who diligently seek Him" (NKJV). The first reward is Himself, His presence in our lives. The choice is yours.

Abram and His Sojourning Faith

By faith Abraham obeyed when he was called to go out to a place he was to receive as an inheritance. He went out, not knowing where he was going. By faith he migrated to the land of promise as if it were foreign, dwelling in tents with Isaac and Jacob—fellow heirs of the same promise. For he was waiting for the city that has foundations, whose architect and builder is God. (Hebrews 11:8–10)

When Abram left Ur and then Haran, there was no set plan except obedience. He had no idea where he was going. God said to get up and get moving, and he went! This was no small ordeal. It wasn't like Abram was a lone drifter who could just exit town riding on a horse or a Harley into the sunset. He had to pull up his roots—everything he'd spent years developing and growing, his security and provision. Simply put, despite the uncertainty and discomfort, he did what God told him to do. This is sojourning faith.

Sojourning Faith Is Willing to Move Forward Without All the Details

When God says to go, He usually doesn't lay out all the specifics. Rather, He gives just enough information for us to take the next step in faith. Because of our fear of the unknown, however, we plead with God to give us *all* the answers before moving forward. *We want to know.* When He doesn't oblige us, we stiffen our necks (become stubborn) instead of trusting Him for the supernatural. When this happens, our relationship with God gets stuck. Like boots deeply entrenched in mire, the longer we stay stuck, the harder it is to get moving again.

Sojourners like Abraham, on the other hand, are quick to act, even if obedience means waiting. That sounds like a paradox, but waiting can be an active state too. Either way, sojourners are moving in faith, saying, "Your kingdom come. Your will be done" (Matthew 6:10 NASB).

The Hebrew phrase *Na'aseh v'Nishma* means "you will do and understand." We need to be willing to do and go! Whether it was leaving his homeland or making a sacrifice, Abraham did not delay. Scripture tells us that he "rose up early in the morning" to build an altar on which to offer Isaac (Genesis 22:3 KJV). If God said to me, "Offer your son," I might delay it a little bit. Not Abraham. One might think that he would have been slow to obey since pain and sacrifice were involved. Yet Abraham responded quickly, and God noted his obedience.

Abraham "awoke," then, according to Rabbi Kook, a highly respected Jewish scholar, he slept during the night. "Evidently, Avraham slept soundly the night before the *Akeidah* [the binding of Isaac]. The peace of mind of this holy soul, of the holy father, the mighty native, did not cease."[7]

He didn't spend the wee hours pacing back and forth trying to bargain with God. Knowing that he was called to sacrifice his son didn't disturb his sleep. It is this kind of calmness in faith that sets him apart from others.

The Talmud states that one must praise Hashem [God] for the bad things as well as the good things. It further requires that this praise be with "simchah"; Rashi [medieval French rabbi] points out in this case "simchah" doesn't mean joy, but with a "perfect heart" (i.e., with acceptance that whatever G-d does is just, even though it may be very distressing and appear to us to be unjust). Equanimity is not easily achieved. We welcome pleasant things but are upset when our wishes are denied or frustrated. Personal losses (whether personal or material) cause us to be depressed. We may think that it is beyond possibility for a person to have the same reaction to adversity that he does when his fondest wishes are fulfilled. For Abraham, there was only one reason for existence—to do the will of G-d.[8]

When we fail to act on what we know we are being asked to do, our faith becomes lukewarm. What does one do when lukewarm or cold? Get in motion. Movement generates body heat. If you want to stay spiritually hot, stay in motion!

Sojourning Faith Serves God with Equanimity

Abraham also served God with *equanimity*. That's a curious word that connotes mental calmness, composure, and evenness of temper, especially in difficult situations. It's the type of faith that allows us to keep our peace even when unforeseen storms of life suddenly appear, threatening to blow us away. Yeshua was the absolute essence of equanimity:

He got into the boat and his disciples followed him. Suddenly a furious storm came up on the lake, so that the waves swept over the boat. But Jesus was sleeping. The disciples went and woke him, saying, "Lord, save us! We're going to drown!"

He replied, "You of little faith, why are you so afraid?" Then he got up and rebuked the winds and the waves, and it was completely calm.

The men were amazed and asked, "What kind of man is this? Even the winds and the waves obey him!" (Matthew 8:23–27 NIV)

Equanimity is rooted in a deep faith that calmly rises above the storms of life and even commands them to be still. Though the waves of our circumstances are beating on our boat, Yeshua calls us to rest. Like Yeshua sleeping on the stormy lake, Abraham could sleep through the night before taking Isaac up the mountain because he knew who was in control of his circumstances. This is sojourning faith. "Rest in the LORD," wrote the psalmist, "and wait patiently for him" (Psalm 37:7 KJV).

Sojourning Faith Always Looks Up

Early the next morning Abraham got up and loaded his donkey. He took with him two of his servants and his son Isaac. When he had cut enough wood for the burnt offering, he set out for the place God had told him about. On the third day Abraham *looked up* and saw the place in the *distance*. He said to his servants, "Stay here with the donkey while I and the boy go over there. We will worship and then we will come back to you." (Genesis 22:3–5 NIV, emphasis added)

Abraham lived a life of firmly *looking up* and onward. No time for distractions. No time for gazing to the right or left. With blinders on his eyes and a guard on his heart, Abraham's face was set like flint on his divine assignment and on the God who always provides. The word "distance" in this verse implies looking forward to the future. So often we live our lives staring in the rearview mirror. Obsession with our past (both good and bad things) distracts us from focusing ahead, causing us to veer off course and swerve out of our assigned lanes. That's why getting us to focus on our past is one of the Enemy's favorite tactics.

Sojourners live in a fresh, synergetic daily relationship with God as they travel through life dependent on Him as their ultimate, ever-present source for life.

Award-winning author and songwriter David M. Edwards wrote, "Too many times we have relied on yesterday's manna to nourish us today, tomorrow, and the rest of the week. God rebuked Israel for trying to stockpile manna! They were not supposed to live on yesterday's provision, yesterday's manifestation, yesterday's visitation. Don't be satisfied with what happened yesterday."[9] And don't get stuck back there either. God made a way for you to get unstuck and move forward with true life. A person who keeps looking back is not fit for the Kingdom (Luke 9:62). That's why the apostle and rabbi Paul told us: "Forgetting those things which are behind and reaching forward to those things which are ahead, I press toward the goal for the prize of the upward call of God in Christ Jesus" (Philippians 3:13–14, paraphrased).

Abraham did not look back; instead, he looked up. Genesis 22:4 tells us a time when he did this: "On the third day Abraham looked up" (NIV). In Jewish tradition the third day is seen as a day of transformation and insight. God created the trees and they sprouted on the third day of Creation. On the third day God provided the lamb to spare Isaac's life. God came down and met Israel at Sinai on the third day. Jonah was spit out from the big fish on the third day. Yeshua rose from the dead on the third day.

In the account of Creation, the third day is called "doubly blessed." A careful reading of Genesis 1:9–13 (the third day of Creation) reveals that it is the day of double blessing—twice during that day, God pronounced it "good." For much of Jewish history, the third day of the week (Tuesday) was considered an especially auspicious day for weddings. This was so because on the third day of Creation, the phrase "and God saw that it was good" appears twice (Genesis 1:10, 12).

When we look to the Lamb of God on the cross who rose on the third day, we are looking up. John compared Yeshua to the bronze serpent on the pole that God instructed Moses to build to cure the people from poisonous snakebites. When they looked upon it, they were healed. It was a look of faith. They had to look up (Numbers 21; John 3:14).

Sojourning Faith Never Goes It Alone

> Abraham took the wood for the burnt offering and placed it on his son Isaac, and he himself carried the fire and the knife. As the two of them went on together, Isaac spoke up and said to his father Abraham, "Father?"
>
> "Yes, my son?" Abraham replied.
>
> "The fire and wood are here," Isaac said, "but where is the lamb for the burnt offering?"
>
> Abraham answered, "God himself will provide the lamb for the burnt offering, my son." And the two of them went on together. (Genesis 22:6–8 NIV)

Let's give Isaac some credit; he suspected what this meant. No lamb meant something was up. And if he had any doubt, it was confirmed when he was bound and laid on the altar. Isaac was not a child at this time as many have believed. According to Jewish tradition, he was a man in his thirties and could have easily resisted his father who was well into his second century of life by then. But he had the faith to trust both his earthly father and his heavenly Father. When Scripture says the two went on together, the Hebrew text implies they were in unity—one heart and one mind.

How can two walk together unless they are agreed (Amos 3:3)? We cannot walk out our faith alone. We cannot fulfill our destiny by ourselves. Two are better than one! We must walk together or else we will waver, backslide, and drift from our faith. We were not created to be Lone Rangers! We were created for community and for a team. One stick is easy to break, but a bundle of sticks tied together is nearly unbreakable.

Sojourning Faith Trusts God to Provide

> Abraham looked up and there in a thicket he saw a ram caught by its horns. He went over and took the ram and sacrificed it as a burnt offering instead of his son. So Abraham called that place The LORD Will Provide. And to this day it is said, "On the mountain of the LORD it will be provided." (Genesis 22:13–14 NIV)

Sojourning faith means being willing to put everything on the altar because we trust God to provide. Genuine faith always trusts God to provide. But how was it possible for Abraham to have that type of trust? He understood that

1. God loved him more than Abraham loved himself;
2. God knew what was best for him, better than he did; and
3. God is good and is faithful to His promises.

By faith, when God tested him, Abraham offered Isaac as a sacrifice. The man who embraced and believed God's promises was about to sacrifice his only son—the promised son. At some point Abraham must have felt his son was going to die. Yet he had enough faith to reason that God could raise Isaac from the dead.

Just as He breathes life into dead situations, the God Who Sees is in the business of resurrecting dead things to keep His promises. Is there something you need to put on the altar and trust God with? Is there something you are holding back? If you put whatever it is on the altar, by faith, God will either raise it back up or give you something new and better in return.

A Note from Kathie

Abram, aka Abraham, is listed in Hebrews 11, the Bible's so-called Hall of Faith chapter. He was described as a "friend of God" (James 2:23) and without a doubt remains a pivotal and profound character in the birth of the Jewish nation and the history of the world.

When God called Abram from the land of Ur, the Scriptures tell us that he immediately left everything comfortable, secure, and convenient in his physical life.

Why? Why would he leave everything for such an unknown destination and an unknowable future?

I can only surmise that he experienced an extraordinary encounter with the living God that left him convinced he had to follow Him.

I'm no Abram, but I, too, experienced such an encounter when I was a twelve-year-old and knew without a doubt in my young mind that I had to follow Jesus. No "if nots" or "maybes."

two

SARAH

Rabbi Jason

Entwined with Abraham's story is that of his wife, half sister, and matriarch of the Jewish people, Sarai (Genesis 11:29, 20:12). Strong, beautiful, independent, and resourceful, she trekked alongside her husband from the beginning when they packed up all their earthly belongings and left Ur without an inkling of where they would end up. Sarah heard the promises to Abraham of land, blessing, and an heir. She, too, trusted in God's faithfulness to guide and sustain them along the arduous journey, ultimately fulfilling His promises.

At birth she was given the name Sarai, which in Hebrew means "princess" or "noblewoman." Perhaps her parents foresaw what she would become, or it was an indication of her family lineage. When God instructed Abraham to change her name to Sarah, He honored her by calling her "the mother of nations," saying that kings would come from her (Genesis 17:15–16). Just like Abraham, Sarah had her struggles, but also like Abraham, she showed resilience and faith under pressure. Sarah understood all too well that women her age could not bear children. Still, she believed God.

23

Laughing *at* God's Promises or *with* Them

Genesis 18:1 says, "ADONAI appeared to [Abraham] at Mamre's large trees while he was sitting in the entrance of his tent during the heat of the day." When Abraham looked up, he saw three men. Immediately he ran from the tent and bowed. Abraham then showed these three men loving hospitality. Then, Genesis 18:10 tells us, "[The LORD] said, 'I will surely return to you at this time next year; and behold, Sarah your wife will have a son.' And Sarah was listening at the tent door, which was behind him" (NASB).

Sarah heard the promise, and what did she do? She laughed. In the beginning it was a laugh of skepticism, and God checked her. "The LORD said to Abraham, 'Why did Sarah laugh, saying, "Shall I indeed bear a child, when I am so old?" Is anything too difficult for the LORD?'" (Genesis 18:13–14 NASB). In the end, however, it became a laugh of faith and thanksgiving.

You may be snickering yourself. What promises has God made to you that caused you to laugh? If we are honest, many of us are guilty of laughing skeptically at some of the promises God has given us.

We either laugh *at* the promises of God, in which case we hinder them from coming to pass, or we laugh *with* them. Ultimately Sarah named her son *Yishaq* (Isaac), which comes from the Hebrew word "to laugh." She said, "Everyone who hears will laugh with me" (Genesis 21:6). And she rejoiced.

Are you laughing at God and His promises, or are you laughing with Him? That is the question we all must ask ourselves. Just as Noah had faith to build an ark when the world around him was scoffing and laughing, Abraham and Sarah had faith to believe that "with God all things are possible" (Mark 10:27 KJV).

For me, the promise "with God all things are possible" is personal. When my parents were finding no success at starting a family, the doctors told them my mother was barren. As you can imagine, this news was devastating, yet my parents knew they served a living God. One night my mother had a prophetic God-dream. In the dream, her father, who had long since passed, appeared to her and told her that everything was going to be all right, that she was going to conceive a son. Within a few months, she was pregnant with me! When I consider the story, I realize that my life is not my own. I was conceived for a divine purpose. So were you.

Weariness Is No Laughing Matter

Even though Sarah had great faith, she had grown weary of waiting on God's timing. Many years before the Lord's final promise to breathe life into Sarah's womb and provide a son within the year, Sarah's growing impatience had led her to devise a scheme to help God out. Charging ahead independently without seeking His will, she decided to give her maidservant, Hagar, to Abraham to jump-start the process (Genesis 16:1–4).

Note to self: trying to help God out almost always gets us into trouble!

Sometimes when we grow impatient, it's because we don't understand God's hidden hand. Though it appears at times that He's not working, He is. Consider what Daniel learned in a vision from God in Daniel 10. After three weeks of fasting, praying, and receiving no answer from God, the prophet who'd been miraculously delivered from a den of hungry lions must have been incredibly frustrated. But in verse 10, the hand of an angel touched Daniel and said,

Don't be afraid, Daniel! For from the first day that you set your heart to understand and to humble yourself before your God, your words were heard.

I have come because of your words. However, the prince of the kingdom of Persia resisted me for 21 days, but behold Michael, one of the chief princes, came to help me because I had been detained there with the kings of Persia. Now I have come to explain to you what will happen to your people in the future days. For the vision concerns days yet to come. (Daniel 10:12–14)

Here again, we *find God's hidden hand*. Often we pray and wonder why God doesn't answer immediately. When He doesn't, we tend to give up and say things like, "What's the use in praying? God's not listening." If we don't say it, we surely think it at times. Does God answer prayer immediately? Absolutely! Yet, like what happened to Daniel, the answers to our prayers are frequently delayed for good reasons we are not aware of. In Sarah and Abraham's life, God spoke, but it took twenty-five years for the answer to come, not just twenty-one days as it did with Daniel.

Despite her weariness and impatience, Sarah is in the great Hall of Faith listed in the New Testament book of Hebrews. "By faith even Sarah herself received ability to conceive when she was barren and past the age, since she considered the One who had made the promise to be faithful" (Hebrews 11:11). Sarah's faith conquered the impossibility of barrenness. She didn't know how God would provide, and she didn't know when, but by faith she conceived in her old age. By faith she trusted God's hidden hand. We need that same kind of faith. Remember, "What is impossible with men," said Yeshua, "is possible with God" (Luke 18:27).

Rabbi Paul gave us more insight. Romans 4:19–22 in the Tree of Life version of the Bible says,

Without becoming weak in faith, he considered his own body—as good as dead, since he was already a hundred years old—and the deadness of

Sarah's womb. Yet he did not waver in unbelief concerning the promise of God. Rather, he was strengthened in faith, giving glory to God. He was fully convinced that what God has promised, He also is able to do. That is why "it was credited to him as righteousness."

Despite moments of failure in their lives, Abraham and Sarah believed in God. They didn't give up despite the improbability of the promise in human understanding. They were *strengthened in faith*. Sarah's faith gave her strength as Abraham's faith did the same for him.

Sarah was weary from waiting, which we can fully understand; we can become weary from waiting on God as well. Next to suffering, however, we learn more from waiting than anything else. We grow as we trust. We understand that even in the darkest places, we can see Yeshua. As we learn more about God and His Word, we realize there are no broken promises in the Bible. Therefore, since we trust Him completely, we wait.

South African writer, teacher, and Christian pastor Andrew Murray wrote,

Patient waiting upon God brings a rich reward; the deliverance is sure; God Himself will put a new song into your mouth. O soul! be not impatient, whether it be in the exercise of prayer and worship that you find it difficult to wait, or in the delay in respect of definite requests, or in the fulfilling of your heart's desire for the revelation of God Himself in a deeper spiritual life—fear not, but rest in the Lord, and wait patiently for Him.[1]

Sarah received a rich reward. God gave her a son, the heir, a forerunner of the Messiah. What reward awaits you as you wait on the Lord? My friend, don't grow weary of waiting. Grow more in Him—who He is, His rich provision, and His love for you.

Sarah's Outer and Inner Beauty

Sarah was one of the most beautiful women in the Scriptures. Genesis 12:11 speaks of her "beautiful appearance" (YLT), and she is also described as "very beautiful" (v. 14 NIV).

The Torah, according to the rabbis, pays tribute to her beauty when it says, "The life of Sarah was one hundred years and twenty years and seven years" (Genesis 23:1).[2] The sages, commenting on the unusual way in which the years of Sarah's life were written, state, "Sinless when she was one hundred as when she was twenty [meaning purity] and as beautiful when she was twenty as when she was seven."[3]

Sarah's beauty and the number of years she lived connect to the beautiful Queen Esther. Sarah lived 127 years, and Queen Esther ruled over 127 provinces with King Xerxes (Esther 1:1). The life stories of Sarah and Esther remind us that beauty is our birthright! God does not do ugly. He not only created the world and said it was "good," He created it beautiful! For many years I had an office in Malibu. Driving through Malibu Canyon and along the Pacific Coast Highway, where the jagged cliffs met the crashing waves, always put a smile on my face. It is breathtaking at times. The overwhelming awe of creation draws us to Adonai because it's a reflection of Him. We must not underestimate or undervalue the significance of beauty!

The Lord is not coming back for an ugly bride but for a beautiful one made in His image. One of the reasons people are not attracted to believers and the church is because we often lack beauty on myriad levels. But God promises to give us beauty for ashes (Isaiah 61:3). And this is what we see in both Sarah and Esther!

Today our celebrity-crazed, social media culture celebrates external beauty. Men and women flaunt themselves to be noticed and make a name for themselves. This is completely opposite of Sarah and Esther. Esther embodied the Hebrew concept "The true honor of the princess is within."[4] The word for "within," *penimah*, is the same as *pnimiyut*, one's inner spiritual makeup. Esther's name alludes to the truth that the true essence of beauty is more than skin deep. It comes from within—that inner, hidden place.

Esther, like Sarah, was even more beautiful on the inside than on the outside. An inner beauty was radiating from Esther that, when coupled with her outer appearance, made her the desire of the king in the same way Sarah was desirable to the kings of Egypt and Gerar. This kind of inner beauty is underscored by the apostle Peter's words in the New Testament:

> Your beauty should not come from outward adornment, such as elaborate hairstyles and the wearing of gold jewelry or fine clothes. Rather, it should be that of your inner self, the unfading beauty of a gentle and quiet spirit, which is of great worth in God's sight. For this is the way the holy women of the past who put their hope in God used to adorn themselves. (1 Peter 3:3–5 NIV)

God wants you to realize the beauty that is your birthright and that you are as lovely as Sarah and Esther. He wants you to radiate with beauty from the inside out. Quiet confidence and peace set us apart from the world and come from His presence living within us.

Spiritual Beauty

In addition to Sarah's and Esther's inner and outer beauty, they had a spiritual beauty. In Jewish tradition there were seven great female prophets.[5] The first was Sarah, as God bore witness to when he told Abraham, "Do whatever Sarah tells you" (Genesis 21:12 NLT). Elaborating further, the Talmud states, "Who were the seven prophetesses? The *Gemara* (part of the Talmud) answers: Sarah, Miriam, Deborah, Hannah, Abigail, Huldah, and Esther."[6]

God has blessed women in general with a greater spiritual sensitivity and discernment. This is alluded to in the Creation account. Man and woman are both created in God's image. But while God created man, He built the woman (Genesis 2:22). The Hebrew word for "build" is *banah*, which shares the same letters as *binah*, meaning "discernment" or "intuition." By God's divine design, women were fashioned to have a heightened level of spiritual and emotional insight, understanding, and discernment. There actually is such a thing as women's intuition! It is for this reason that traditional Judaism believes that generally the matriarchs were greater than the patriarchs in matters of prophecy. When women are not respected and their voices not valued, it not only dishonors and displeases the Lord, but it is to the detriment of family and the church.

God wants to beautify His bride from the inside out.

The Connection Between Beauty and Joy

There is a connection between beauty and joy. Poet John Keats wrote,

> A thing of beauty is a joy forever,
> Its loveliness increases, it will never
> Pass into nothingness, but still will keep
> A bower quiet for us, and a sleep,
> Full of sweet dreams and health and quiet breathing.[7]

A key part of God's beauty is to give us a radiant joy that rises from within our core, despite our outward circumstance. We can find this concept in the book of Esther:

> Mordecai went out from the king's presence in blue and white royal robes, with a large gold crown, and also a purple robe of fine linen. The city of Shushan shouted and rejoiced. For the Jews there was light and gladness, *joy* and honor. Throughout every province and throughout every city, wherever the king's edict and his law went, the Jews had gladness and *joy*, banquets and holidays. Many peoples of the land became Jews, because the fear of the Jews had overcome them. (Esther 8:15–17, emphasis added)

If we want to be light and attractive and beautiful, then we must live our lives with a contagious, infectious joy. There are those who illuminate the spaces they enter. Rooms light up with their presence as their joy and laughter shift the atmosphere. Then there are those who emit gloom and heaviness from all the baggage they are lugging. Like a thick blanket, it weighs down the atmosphere and those around. Which person are you going to be? One of light and joy, or gloom and heaviness? We have a choice. Sarah needed to wait, but her waiting led to blessing, and she named her son Isaac—"Laughter." Though she experienced weariness and impatience, by faith she ultimately shed the blanket of heaviness and let the joy within her rise.

We are called to *carry* the Kingdom, and the Kingdom that Yeshua came to bring is joyous. Rabbi Paul wrote, "For the kingdom of God is not about eating and drinking, but righteousness and *shalom* and joy in the *Ruach ha-Kodesh* [Spirit of God]" (Romans 14:17).

Joy and silliness are signs that the Spirit of God and His Kingdom is in our midst! You cannot be fully filled with the Spirit and live continually from a place of sadness. It's the fullness of the Spirit that brings the fullness of joy!

And from where does this joy come? From the Holy Spirit. "The disciples were filled with *joy* and with the Holy Spirit" (Acts 13:52 NIV, emphasis added). Although at this time, Paul and Barnabas and the disciples at Antioch were experiencing severe persecution and hardship, through the Holy Spirit of Yeshua inside them, their sadness was changed to joy—from fear into faith.

Although Sarah had a significant amount of difficulty in her life, she was able to accept everything that happened with joy because of her ultimate belief in God's goodness and sovereignty. The apostle and rabbi Paul, who suffered greatly for the sake of Messiah, also knew this secret; for true joy is based on the belief that "in all things God works for the good of those who love him, who have been called according to his purpose" (Romans 8:28 NIV). If we really believe this like Sarah and Paul did, we will also live a positive, joyous, faith-filled life worth emulating. Then it will be said of us as it was of Sarah, "that all our years were equal in goodness."[8]

A Note from Kathie

Even though Scripture tells us that Sarah was extremely beautiful, so desirable that even the king coveted her, she traveled alongside her husband on this epic journey with her shame of infertility.

She heard the promise God made to Abram to make him the father of a great nation, yet she laughed at the improbability of such a notion. It didn't matter that she was still extraordinarily beautiful. She was still barren and way past her childbearing years.

Sarah became impatient with God. Haven't we all? And she made a foolish choice because of her frustrated desires to become a mother. It almost ended in tragedy, but Adonai intervened as He always does and brought beauty from the ashes of her mistakes.

One thousand years after Abraham and Sarah welcomed the promised son, Isaac, God called a different man to deliver God's people, now called the Hebrews, from the suffering of slavery under the pharaoh of Egypt.

three

MOSES

Rabbi Jason

In my book *Mysteries of the Messiah*, I wrote about another critical figure in Israel's history:

> Moses, the greatest prophet of the Hebrew Bible and central figure in Judaism, was used by God not only to free Israel from slavery to the greatest superpower of its day but also to give the Ten Commandments and the Torah to the Hebrew people. No leader or prophet is as loved and revered by the Jewish people as Moses.[1]

As He did with Abraham and Sarah, God asked Moses to step out in faith and trust Him with a tremendous challenge. Though sometimes with hesitation, Moses obeyed and moved out into God's will and way. He often didn't know the *how—How are we all going to cross this sea? How will I feed all these people? How will we get water?* And he often didn't know *when—When will Pharaoh let us go and release the people from slavery? When will we get to the Promised Land?* But it was the not knowing that led him to trust God.

"I Am Not the Man You Need Me to Be"

Now Moses was tending the flock of his father-in-law Jethro, the priest of Midian. So he led the flock to the farthest end of the wilderness, coming to the mountain of God, Horeb. Then the angel of ADONAI appeared to him in a flame of fire from within a bush. So he looked and saw the bush burning with fire, yet it was not consumed. Moses thought, "I will go now, and see this great sight. Why is the bush not burnt?" (Exodus 3:1–3)

Can you imagine this scene? Moses was quietly tending his father-in-law's sheep on a typical sunny and warm day. Then "an angel of ADONAI" appeared to him in a bush that was on fire but not consumed. An angel would have been different enough, but a bush that burns without burning up? That would be something to change the course of your day.

In Southern California, where I live, we often have horrific fires. These are not merely forest fires; they're often called firestorms. The flames roar through mountainous terrain fueled by extremely dry and thick underbrush. As the raging fires burn out of control, they consume the area and everything in their paths—homes, cars, in some cases, entire communities. That's not what Moses experienced.

This thornbush kept burning yet stayed perfectly intact. By appearing in this unusual thornbush, God told Israel that He had heard their cries and identified with their suffering. When Moses shared this reality with his enslaved brothers and sisters, they were overwhelmed (Exodus 4:30–31).

About fifteen hundred years later, thorns would be used once again with a prophet greater than Moses (Deuteronomy 18:18)—with the Messiah—for an even greater exodus. As you will recall, in the person of Yeshua, the Lord had a crown of thorns placed upon His head right before He died as the Passover Lamb (Matthew 27:29). He did this to demonstrate how much He was willing to identify with us and feel human pain so He could set us free from the slavery caused by sin and death. The crown of thorns on Yeshua's head, and the cross in general, declares loudly that the Lord loves and cares for you and is willing to feel your pain.

After hearing what God asked him to do, "Moses said to God, 'Who am I, that I should go to Pharaoh, and bring *Bnei-Yisrael* [Children of Israel] out of Egypt?'" (Exodus 3:11). Through most of the remainder of Exodus chapter 3, God gave Moses reassurance and further detailed what He wanted him to do. Moses wasn't convinced. Then, in chapter 4, Moses said, "But look, they will not believe me or listen to my voice. They will say, 'ADONAI has not appeared to you'" (v. 1).

As the story unfolds in chapter 4, God showed Moses great wonders and signs. After seeing a bush that didn't burn up, Moses still had apprehension and questioned God. So, God had Moses' hand turn leprous, then back to normal. Next, Moses watched his shepherd's staff become a snake, then turn back to his original staff.

God was trying to help Moses do what He had called him to do. We can't be too critical of this great man of God because we, too, often hear God's calling and make excuses. We don't move on to what God has for us. We don't see the greater purpose. God didn't need Moses, but He wanted Moses to see that he needed God. It was better for Moses to feel distressed with God than be comfortable in Midian.

Moses offered many excuses. One was about his identity. God asked him to throw down his own identity (the shepherd's staff) and pick up a snake (4:3). He wanted Moses to recognize his real identity. It was not as a shepherd, but as a son—not a son of Pharaoh, but a son of Adonai, the One True God.

Moses' insecurity was another issue. He likely felt he was too old for such a mission. So God healed his hands to show Moses how He can overcome and heal anything, even the dreaded disease of leprosy (vv. 6–7). Why would age be a problem when God would be his source of strength to accomplish his assignment?

Moses also felt he was inadequate, that he didn't possess the speaking skills needed to confront the world's most powerful man (v. 10). Moses forgot who gave him his voice and had to realize that excuses don't make sense to the Creator of everything. God delights in using our weaknesses. He can use us when we are not educated or trained. He can use us when we are afraid. But God cannot use us when we don't believe Him. If God says we can, we can. We need to get our focus off what we are or are not and onto who He is.

Moses became stubborn (v. 13). If you want to make God angry, just keep stubbornly believing that He cannot do great things through you. Every one of us is alive because God has something for us to do that is far better than any plans we could come up with ourselves. Like Moses, we need to submit to God, step out in faith, take one step at a time—without overthinking or paying attention to people—and trust Him.

But there's more! God wasn't angry with Moses because of his weaknesses and flaws. It was Moses' unbelief that concerned God. "Without faith," penned Rabbi Paul, "it is impossible to please Him" (Hebrews 11:6 NASB). "Impossible" is a strong word, but it's clear-cut. Faith pleases God. Unbelief doesn't. Pretty simple. That's because unbelief leads to disobedience. Instead of submitting to what God called us to do and relying on Him for strength and wisdom, we argue and stubbornly dig in our heels. When we do, we cheat ourselves and live below our potential.

Moses finally agreed to go to Pharaoh and plead for the people's release. Though he wavered, he did obey what God called him to do. By God's power, he performed many miracles. Pharaoh's heart was hard, so God sent plagues to convince him to let His people go. Pharaoh eventually relented, only to change his mind and pursue the Children of Israel to the edge of the Red Sea. Moses lifted his staff, and God caused the winds to separate the sea, creating a dry path to freedom. God's people walked through to safety. When Moses lowered his staff, the waves collapsed, consuming Pharaoh's chariots. They perished in the depths of the waters. And so, Israel continued their journey into the heart—and the harshness—of the wilderness (Exodus 5–14).

"I Am the Man Who Trusts You, Lord"

As Moses led the Children of Israel into the wilderness, his trust in the Lord evidenced itself in many ways. Desperate for healing after centuries of abuse in Egypt, the Children of Israel needed to rebuild their relationships with God and with one another. They were not only physically broken from years of hard labor and slavery but also spiritually broken from constant exposure to Egyptian culture and idol worship.

Moses led the people to Mount Sinai, where God gave them the Ten Commandments written with His finger on tablets of stone (Exodus 31:18). The Ten Commandments are the foundation of the Torah and historically the foundation of Jews, Christians, and most of Western civilization. The Ten Commandments became the first step toward removing the chaos the people felt from leaving Egypt.

Moses was the man God entrusted to give the people the Ten Commandments. But why did God choose Moses in the first place? Because he was humble and a man of faith.

Testing frequently strengthens faith. Severe tests often challenged Moses' faith. He obediently assumed the mission God called him to do, and it tested him. Just because God calls and we obey doesn't guarantee smooth sailing. Sometimes the middle of a storm is right in the middle of God's will. Moses faced the hard-hearted Pharaoh, yet his faith remained and was strengthened. The people doubted him. They grumbled about food, water, and living conditions. Craving to return to the comfort of slavery, they accused Moses of bringing them into the wilderness to suffer (Numbers 14:2). Can slavery be comfortable? How often do we choose to live in our bondage because the journey to freedom is too uncomfortable? Despite the people's rebellion, Moses' faith remained, bearing the strain of criticism and rejection.

The first time Moses brought down the Ten Commandments from Mount Sinai, he found the people worshiping a golden calf. Horrified and angry, he slammed down the tablets, shattering them. God told him to go back up the mountain so they could talk. Because of his faith and trust in God, Moses obeyed, and God wrote the second set of tablets.

Despite his proven faith and trust in God, Moses was still human and capable of thinking he knew better than God at times. As the people neared the end of their journey, they discovered there was no water at Kadesh in the wilderness of Zin. They raised their voices and complained against Moses, so the Lord instructed him, "Take the staff and gather the assembly, you and your brother Aaron. Speak to the rock before their eyes, and it will give out its water. You will bring out water from the rock, and you will give the community something to drink, along with their livestock" (Numbers 20:8). Unfortunately Moses' anger with the whining Hebrews got the best of him, and as a result he uncharacteristically deviated from God's instructions. Instead of speaking to the rock, he struck it with his staff. Because of his disobedience, Moses suffered severe consequences (Numbers 20:10–12). Both he and Aaron would die on the far side of the Jordan, in the land of Moab, having never set foot in the Promised Land.

There are many thoughts about why, at this point, Moses didn't listen to God. One commentator wrote,

> Through his subtle disobedience, however, Moses misrepresented God's gracious intentions toward Israel. Perhaps he is thinking of their entire history of complaint, and God's earlier acts of judgment against them. Perhaps Moses pictures waters gushing forth from the rock to sweep away the worst complainers, just as the Lord had earlier provided so much quail meat to those who complained about food that they choked upon it (Num. 11).[2]

Maybe Moses could not fully understand God's kindness toward a rebellious people. In any case, God told Moses, "Because you did not trust in Me so as to esteem Me as holy in the eyes of *Bnei-Yisrael* [Children of Israel], therefore you will not bring this assembly into the land that I have given to them" (Numbers 20:12).

Moses was the man who had obediently climbed to the heights of Mount Sinai and brought down the Ten Commandments. Now he obediently climbed to the top of a different mountain, Mount Nebo (Deuteronomy 32:49), and he looked out upon the land God had promised Abram centuries before. He would never taste of its sweet fruit or sleep in the Promised Land's beauty beneath the stars. Yet God would still reward his faithfulness, for Moses would soon wake up in the true Promised Land—heaven!

Scripture does tell us, however, of one occasion when Moses entered the land of Canaan—after his death! In Matthew 17 Yeshua took Peter, Jacob, and John to a high mountain.[3] Yeshua was "transfigured before them; His face shone like the sun, and His clothes became as white as the light" (v. 2). And Scripture tells us there were two witnesses besides the three apostles— Elijah and Moses!

Why Moses? Moses was a man of faith. He was arguably the most outstanding leader in human history, ruling the people in God's name. *The Leadership Bible* explains, "When God directed him to lead in a difficult situation, Moses hesitated before he obeyed—but he did obey. Like Moses, all leaders will occasionally face tough challenges and seemingly impossible situations. At such times they need to follow Moses' lead: Assess the situation, take their fears to God, listen for His response, and then obey."[4] Moses didn't know *how*, and he didn't know *when*. But he asked God questions, listened, and obeyed.

On that unknown mountain, Moses' faith put him in front of the Messiah. God allowed him an opportunity to witness the deity of Yeshua in His full, radiant display. Moses then knew the full story, witnessing the fullness of the Law standing before him.

Finding Your Spiritual Song

Each of us has a unique spiritual song that only we can sing. God has planted it inside us, and we need to find it. Often in life it is easy to lose our song, to lose ourselves, and to start singing somebody else's song. A song is something we sing repeatedly, and it becomes a meditation, something that is internalized within us. If I were to throw out a few words to a popular song, a lot of you could easily complete the lyric because you have recently sung it or often heard it. That is the power of song and the power of living in harmony with the song that God has created us to sing.

Moses Sings His Song

Moses learned to sing two different songs. Growing up in Pharaoh's house, he learned his first song from his adopted mother. Later Moses would learn a song from his biological mother, Jochebed. At some point in his life, Moses had to decide which song he was going to sing and to which song he would attune his life. If Moses stayed in Pharaoh's house, he would have lost his true song and his life's true purpose. God didn't call him to be the prince of Egypt but rather a man of faith and the shepherd of Israel.

If we try to sing someone else's song, it is like being in slavery. We must make that transition in our lives and sing the song God created for us to sing. But to be able to sing that song takes at least two things: practice and preparation.

It took forty years at Pharaoh's house and another forty years as a shepherd before Moses could begin to sing his own song. It took two-thirds of his life to *prepare him* for the final one-third. Friends, if you are in a season of preparation, do not get discouraged because it seems to be taking so long. Often it takes significant time for God to mold us into the people we need to be to be most effective when our moment comes. As the old saying goes, practice makes perfect.

Sharpening Our Axes

In a 1977 interview with *Christianity Today*, Billy Graham said, "One of my great regrets is that I have not studied enough. I wish I had studied more and preached less. People have pressured me into speaking to groups when I should have been studying and preparing."[5]

Will Sweeney, a noted preacher of the first half of the twentieth century, felt the same. He said, "God can cut a lot of wood with a dull ax, but He can cut a lot more wood with a sharp one! What God and His church need today is more sharp axes!"[6]

The season of preparation is a time for us to sharpen our axes. Even if it takes more time to get to the point where you begin to cut down trees, it is easier to cut if your ax is sharp. There is less resistance. It goes a lot smoother. We need God to sharpen our axes like iron sharpens iron (Proverbs 27:17). This is often accomplished through relationships with one another. It's the education we get from having a teachable spirit while going through challenging life situations.

God prepared Moses in all these ways and gave him a song of faith and endurance.

Overcoming Stage Fright

You may have heard the phrase "Feel the fear and do it anyway." That was Moses. He trusted the God of the *here and now* and sometimes did it afraid; he didn't let fear paralyze him. Fear can rob us of our ability to go out and sing our song. It's important that we make the decision not to be paralyzed by fear of failure, by fear of rejection, or by fear of looking stupid. Fear cannot dominate our lives if we are going to be all God wants us to be. As my friend Shawn Bolz says, we are going to have to risk a little holy embarrassment. When you think about it, what do you have to lose?

If we are going to be fearful of anything, it should be fear of coming to the end of our lives and thinking, *What if?* or *If only . . .* We should not be afraid that we tried something, and it did not happen. Success is getting up one more time. It's failing forward. Falling builds strength and integrity in us. The issue is not falling; it is how we respond when we do, because we *will* fall. Moses fell a couple of times, but he got up and trusted God to move ahead.

It's not only fear that robs us of the ability to sing our song but also depression and discouragement. "The joy of the LORD is your strength," wrote Nehemiah (8:10 NIV). Depression is a joy killer that destroys our strength. It's no wonder depression and discouragement are two of the Enemy's favorite weapons against us. I believe most depression is anger turned inward. We become angry at our circumstances, angry with God, and often we are the angriest with ourselves. When anger turns into self-hatred, it kills our joy and our desire to serve Messiah, and it mutes the song within us. God made you unique and like no other. He created you for good works that He prepared beforehand that you should walk in (Ephesians 2:10). Don't allow anger to keep you from singing your song.

Moses chose to sing the song God called him to sing. He faced incredible odds and challenges, but, like Messiah, he led his people out of exile. He spoke with God, and despite severe challenges, not knowing how or when, Moses trusted God.

A Note from Kathie

The story of the deliverance of the Hebrews from Pharaoh's ruthless hand and the subsequent forty-year journey to the Promised Land is perhaps the most famous narrative in the whole Bible, outside of the birth and life of the Messiah, Yeshua, many centuries later.

By the time God appeared to Moses at the burning bush and sent him off to free the Hebrew slaves, Moses was eighty years old, well beyond what anyone today would consider hero material (Exodus 7:7). In fact, not even Moses thought he was up to the task. When God approached him at the burning bush, he was a stuttering, fearful shepherd totally convinced that he was not capable of doing what God was calling him to do. And yet when he finally obeyed God's calling, he became one of the greatest heroes in the entire Bible.

four

JOSHUA

Rabbi Jason

Moses knew that his time to depart this world was drawing near. He wanted to make sure his family, the Jewish people, would have a shepherd to guide them in spiritual matters and to lead them into the Promised Land. He asked the Lord to "appoint a man over the community to go out and come in before them, who will lead them out and bring them out so that the people of ADONAI will not be like sheep without a shepherd" (Numbers 27:16–17). God responded by telling Moses to appoint Joshua, son of Nun (v. 18).

Why was Joshua chosen to lead the Children of Israel in the battles and mission to possess the Promised Land? What can we learn from him that can help us in our battles to possess our personal promised lands?

How Do You Replace a Legend?

Joshua could not have received a higher honor than to take Moses' place. But Moses was a tough act to follow. He was the greatest prophet and spiritual leader in the Old Testament. God spoke to him face-to-face. The number and nature of the miracles that Moses performed were without parallel until Yeshua came.

Joshua couldn't rise to the level of Moses. In the closing line of Deuteronomy, Joshua wrote concerning Moses, "There has not risen again a prophet in Israel like Moses, whom ADONAI knew face-to-face, with all the signs and wonders ADONAI sent him to do in the land of Egypt—to Pharaoh, all his servants, and all his land—by the strong hand and great awe that Moses did in the sight of all Israel" (Deuteronomy 34:10–12). Although Joshua could not equal Moses in his spiritual stature, he was equal to Moses in his zeal for the Lord, zeal for His Word, and zeal to serve.

Joshua's Zeal for the Lord

"Arise, you and all these people" (Joshua 1:2). If we're going to accomplish anything, the first thing we must do is arise. Joshua's zeal led him to arise and obey the Lord. He didn't dwell on the circumstances. He didn't "wait and see." He got up and led the people.

Joshua's zeal is what singled him out. We can define "zeal" as enthusiastic, energetic, and proactive action done in the service of God and fulfillment of His commandments. Merriam-Webster.com defines "zeal" as "a strong feeling of interest and enthusiasm that makes someone very eager or determined to do something."[1] In line with this definition, the ancient rabbis gave a memorable and vivid description of zeal when they said, "Be fierce as a leopard, light as an eagle, swift and as strong as a lion to do the will of your Father in Heaven."[2] Zeal is foundational to all leadership and greatness for God. It is essential for helping develop the fruit of the Spirit, character traits, and spiritual gifts. As Paul wrote, "eagerly desire spiritual gifts" (1 Corinthians 14:1).

Zeal is key to overcoming both laziness and lethargy. Zeal for the Lord causes us to go the extra mile and sacrifice our service to the Lord. This type of zeal marked the life and ministry of Yeshua, to whom the disciples applied the verse, "Zeal for your House will consume Me!" (John 2:17; Psalm 69:10).

Joshua was so zealous for the Lord that he "did not depart from the tabernacle" (Exodus 33:11 NKJV). As a young man, Joshua would remain behind in the Tent of Meeting tarrying with the Lord, keeping charge over it, and in all probability assisting those who came to seek God whenever Moses was away. It's a bit shocking to think that Joshua, and not Aaron, the high priest, or one of the chief priests, was charged with this responsibility. It was Joshua's zeal for the Lord that singled him out.

Joshua's Zeal for God's Word

Passion for God's Word consumed Joshua, which translated as a love for *Adonai* Himself. Studying and meditating on the Torah was his lifeblood. Hungry to learn and grow in spiritual wisdom, Joshua's passion and zeal for God's Word set him apart.

In Jewish tradition, Moses secretly wanted one of his sons to succeed him as the next leader of Israel. But according to the rabbis,[3] "God said to Moses, 'The one who guards the fig tree eats the fruit.' Your sons sat idly by and did not study the Torah."[4] Joshua was completely different as a leader. He engrossed himself in the words of the Torah. One reason Joshua did not leave the tent much was that he was busy sitting and studying Torah. He didn't leave what he studied in the tent either. Instead Joshua took it outside where he lived among the people. As Joshua prepared to lead the Children of Israel into the Promised Land, the Lord encouraged him to continue in his love for and devotion to the Word: "This book of the *Torah* should not depart from your mouth—you are to meditate on it day and night, so that you may be careful to do everything written in it. For then you will make your ways prosperous and then you will be successful" (Joshua 1:8). *The Complete Jewish Study Bible* renders this verse a bit differently: "Keep this book of the Torah on your lips and meditate on it day and night." Their commentary on the passage says,

> The phrase "on your lips" refers to the custom of muttering while studying or reflecting. The Hebrew word *hagah*, translated "meditate," literally means to "mutter." When one continually mutters God's Word, one is constantly thinking about it. Meditation is the practical study of the Torah for the purpose of observing it in thought and action, which would be followed by blessings.[5]

God gave this exhortation to Joshua at that moment because leadership is often wearisome. Joshua had to make sure that in all his responsibilities he never lost his zeal for study and meditation on the Word, for it was vital to his success.

Joshua was a true disciple and the example of the disciple par excellence in the Old Testament. Both *talmid*, the Hebrew word for "disciple," as well as the New Testament Greek word *mathetes*, are best translated as "learner." Disciples are learners. You can't be a true intimate lover of God if you are not a lover of His Word. Loving and learning go hand in hand. Great leaders are great learners. Joshua was a committed learner before becoming Israel's leader. His zeal to learn far surpassed that of all others, including Moses' own sons. A passion for learning should always precede the pursuit of leadership. Joshua was the embodiment of this.

Being a learner helped Joshua to trust God in all situations. After assuming leadership from Moses, he most likely stood by the Jordan humbled and afraid. Perhaps he doubted that he was the man to lead the nation and conquer the land. But he knew the Torah. He learned God's promises and knew the Lord never broke them. He didn't know how or when God's plans for the Children of Israel would develop, but he learned to trust God in all things. His study and meditation on God's Word took away the *how* and *when* doubts.

There is another reason the Lord exhorted Joshua more than once to meditate on the Torah day and night. God wanted him to grasp that the battles, temptations, and tests he faced were never only physical. They were, first and foremost, spiritual. God wants us to grasp this too. The ability to face spiritual battles is one reason Rabbi Paul referred to the Word of God as the sword of the Spirit (Ephesians 6:17). If our sword is not sharp, it's nearly impossible to overcome the spiritual, emotional, and physical attacks we face when trying to possess our own personal promised lands. Even Yeshua faced trials and temptations in the wilderness. He overcame them by quoting Scripture to Satan, who was trying to lead Him astray (Matthew 4:10). We will not have the courage, wisdom, or strength to stand and overcome unless we immerse ourselves in Scripture. It is crucial to overcoming and succeeding.

A Change of Name

Joshua's name further exemplifies the truth of being a person of God's Word. At some point around the time when Joshua left with the others to spy out the land of Canaan, Moses had actually changed Joshua's name from Hoshea: "These are the names of the men Moses sent to investigate the land. (Now he gave Hoshea son of Nun, the name Joshua.)" (Numbers 13:16). Moses changed Joshua's name from Hoshea to Yehoshua by adding the Hebrew letter *yud* (י) to the beginning of his name. Why was this particular letter added?

The letter *yud* represents the divine name *Jehovah*, which in Hebrew is spelled *yud-hei-vav-hei* (יהוה). It is common not to write the full name of God out of respect. Instead the four-letter name of God, known as the Tetragrammaton (meaning "four letters"), is abbreviated by writing two letter *yuds* together. The name *Jehovah* is associated with God's covenantal love and faithfulness. Leading is challenging, and adding the letter *yud* to Joshua's name served as a promise that the Lord would always be with Joshua through those challenges.

But of course, there is more. The *yud* also represents God's hand. The name *yud* comes from the Hebrew word *yad*, which means "hand." It was the Lord's hand that delivered Israel from the Egyptians; He'd promised Moses He would redeem Israel "by a mighty hand and by an outstretched arm" (Deuteronomy 5:15 NASB). What's amazing is that the earliest form of Hebrew pictograph of this letter is an arm with a hand.

The only way for Joshua to be successful was for the Lord's hand to work through him and deliver the Canaanites into his hands as God's hand had delivered the Egyptians into the hands of Moses.

Interestingly, at the end of the Torah, Moses called Joshua by his original name: "Moses came and spoke all the words of this song in the ears of the people, he, and Hoshea the son of Nun" (Deuteronomy 32:44 JPS). Why did Moses, right before his passing, suddenly use Joshua's original birth name? It seems strange because throughout the five books of Moses, except for two places, he was called Joshua.

By nature, Joshua seemed to be more of a private and contemplative man. He was happy sitting at the feet of Moses, serving him, and learning God's Word. He loved to sit in the house of God, soaking in the Lord's presence and delving deeper into the depths of Torah. Perhaps Joshua was reticent about the burden of leadership that was about to rest so heavily upon his shoulders.

Perhaps Joshua secretly desired to go back to his old life. Using his old name this one last time, the Lord reminded him where he came from and where he was going. Through Moses, the Lord changed his name to Joshua, which means "the Lord saves." Now he needed more of the strength of the Lord to lead the people successfully.

Moses may have used Joshua's birth name a final time to communicate that the old Joshua had to die and be buried completely. He could no longer be Hoshea but must fully embrace and step into the full meaning of his God-given name, Joshua. He could never go back to being Hoshea, no matter how challenging, stressful, or out of his comfort zone his life might be. His old name was eulogized, remembered one last time before being buried with Moses. He was never to go back to his old way of being, no matter how challenging things became.

Every one of us has the propensity to return to what feels comfortable when things become stressful and overwhelming. Devastated after the crucifixion of Yeshua, Peter and the apostles went fishing (John 21:1–14). They went back to what was familiar. But they caught no fish. The word for "fish" comes from the same Hebrew root for "fear." If we retreat to our old patterns in fear instead of forging forward in faith, our lives will be left as empty as the disciples' nets were that morning. When we faithfully follow the voice of the Lord, however, He fills our nets. After Yeshua had risen, He strolled along the shore of Galilee as Peter and some others were fishing with no success. Unrecognizable to them, He called out that they should cast their nets on the other side. When they reluctantly obeyed and the catch was uncontainable, they knew who He was! Yeshua did for them what they could not do for themselves, which was turn failure and frustration into success.

When God calls us outside our comfort zones, we must guard against going back to our old ways. The Israelites wanted to return to their former lives as slaves. Joshua wished to live a quieter private life, and the disciples went fishing.

The Lord essentially told Joshua, *You must let Hoshea die; you will never be that person ever again. You must step up and into your new name, representing my calling and purpose for your life. You must be zealous, strong, and courageous. I am with you and will empower you and the Children of Israel to conquer the land.* As the Lord promised to be with Joshua, so the Lord promises to be with us: "I will never leave you or forsake you" (Hebrews 13:5), and "Remember! I am with you always, even to the end of the age" (Matthew 28:20). This promise should fill us with zeal and courage to pursue God's promises and purposes for our lives without ever losing heart and wanting to go back to Egypt—the old way of seeing and being, the place of slavery.

Joshua's Zeal to Serve

Another mark of an authentic disciple and leader is that they lead from a place of servanthood. A text called *Bamidbar Rabbah*, a twelfth-century *midrash* (or interpretation)[6] on the book of Numbers, tells us, "Joshua served you faithfully and showed you great honour. It was he who rose early in the morning and remained late at night at your House of Assembly. He used to arrange the benches and spread the mats. Seeing that he has served you with all his might, he is worthy to serve Israel, for he shall not lose his reward."[7]

Joshua spent his time not only studying in "the tent" but also serving

Moses. True leaders do not wait to be asked to help. They see a need and begin to fill it. Like Joshua, they are as zealous to serve in small things as they are in large things. Seeking only an audience of One, they don't do what they do for applause or hopes of promotion, but from their genuine love for the Lord.

Messiah Yeshua was one of the most outstanding examples of what it means to be a servant leader. Often exhausted, He ministered to the multitudes because of His love for the Father and His people. Moved by their pain, He ministered to the poor and wealthy alike with the same zeal. No respecter of persons, yet respecting all persons, Yeshua was passionate about serving. Concerning Himself, He said:

- "Even the Son of Man did not come to be served, but to serve, and to give his life as a ransom for many" (Mark 10:45 NIV).
- "I have come down from heaven not to do my will but to do the will of him who sent me" (John 6:38 NIV).
- "Who is greater, the one who is at the table or the one who serves? Is it not the one who is at the table? But I am among you as one who serves" (Luke 22:27 NIV).

Yeshua was teaching us about genuine servant leaders. They do not seek to be served. Their goal is to serve others. They seek the Father's will, not their own, and they don't overtly promote themselves.

If we are truly Yeshua's disciples, we must strive to be like Him.

Like Joshua, Yeshua was just as zealous—even more so—to minister to the nobodies. We should be as well. I like how *The Message* puts it: "God deliberately chose men and women that the culture overlooks and exploits and abuses, chose these 'nobodies' to expose the hollow pretensions of the 'somebodies'" (1 Corinthians 1:28). Yeshua loved serving and ministering as much to one individual as to the multitude. God is all about the "ones," and every person is valuable to Him.

There is another important insight to be learned as we read about Joshua and service. When we are faithful in the small things, God will trust us with more. Joshua began by arranging benches, but this is what prepared him to replace Moses as the leader of Israel. Yeshua sought the Lord and was willing to serve in secret. It was His willingness to serve in the small things and sacrifice for others that played a compelling role in His exaltation:

> Have this attitude in yourselves, which also was in Messiah Yeshua,
>
> Who, though existing in the form of God,
>
> did not consider being equal to God a thing to be grasped.
>
> But He emptied Himself—
>
> taking on the form of a slave,
>
> becoming the likeness of men
>
> He humbled Himself—
>
> becoming obedient to the point of death,
>
> even death on a cross.
>
> For this reason God highly exalted Him. (Philippians 2:5–9)

This should be the song of all our hearts if we truly want to be great like Joshua and Yeshua.

Zeal in the New Testament

Zeal also marked the life and ministry of Yeshua, of whom the disciples applied the verse, "Zeal for your House will consume me!" (John 2:17; Psalm

69:10). The disciples also had incredible zeal. We can see their zeal as they continued to boldly proclaim the Gospel of good news despite persecution, imprisonment, and beatings:

> They called them in and ordered them not to speak or teach at all in the name of *Yeshua*. But Peter and John replied, "Whether it is right in the sight of God to listen to you rather than to God, you decide. For we cannot stop speaking about what we have seen and heard." (Acts 4:18–20)

> When they had brought them, they placed them before the Sanhedrin. The *kohen gadol* [High Priests] questioned them, saying, "We gave you strict orders not to teach in this name—and look, you have filled Jerusalem with your teaching, and you intend to bring on us the blood of this Man!"
> Peter and the emissaries replied, "We must obey God rather than men...."
> [The Sanhedrin] called in the emissaries, flogged them, ordered them not to continue speaking in the name of *Yeshua*, and let them go.
> So they left the presence of the Sanhedrin, rejoicing that they were considered worthy to be dishonored on account of His name. And every day, in the Temple and from house to house, they never stopped teaching and proclaiming *Yeshua* as the Messiah. (Acts 5:27–29, 40–42)

Even the disciples of the disciples had this same type of zeal for the Word. James and the elders of the messianic Jerusalem community (the Jerusalem church) said to Paul, "You see, brother, how many myriads there are among the Jewish people who have believed—and they are all zealous for the *Torah*" (Acts 21:20).

Most people are zealous for something. Some people are zealous for their favorite sports teams. They are willing to paint their bodies, sit for hours in the heat or in freezing cold, and devote countless hours to cheering on their team. Others are zealous for their family. They are willing to make any sacrifice. Still, some burn with zeal to be successful in their careers. There is nothing inherently wrong with any of the above, as long as we have even more zeal for the Lord. We need to ask ourselves, *Am I consumed with zeal for the Lord like Yeshua and Joshua?*

A Note from Kathie

After Moses' death on Mount Nebo, his faithful follower Joshua was named the new leader of the Hebrews and called to lead the charge to conquer Canaan, the "land flowing with milk and honey" God had promised Abram centuries before (Exodus 3:8). Not coincidentally, Joshua was about eighty years old at this time, the same age Moses was when the Lord met him at the burning bush.[8]

I'm nowhere near eighty yet, but I find great comfort in these stories of God's incredible faithfulness to fulfill His promises, even using people well past their prime to accomplish them.

It's equally thrilling that He chose the very young as well, as He did many centuries later with a betrothed, barely teenage girl from Nazareth.

five

MARY

Rabbi Jason

Fifteen hundred years later, God would choose perhaps His most unlikely vessel to set into motion the salvation of mankind: a teenage girl named Mary.

Her Hebrew name was Miriam, and she was a young Jewish girl of the tribe of Judah. A descendant of David, and a virgin herself, she was betrothed to a carpenter named Joseph (Isaiah 7:14; Matthew 13:55). Both were poor (Leviticus 12:8; Luke 2:24).

One ordinary day, while Mary was living in the village of Nazareth, God sent the angel Gabriel to pay her a visit.

Coming to her, the angel said, "*Shalom*, favored one! ADONAI is with you." But at the message, she was perplexed and kept wondering what kind of greeting this might be. The angel spoke to her, "Do not be afraid, Miriam, for you have found favor with God. Behold, you will become pregnant and give birth to a son, and you shall call His name *Yeshua*. He will be great and will be called *Ben-Elyon* [Son of God]. ADONAI *Elohim* will give Him the throne of David, His father. He shall reign over the house of Jacob for all eternity, and His kingdom will be without end."

Miriam said to the angel, "How can this be, since I am not intimate with a man?"

And responding, the angel said to her, "The *Ruach ha-Kodesh* [Holy Spirit] will come upon you, and the power of *Elyon* [God Most High] will overshadow you. Therefore, the Holy One being born will be called *Ben-Elohim* [Son of God]. Behold, even your relative Elizabeth has conceived a son in her old age; and the one who was called barren is six months pregnant. For nothing will be impossible with God."

So Miriam said, "Behold, the servant of ADONAI. Let it be done to me according to your word." And the angel left her. (Luke 1:28–38)

What About the Wedding?

Mary thought she was waiting for a wedding, but something came to her that was far different—an improbable event she never would have dreamed of. A holy interruption.

In ancient Jewish practice, girls were typically engaged around twelve or thirteen and then married at the end of a one-year betrothal period. The couple's parents arranged the betrothal, which was "a more binding arrangement than our modern-day engagement."[1] Truly, "only death or divorce could break the betrothal commitment."[2] During the year, the couple lived separately without having sexual relations. The young woman would prove her purity, while the young man prepared their future home.

It's easy to understand Mary's dilemma. At the time she was to demonstrate her wholesomeness, an angel gave her the news that she was going to have a baby.

Mary's Humility

Much about Mary and her relationship with God is revealed when we read about her response to the angel. Imagine a bright, glowing angel showing up at your bedside or in your living room and announcing, "You have found favor with God." Isn't that something we all long to hear? Along with, "Well done, good and faithful servant!" (Matthew 25:21). I'm sure those words caused Mary's spirit to leap within her. But look at her response. Author and pastor Warren Wiersbe wrote this:

> Mary's response reveals her humility and honesty before God. She certainly never expected to see an angel and receive special favors from heaven. There was nothing unique about her that such things should happen. If she had been different from other Jewish girls, as some theologians claim she was, then she might have said, "Well, it's about time! I've been expecting you!" No, all of this was a surprise to her.[3]

Mary showed tremendous humility of heart considering everything that was happening to her—things that would cause many to get puffed up. We find this same humble quality in Yeshua.

> Who, though existing in the form of God, did not consider being equal to God a thing to be grasped. But He emptied Himself—taking on the form of a slave, becoming the likeness of men and being found in appearance as a man. *He humbled Himself—becoming obedient to the point of death,* even death on a cross. For this reason God highly exalted Him and gave Him the name that is above every name. (Philippians 2:6–9, emphasis added)

In this passage we see that equality with God was not something Yeshua clung to, even though He had every right to do so. He was deity in flesh. Instead He offered up His divine privileges and took the humble position of a servant. Yeshua made the ultimate sacrifice, leaving the unspeakable riches and position of His home in heaven to come to earth for you and me, not just to experience life as we know it, but to suffer and die in our place. Our minds can't wrap around even a microscopic fraction of what that entails.

Humility is also receiving. Probably understanding some, though not all, of the misunderstanding and scorn that would surely come, Mary embraced God's new vision for her life without complaining or sarcasm.

God requires faith, but "nothing stirs God's heart more than a humble heart and a merciful spirit," as former New York gang member Nicky Cruz wrote.[4] "God resists the proud, but gives grace to the humble" (1 Peter 5:5 NKJV). You want God's grace? Become humble. Mary was humble in spirit.

Humility allows those greater than we are to do what God has called them to do. As John the Baptist, *Yochanan HaMatbil* in Hebrew, said concerning Yeshua, the *Mashiach* (*Messiah* in Hebrew), "He must increase, while I must decrease" (John 3:30). Being willing to decrease so that others can increase is the essence of humility. It's important to note, however, that I'm not talking about self-abasing. A truly humble person is secure and confident in God's love. They know who they are. Those who are insecure may put themselves down a lot, but it's because they are focusing on themselves too much. Genuine humility is not thinking less of ourselves. It's thinking of ourselves less. Nowhere in Scripture do we see that Mary tried to be greater than her Son. She didn't stand in His way but let Him increase as God opened the door for His ministry on earth.

It also takes humility for us to be completely transparent before others, allowing them to speak into our lives, encourage us, sharpen us if needed, and help us in our own journeys. Notice that when the angel ended his time with Mary, he said, "Nothing will be impossible with God" (Luke 1:37). Mary needed to be transparent to receive that word and then live by it.

Just as God metaphorically gave Abraham, Sarah, Moses, and Joshua songs to sing, He put a song in Mary too. Luke 1:46–56 records how Mary humbly bowed her head and worshiped God. This passage is often referred to as Mary's Magnificat, or the Song of Mary. In it, she genuinely and lovingly magnifies the Lord. In verses 46 and 47, we find the key to Mary's humility. "My soul magnifies the Lord, and my spirit has rejoiced in God my Savior" (NKJV). Notice whom Mary magnified and how she referred to Him—God and Savior. R. Kent Hughes, author and former senior pastor of College Church in Wheaton, Illinois, wrote, "Magnifying the Lord, making great the Lord with our entire spirit and soul—that is what God desires in our lives today."[5] Charles Spurgeon understood this, as his own experience of complete enjoyment testified: "I like, sometimes, to leave off praying and singing, and to sit still, and just gaze upward till my inmost soul has seen my Lord; then I say, 'He is inexpressively lovely; yea he is altogether lovely.'"[6]

Another aspect of humility is kindness. It's difficult to be proud and be full of compassion and kindness because the proud are focused primarily on themselves. There's a difference between being nice and being kind. "Niceness" is being polite and treating others with decency. "Kindness" kicks it up a notch. It's when you feel for others and demonstrate it through your actions. In Jewish thought, water is associated with kindness (the Hebrew word chesed is often translated as "lovingkindness" in the Bible). When Jewish people think of kindness and water (mar in Hebrew), they often think of Miriam, Moses' sister (as we mentioned, Mary's name in Hebrew is Miriam).

Miriam is associated with kindness because of her special acts in serving as a midwife. She devoted herself to the needs of her people and spared many infants from the evil decrees of Pharaoh.[7]

Her connection with water includes saving Moses at the Nile (Exodus 2:4, 7–9), leading worship and singing praises after the Children of Israel crossed the Red Sea (Exodus 15:20–21), and providing water for the traveling people from a wilderness spring named "the well of Miriam" (Exodus 17:6).

In John 2 we find a story involving Mary and water as well, in Yeshua's first miracle, which teaches us more about Mary's humility.

The story unfolds with Mary and Yeshua at a wedding celebration where the host has run out of wine—an embarrassing situation. Mary saw the need (as Moses' sister Miriam did with the midwives) and went to Yeshua for help. She boldly told the servants, "Do whatever He tells you" (John 2:5). Yeshua instructed the servants to fill six large pots with water, and then He turned the water into incredible wine.

Water into wine was an amazing miracle, but our lesson from Mary is her boldness, or *chutzpah*. What is *chutzpah*? It's "holy boldness, audacity." Mary and Miriam both teach us that we cannot accomplish anything great without faith and *chutzpah*.

One night I had a dream that I was standing at a movie premiere in Hollywood. There were two giant spotlights in the sky, and the next thing I knew, those lights were turned toward me, and I became blinded. So I asked that the lights would be turned back toward the sky.

I felt God say to me, *If you remain small in your own sight, you will remain great in Mine. If you become big in your own sight, you will become small on your own.*

If you try to take the glory and shine it on yourself, you will become blinded. If you keep your eyes fixed on God, however, and keep the light turned upward, you will know humility and be successful. It is the reason God chose Moses—he was the humblest man in all the earth (Numbers 12:3), both meek and humble. It was the reason He chose Mary. Meekness is not weakness; it is power under restraint.

Faith, *chutzpah*, and humility together lead to God's favor. To walk in our divine assignments and sing our unique songs, we will need to seek God's presence, understanding that He is the source of favor to open the doors that only He can open—doors that no man can shut. With both Miriam and Mary, they by themselves could not alone do what needed to be done. We need to constantly remind ourselves that we are the same. We cannot fulfill our divine assignments on our own. It is God's favor that opens doors, and that favor often comes in the form of a person helping us reach the next level or just get across the ditch. Two are better than one because if either of them falls, one can help the other up (Ecclesiastes 4:9–12).

Humility is not weakness. It's knowing that you are in God's control and, when the situation calls for it—whether your brother needs saving or the wedding needs wine—having the *chutzpah* to do what God has asked you to do.

The smaller we make ourselves, the bigger we make God.

Mary's Obedience

Upon the angel's visit, Mary immediately obeyed God's will in her life. She said, "Behold the servant of ADONAI. Let it be done to me according to your word" (Luke 1:38). Despite the shock of the encounter with the angel, Mary was not afraid to ask questions; however, before the angel departed, she chose obedience.

Think of what obedience meant to this young girl. She needed to confront Joseph and risk a divorce. She had to face her neighbors, whose imaginations must have run wild. She had to confront her parents and Joseph's parents. But through all this confrontation and gossip, she was able to cling to the angel's promise to her and to Joseph's loyalty to her after his own angelic visit (Matthew 1:18–25). She remained obedient to God's calling on her life.

I find it interesting that Mary obeyed without hesitation. Responding immediately and affirmatively to the Lord, she needed no time for deliberation. Obedience was her delight. Looking back at the times God has called me to do something, I have to ask, *Did I react like Mary?* Not all the time. There were moments of hesitation. I wonder what blessings from God I lost. Is slow obedience disobedience?

Mary obeyed without any selfish motives, looking to the future and what God would do in her life. She didn't know *how*, and she didn't know *when*, yet she didn't try to figure everything out. Commenting on Mary's obedience, Anglican commentator William Barclay wrote, "Mary's submission is a very lovely thing. 'Whatever God says, I accept.' Mary had learned to forget the world's commonest prayer—'Your will be *changed*'—and to pray the world's greatest prayer—'Your will be *done*.'"[8]

Today we often regard obedience as a weakness. We feel we need to assert ourselves within the freedom to be "me." Mary's example should correct our thinking. She is a beautiful model of obedience. Mary joyfully accepted the will of the Father (Luke 1:46–56). In Scripture we can almost see that His will became her will. She willingly yielded to what God wanted for her instead of fighting for her self-defined life direction. Author and speaker Janet Chester Bly wrote about Mary, "Few in biblical history exhibit such immediate obedience and complete trust in God."[9]

Mary's Patience

Instant gratification and impatience have become the culture's norm. "Faster is better" is its mantra. We want what we want, and we want it yesterday—faster phones, faster networks, faster weight loss, and fast food. God forbid we get stuck in line somewhere for more than five minutes! Unfortunately, because of our internet-paced living, people and relationships become casualties. But this is not God's way. We know the passage by heart: "Love is patient, love is kind . . ." (1 Corinthians 13:4). Just as we saw that one can't be proud and have loving-kindness, it's also impossible to have loving-kindness without patience. The two go hand in hand. When we study Mary, we find she was not only a humble and obedient woman, but she also had remarkable patience.

The Hebrew word for "patience" is *savlanut*, which has the same root as the words for "burdens" (*sivlot*) and "porter" (*sabbal*).[10] "Patience can therefore be understood as the ability to carry a burden. That burden can often be time, or the burden of waiting."[11] We feel stretched for time; we hate waiting on a delayed flight or even for a file to download. We refuse to carry the burden.

One of the foremost characteristics of the great men and women of faith was patience. Abraham waited twenty-five years for the son of promise! Moses spent forty years in the desert before God called him. When God calls us or gives us a promise, we often think it's going to be *right now*! But God's view of time is different from ours. Mary, too, was a person with patience.

The word "longsuffering" is often associated with patience. While it has a similar meaning, longsuffering has to do with the longevity of patience. It's patience with plenty of persistence. Peter reassured us that the Lord is "longsuffering toward us, not willing that any should perish" (2 Peter 3:9 NKJV). Mary was patient and longsuffering, as we'll discover below.

Why are these qualities so important for us? If we don't learn to be longsuffering and patient, we will never be able to foster growth and transformation in our lives. It takes time to grow, and time connects directly to patience. If we don't learn to be patient, we will become angry, critical, and judgmental, and we won't be able to give God's love.

Here's a God-story. We saw earlier that Mary's Hebrew name was Miriam. The woman I married is named Miriam, too, and just as Miriam in the Bible was longsuffering, so is the woman I married. My Miriam is a well-known worship leader for Hillsong. For years while she was serving the Lord, she didn't chase after a dating relationship but did want to find her soul mate. She waited faithfully, and time seemed to be running out. One day, while doing some routine cleaning, Miriam was inwardly crying out to God. Listen to her own words.

I prayed, *God, your will be done, and help me to laugh, whatever your will is.* I just knew my prayer, whatever I'd cried, went straight to the throne room. Then I kind of forgot about it, wiped my eyes, and went back to doing what I was doing. A couple of hours later, as I was just going about my day, I heard the word "longsuffering." It was like someone spoke it directly into my ears. I stood there going, "Wow, wow, wow!" I hadn't expected that. God bypassed my mind and spoke straight in my spirit, louder than my mind and very, very clearly. I literally heard His voice, audibly, but not with my natural ears, louder than my natural ears—just louder.

God had told her not to be discouraged, that she needed longsuffering and patience in waiting for the promise. But God is amazingly even more specific than we sometimes think. Many years later, God brought Miriam and me together, and Miriam found out that my last name, Sobel, in Hebrew means "longsuffering." God knew her heart's desire and gave her His word for a promise.

Young Mary understood longsuffering and patience as well. She waited nine months for the birth of Yeshua, and nothing different happened. After He was born, He didn't fly around the manger or walk through walls. Not long after, however, Mary witnessed a remarkable and confirming event.

Because they followed the Torah, Joseph and Mary brought Yeshua to the temple to fulfill obligations of Jewish parents (traditionally done thirty days after the child's birth). They brought Him for two reasons: First, to ceremonially cleanse the mother with the proper sacrifices (Leviticus 12:1–8). Second, for the redemption of the firstborn son (*pidyon ha'ben*) ritual (Exodus 22:28–29).

In accordance with ancient tradition, the young couple placed their son in the arms of the priest who asked the relevant questions about their desire to redeem their boy. As the shekels were exchanged, the Cohen [priest] would "bless God" with the traditional blessings. Yosef [Joseph] and Miryam [Mary] were amazed as they heard the priest add a few of his own prophetic comments inspired by the *Ruakh HaKodesh* [Holy Spirit]. This son would be yeshu'ah (a word play on the name "Yeshua"), salvation for many in Israel as well as a light to non-Jews.[12]

We can read about this encounter in Luke 2:25–33. The Holy Spirit had revealed to a priest named Simeon that he would not die before seeing the Messiah. When Mary and Joseph brought Yeshua to the temple, Simeon blessed Him, saying, "Now may You let Your servant go in peace, O Sovereign Master, according to Your word. For my eyes have seen Your salvation, which You have prepared in the presence of all peoples; 'A light of revelation to the nations' and the glory of Your people Israel" (Luke 2:29–32).

Both Mary and Joseph marveled at the things that were said about their Son (Luke 2:33). Mary's trust and patience were confirmed by Simeon's declaration about the newborn Yeshua.

It would be a long twelve years, though, before Mary could witness even a small part of her Son's ministry. Mary and Joseph were raising Yeshua by the Torah and regularly participated in the required festivals (Luke 2:39). Beginning at Luke 2:41, we find a twelve-year-old Yeshua fulfilling the journey to Jerusalem to observe the festivals—in this case, Passover. Yeshua showed His desire to serve God. Unbeknownst to his parents, who had already left on the journey home, He spent three full days in the temple, discussing the Torah with the rabbis (Luke 2:43–50).

A critical passage speaks once again to Mary's patience after the three days, when Mary and Joseph found their Son.

> When His parents saw *Yeshua*, they were overwhelmed. And His mother said to Him, "Child, why did you do this to us? Look! Your father and I were searching for You frantically!"
>
> He said to them, "Why were you searching for Me? Didn't you know that I must be about the things of My Father?" But they did not grasp the message He was telling them. (Luke 2:48–50)

After this remarkable event at the temple, we don't find Mary rushing Yeshua into ministry. Instead she waited for God's leading. She remained patient for God's promises to come to pass in God's own time. There is danger in trying to force God's promises and speed up the process. As we learned with Sarah and Hagar, it's never good to try to take matters into our own hands. Mary understood the God of the How and When, and she lived with a patient heart.

While the Bible doesn't give us many clues about Yeshua from ages twelve to thirty, we can assume He lived in Nazareth with Mary. Many suppose that Joseph, Yeshua's father, died sometime during these years. While he and Mary did have other children, and Yeshua learned a trade from him, Joseph probably didn't see his Son go into public ministry. With Joseph's death, Mary became a single mom raising not only Yeshua but also her other children alone. Here again we find Mary's longsuffering quality. She didn't know when her Son would go into what God called Him to do. She had to wait.

Finally Yeshua's ministry began. He was victorious over Satan's attempts to derail Him from what God had called Him to do. After His time in the wilderness, Yeshua returned to Galilee with great spiritual power and began to teach (Luke 4:14). While the people spurned Him, Mary knew her Son would be leaving home, and she would need to draw upon her patience. The same way David of old had encouraged himself in the Lord, she perhaps remembered those early years when the angel spoke and she miraculously conceived, and when John the Baptist leaped inside Elizabeth's womb. During seasons of patient waiting, it is important for us, as well, to remember what God has done—the words He has spoken.

Mary had to watch her Son be rejected by Jewish leaders and people. He was disrespected in His hometown (Mark 6:4). While she did not always follow her Son in His travels, Mary sometimes heard Him preach, and she may have been in the synagogue when Yeshua read Isaiah's prophecy (Luke 4:18–30). She observed the harsh hostility of her fellow citizens who drove Yeshua from the temple. She went with Him to the wedding feast at Cana, and it's there we find her complete faith in her Son when she told the servants, "Do whatever He tells you" (John 2:5). Witnessing that criticism must have been difficult for Mary, but her patience and longsuffering spirit kept her eyes focused on God's plan, not hers.

The most extended wait of Mary's life was the three days after Yeshua's crucifixion. I can't imagine the agony of seeing her Son on that cross. But Mary was patient. She knew her Son's teaching deeply. Mary knew He was a unique child of God. She knew He was Messiah. She knew God's promises concerning her Son, so she waited.

Mary clung to God's promises. She trusted Him with the how and the when. Yeshua's mother bore God's only Son and had no idea what lay ahead in the future for this precious little child. She watched Him grow and learn. She saw Him discuss the Torah with the rabbis, and she saw Him leave to embark on the most extraordinary three years of anyone's life.

Mary, Sarah, and the Role of Women

It must have been a shocker for Mary to be told that as a virgin she would conceive the Messiah by the Holy Spirit. Mary's supernatural conception was unique, and it was tied to an ancient promise. The first direct messianic prophecy or promise in the Bible is found in Genesis 3:15. Eve, the first woman, set the Fall in motion, but it would be through the woman that the hope of redemption would be birthed. "I will put animosity between you and the woman—between your seed and her seed."

What is fascinating about this messianic promise is that women don't have any seed. Throughout the Bible, except for this passage, seed is associated with men, as in the "seed of Abraham" (Psalm 105:6; John 8:33, 37), "the seed of Jacob" (Jeremiah 33:26 KJV), and "the seed of David" (1 Kings 11:39 KJV). By referring to the Messiah as the seed of the woman, this passage alludes to a mystery that would later be revealed in more detail in Isaiah 7:14: "Behold, the virgin will conceive. When she is giving birth to a son, she will call his name Immanuel."

But there is more! Sarah, who is both the mother of faith and the matriarch of Israel, also supernaturally conceived, for it is impossible for a woman of ninety to bear a child. The Lord performed a miracle, according to Jewish tradition, supernaturally renewing Sarah internally so she could conceive and bear a son. What the Lord did for Mary was an even greater miracle, though. Never before and never since has a virgin conceived. But not only Sarah struggled with being barren; so did Rebekah and Rachel.

What is the connection between all these great women of faith? In all these cases, the Lord wanted to demonstrate that only He could fulfill and bring about the line of the promised "seed of the woman." The bigger lesson for all of us is how the Lord has the power to transform our barrenness into birthing. No matter how long you have struggled to birth your promise or how improbable it might seem, nothing is impossible with God! If you believe, you can conceive and receive His promise. What the Lord did for Mary and the matriarchs He can do for you. In the same way that only the Lord could bring about the promise of the seed, you must depend on the Lord to do what no one else can do for you!

Mary's giving birth to the promised Seed also points to another important truth: God always intended women to play a central role in His plan of redemption. The most defining spiritual event in the history of the Jewish people was the exodus from Egypt. Jewish tradition says that Israel was redeemed from slavery because of righteous women.[13] This makes a lot of sense. Women played a critical role in the book of Exodus and the Passover story. It was the midwives who risked their lives by lying to Pharaoh to save Jewish baby boys. Moses' mom risked her life and her family member's lives

THE GOD OF THE WAY

to hide Moses for three months. Miriam, his sister, placed the baby Moses in the Nile and watched over him until he was safe. Pharaoh's daughter seemingly defied her father's orders by rescuing Moses and raising him as her own son. Without these godly women of faith, Israel never would have survived, let alone left Egypt!

In the New Testament, women also play a crucial role. Mary the mother of Yeshua was named after Moses' sister. Again, Mary's biblical name was Miriam in Hebrew. Her name was changed as the Bible was translated into Latin and then English. Mary is the New Testament Miriam who is called to watch over and protect the baby Yeshua in the same way Moses' sister watched over Moses. It was Mary who caused Yeshua to perform His first miracle of turning water into wine.

Yeshua elevated everyone around Him, including women. He valued them. Think of His interactions with the Samaritan woman, the woman caught in adultery, and Mary Magdalene. He chose each of them to play key roles. Women were the key supporters of Yeshua's ministry. All of Yeshua's male disciples, apart from John, abandoned Yeshua while He hung on the cross. Only the women remained with Him and risked their lives to be with Him until the end. It was Mary Magdalene who found the empty tomb, encountered an "angel of ADONAI" who told her that Yeshua had risen (Matthew 28:2), and became the first to proclaim the good news on that first Resurrection Sunday!

In the same way, women must be valued and empowered in the body of Messiah today. Women have a critical role to play in the church. We must encourage women to use their God-given spiritual and natural gifts for the Kingdom! If we fail to do so, we fail to follow in the footsteps of Yeshua.

We can learn so much from Mary—humility, obedience, and patience. But perhaps Cora Jakes Coleman, in her introduction to Sarah Jakes's book

Dear Mary: Lessons from the Mother of Jesus for the Modern Mom, summed up best all that Mary taught us:

> Your ability to allow God to bless you with something indescribable later gave us the ability to receive and understand indescribable blessings. As women, we now seek the impossible because you had the faith to birth the One who makes all things possible in an impossible way. A mother's love is indescribable, but a mother's sacrifice is priceless. You lovingly raised your child, preparing Him for His assignment of bringing salvation to the world, knowing fully that it would break your heart. . . . You taught us that mothering is not about us, but rather about guiding and nurturing our children so they are able to walk in God's chosen purpose for their lives.[14]

Oh, God of the How and When, only You know how, only You know when.

A Note from Kathie

Mary was most likely a young teenage girl when the angel Gabriel visited her in Nazareth with a startling message: she had been chosen by God to give birth to the long-awaited Messiah, whom the prophets had foretold for centuries.

In Isaiah 7:14 we are told that a "virgin will conceive and give birth" to this Redeemer of the world (NIV). The fact that this young peasant girl's response to the angel was, "I am the Lord's servant. Let it be unto me as you have said" is astonishing to me (Luke 1:38, paraphrase)!

She—like Abraham and Sarah and Moses and Joshua before

her—was willing to give up everything she knew and depended on to obey the calling of God in her life to journey into an unknown future.

When we *believe*, miracles abound.

Part Two

THE GOD OF HIS WORD

Kathie

My passion for understanding the Scriptures is rooted in my desire to know what the Hebrew in the Old Testament and the Greek in the New Testament *actually say*. Too much damage has been done over the centuries by the erosion of the source texts by sloppy and misleading translations.

Psalm 18:30 says, "As for God, His way is perfect; the word of the LORD is flawless" (BSB).

But that applies only to the original words the authors used. So, as I've grown in my knowledge and understanding of the Scriptures through decades of study and rabbinical trips to the Holy Land to deepen my experience, I've grown ever more passionate to pass along what many teachers, who have vastly more knowledge and insight than I do, have shared with me. For example, take the startling declaration in John 1:1 and all it truly means.

The apostle John began his gospel by revealing to us, "In the beginning was the Word, and the Word was with God, and the Word was God" (NKJV).

John was stating that Jesus was not only with God at the beginning of

Creation but also created all things. Genesis 1:26 refers to the plurality of God at Creation as well when it says, "Let Us make man in Our image, after Our likeness! Let them rule over the fish of the sea, over the flying creatures of the sky, over the livestock, over the whole earth, and over every crawling creature that crawls on the land."

This is profound in every way. Together Jehovah God (Adonai), Jesus (His only begotten Son), and the Holy Spirit (the *Ruach*, or "breath" of God) all worked together to bring all things to pass and still work together to sustain all things.

John 1:14 continues with more eye-popping revelations. "The Word become flesh and dwelt among us" (ESV). The Word who spoke all of creation into existence is the same Word who followed the will of His Father to come to earth in human form and be born to a virginal teenage peasant girl in order to provide the ultimate sacrifice of His blood for the salvation of all of humankind.

Who among us can even begin to fathom the depth of the mystery of such a cosmic event? Only the Creator Himself. But the Bible tells us in John 14:7–9 that Jesus is the reflection of the face of the Father. When we see Jesus, we literally see God incarnate.

Jesus, the Rabbi, walked the earth He created so He could teach us how to walk in this world as He did. He promised us that if we believed in Him and the One who sent Him, we, too, could do all things in His name. We, too, could learn how to truly love and truly forgive. We, too, could have the strength to carry our own cross and to sacrifice our own will for the Father's.

And ultimately, because of Jesus' death, we, too, could be resurrected into eternal life with our Creator.

I am stunned by God's grace, overwhelmed by His incomprehensible love for me, because I know I don't deserve it. Isaiah 64:6 tells us that our righteousness is like filthy rags. The Hebrew word for "filthy rags" refers to menstrual rags. Being a woman, I am completely familiar with what that means.

But the Bible also tells us in Isaiah 1:18 that Jesus has forgiven us of all unrighteousness and made us as white as snow—completely new creatures.

I don't worship a God I have to visit in a building once a week. No, in Him I "live and move and have [my] being" (Acts 17:28 NIV).

Every second of every hour of every day of my existence, He is the giver of "every good gift and every perfect gift" and the lover of my very soul (James 1:17).

Jehovah Elohim is Hebrew for God, the Creator. He created us in His image; therefore, we are created to become cocreators with Him.

God put Adam and Eve in the Garden of Eden to work after His work was finished and to have dominion over everything God had entrusted to them. That truth has *never changed*. You and I were also created to cocreate with *Jehovah Elohim*! Our work should still reflect our relationship with the living God we worship—the Holy (*Kadosh*) God but also Abba Father, the loving and compassionate God who longs to protect and guide His children into all blessing.

six

JEHOVAH ELOHIM: CREATOR GOD OF EVERYTHING WE SEE

Rabbi Jason

Being around creative people lights my fire. Painters, actors, singers, and musicians, to name a few, use their gifts to reach deeply into our emotions, touching those hidden spots within our souls, causing us to cry, laugh, and remember. They inspire me. They encourage the world.

As a small child, renowned composer and conductor Leonard Bernstein wasn't interested in music until his aunt gave her piano to his family. When Leonard sat down at the keys, things just clicked. With a natural ear for music, he could hear a song on the radio and immediately recite the tune on the piano. It was a rare gift.

Leonard Bernstein was a creator. He wrote several musicals, including his most famous *West Side Story* (1957), and he conducted world-famous symphonies for which he won countless awards and accolades. But nothing he created compared to the works of God.[1]

There are two primary names for God in the Creation account. The first is *Elohim*. "In the beginning [*Elohim*] created the heavens and the earth" (Genesis 1:1). In Jewish thought, *Elohim* is associated with God as the Creator who providentially cares for His creation. As the Maker and Master of the universe, *Elohim* is revealed in and through nature. "The heavens declare the glory of God [*El*, which is the singular form of *Elohim*]," wrote the psalmist, "and the sky shows His handiwork" (Psalm 19:2). He is the all-powerful God who exercises complete authority over all creation.

Elohim is also associated with God's attribute of strict justice, or *middat hadin* in Hebrew. *Elohim* is both the First Cause of Creation and the Supreme Judge and Ruler of the universe. Initially God wanted to create the world according to strict justice but knew the world wouldn't be able to endure it. The divine attribute of strict justice, *middat hadin*, is connected to God holding the world accountable and judging people according to His general revelation in creation and special revelation in Scripture. For this reason, *Elohim* is the name of God used in the account of the giving of the Ten Commandments (Exodus 20). Judgment is the natural result when God withdraws His grace and kindness and allows people to reap what they sow. When God's divine quality of strict justice deals with a person or nation, measure for measure, that person experiences the expected consequences for their actions apart from God's attribute of mercy.

The Powerful Name of God

The Hebrew word for "name" most often means "sign" or "distinctive mark." It's the idea that a person's name carries with it the nature of the person, describing their essential character. For example, "'Noah' means 'one who brings relief and comfort' (Genesis 5:29); 'Jesus' means 'savior' (Matthew 1:21)."[2]

Elohim derives from the Hebrew word *El*, which can mean "power" or "might." For example, we find its use in Genesis 31:29 when Laban confronted Jacob, saying, "It is in the power [*b'el*] of my hand to do evil with you." *Elohim* describes God as an all-powerful Omnipotent One who has absolute power and control over everything. This thought is underscored because, in the alphanumeric nature of the Hebrew alphabet, both *Elohim* and *hateva* (nature) have the same numerical value of 86 in their letters.[3] *Elohim*/86 is the One who created and has complete power over all creation (nature/*hateva*/86).

One Bible encyclopedia says, "*Elohim* is best understood as expressing intensity. God makes himself known by this name as the Lord of intense and extensive glory and richness as he exercises his preeminence and power in the created cosmos."[4]

There is another significant connection between *Elohim*/God/86 and nature/*hateva*/86. The Ten Commandments state, "I am the LORD your God. . . . You shall have no other gods before me" (Exodus 20:2–3 NIV). Strangely, the word used for "other gods" in this verse is also *elohim*. This doesn't seem to make sense until one understands that those who worshiped idols in biblical times ascribed divinity and power to them (connected to the *El* and *Elohim*/86) of nature/*hateva*/86.

At the root of all this is the numerical connection between nature and God. The power/86 of God/86 is concealed in creation, nature/86! Creation demonstrates the power and goodness of God our Creator, but sin impacted the ability to distinguish between the Creator and the creation. As Paul wrote,

The wrath of God is revealed from heaven against all ungodliness and unrighteousness of men. In unrighteousness they suppress the truth, because what can be known about God is plain to them—for God has shown it to them. His invisible attributes—His eternal power and His divine nature—have been clearly seen ever since the creation of the world, being understood through the things that have been made. So people are without excuse—for even though they knew God, they did not glorify Him as God or give Him thanks. Instead, their thinking became futile, and their senseless hearts were made dark. Claiming to be wise, they became fools. They exchanged the glory of the immortal God for an image in the form of mortal man and birds and four-footed beasts and creeping things. (Romans 1:18–23)

Here again, there's a connection between the name *Elohim*, God as Creator, and God as Judge, as Paul related in the above passage. In Jewish thought, *Elohim* represents God's attribute of justice, and *YHVH/Jehovah/* Lord represents His attribute of mercy and kindness.

Jehovah, YHVH, and the LORD

The second name of God found in the Creation account is *YHVH*. Christians often translate this name as *Jehovah*: "These are the genealogical records of the heavens and the earth when they were created, at the time when ADONAI *Elohim* [Lord God, or *Jehovah Elohim*] made land and sky" (Genesis 2:4). *YHVH*, or *Jehovah*, is the personal covenantal name of God. *Jehovah/YHVH*, or *Adonai*, as Jews translate and pronounce the divine name, portrays God's relational and personal or emotional aspects. It is not *Elohim* but *Jehovah Elohim* who created humanity because *Jehovah/YHVH* is God revealed and personally encountered throughout history.

It is Jehovah who established and entered a covenant with the Children of Israel at Mount Sinai: "ADONAI [the Lord] came down onto Mount Sinai"

(Exodus 19:20). It is primarily by the name *Jehovah* that God lovingly involves Himself in the lives of His people.

Jehovah also points to God as the Redeemer. When God appeared to Moses in the burning bush and called him to redeem the Children of Israel, He revealed His name to Moses as *YHVH/Jehovah* (Exodus 3:2–14).

God's appearance in a burning bush was essential for a complete understanding of God. While the name *Elohim* is associated with His strict justice and authority, *Jehovah/YHVH* is associated with *middat ha-rachamim*— God's attribute of mercy. How does this directly connect to the burning bush? The thornbush represented the painful exile of Israel as slaves in Egypt. God's appearance in the bush made of thorns was *Jehovah*, who saw and identified with the suffering and afflictions of His people. His appearance in the burning bush also represented *Elohim*, the supreme, all-powerful Judge. *Elohim* judged the Egyptians and executed justice for the way they cruelly treated His children. Jehovah not only heard the cries of the people but also identified with their hurts and would act justly on their behalf. Biblical text scholar Akiva Mattenson wrote,

> Thus, what constitutes divine strength, what makes God unique and incomparable, is a capacity for compassion. This compassion sits in an uncomfortable tension with the rage that lights God against the enemies of Israel and the stern judgment that calls for unmitigated punishment. Yet it is precisely this tension that marks divine compassion as a strength. For it is only in mightily subduing a predilection for unmitigated judgment that God's compassion emerges victorious.[5]

God's compassion moved Him to redeem His people. What *Jehovah Elohim* did for Israel, He will do for you too!

This extraordinary compassion connects directly to Creation and highlights one of the primary reasons Yeshua-Jesus had to die on the cross. It is not uncommon for people to question, was it really necessary for God to sacrifice His Son to deal with the issue of sin? Couldn't there have been a simpler, kinder, gentler way of dealing with it? For God's approach to make sense, we must understand how God created the world. Commenting on the two names of God used in the Creation, the famous rabbinic commentator Rashi stated,

> God (Elohim—God's name traditionally associated with His trait of strict judgment) created: But it does not say "of the Lord's creation of" (i.e., it should say "of the Lord God's creation of" as below 2:4 "on the day that the Lord God made earth and heaven") for in the beginning it was God's intention to create it with the Divine Standard of Justice, but God perceived that the world would not endure; so God preceded it with the Divine Standard of Mercy, allying it with the Divine Standard of Justice, and that is the reason it is written: "on the day the Lord God made earth and heaven."[6]

Ultimately God decreed that mercy should overcome strict justice. How can this be? How is it possible without God violating His attribute of justice? Remember, God is not human. He, *Elohim*, spoke creation into existence out of nothing. With Him, all things are possible, including mercy and justice. God makes a way where there is no way (Isaiah 43).

We get a beautiful picture of mercy and justice working together in a story found in Jewish tradition concerning King David. As the ruler of Israel, David would act as a judge at times. In some instances he had to rule against a poor person who could not afford to pay the judgment against them. David executed strict justice by awarding money to the one to whom it was rightfully owed. He also demonstrated mercy by personally making the payment for the poor person who did not have the means to make it.[7] In this way, David embodied both the justice and mercy of God.

Messiah, Justice, and Mercy

Scripture is clear: "The wages of sin is death" (Romans 6:23 NIV). Sin creates a debt that must be repaid. The problem is it is massively more than any individual can repay. In reality, it is impossible. A person may think they are good enough, but not according to the Bible. "There is none righteous," wrote Rabbi Paul, "no, not one. . . . For all have sinned and fall short of the glory of God" (Romans 3:10, 23 NKJV).

Therefore, because the wages of sin is death, a person who sins—which is each one of us—deserves to die according to God's strict justice. Thankfully Yeshua Messiah reveals God's justice, but not as the world understands or expresses it. Yeshua's ministry and death unveil both God's attribute of justice and the mercy associated with the other divine name used in the Creation account, *YHVH* (the LORD). Yeshua's death paid the debt of sin we could not afford and thereby satisfied God's strict justice and demonstrated God's mercy. God is so good! He made a way for us where it seemed there was no way.

The first-century people did not fully comprehend either aspect that Messiah came to reveal. The religious leaders wanted Yeshua to demonstrate that He was the Messiah by embodying the attributes of *Elohim*—the power of God to judge the Gentiles and sinners who oppressed and corrupted Israel. Yet to their dismay, the masses flocked to Him when He embodied the compassionate characteristics of *YHVH* as He fed, healed, and cared for the people.

The people had a glimpse of both attributes of God, but most could not understand who Yeshua was because His hidden divinity as *Elohim* made it difficult for them to see beyond His physical being. Yeshua hid His true identity the way God as Creator hides Himself in nature. The Divine was clothed and concealed in the garments of *gashmius* (the Hebrew word for "physicality"). At the resurrection, however, Jesus revealed Himself to those who have eyes to see Him as both *Elohim* and *YHVH*. It is for this reason that "God highly exalted Him and gave Him the name that is above every name, that at the name of *Yeshua* every knee should bow, in heaven and on the earth and under the earth, and every tongue profess that *Yeshua* the Messiah is Lord—to the glory of God the Father" (Philippians 2:9–11). He is truly worthy of our worship!

Practically speaking, Scripture calls us to model our daily lives after Messiah. Part of our worship of Him is being people who advocate, stand for, and embody the justice and righteousness of God, which are the foundation of His throne and a healthy society. Too often, though, as believers, we are judgmental and harsh in the name of righteousness and justice. When modeling the Lord, however, we must learn to balance justice *with* mercy. How can we ask God to treat us with mercy and grace if we aren't willing to do the same with others? Becoming less judgmental and richer in kindness—especially to those who have wronged us and live in sin—goes against our natural bent. As Rabbi Paul wrote, "But you, O man—judging those practicing such things yet doing the same—do you suppose that you will escape the judgment of God? Or do you belittle the riches of His kindness and tolerance and patience—not realizing that God's kindness leads you to repentance?" (Romans 2:3–4). God's Word calls us to treat and judge people with the same measure He uses to deal with us.

God's name *Jehovah Elohim* is our source of hope and strength. *Elohim* the Almighty, Powerful One is watching over and providentially guiding the events of your life and all of history. *Jehovah* sees and feels your pain. He is your Redeemer who, out of His great mercy and compassion, not only died for your sin but also wants to have a personal relationship with you. He deeply desires to come near and be your ever-present help in times of trouble (Psalm 46:1).

Tim Keller wrote, "While God's ways are often just as opaque to us as a parent's are to an infant, still we trust that our heavenly Father is caring for us and present with us to guide and protect in all the circumstances of life."[8]

The God of Order

The more I study the Bible, the more I find that God creates order and direction out of lifeless chaos. He is in control and seeks to point us in the direction He has for us. Before I knew Yeshua, I was lifeless. Yes, I desperately sought spiritual wholeness through Judaism and Buddhism, but thank goodness God had other plans for me. He took this lifeless Jew-Bu and made him a new creation. Yeshua brought order to my disordered life and gave me clear direction. He will do the same for you if you let Him. Just as He spoke over the chaos in the very beginning when He created *seder* (order), He can speak over your life. Rabbi Paul wrote, "If anyone is in Messiah, he is a new creation. The old things have passed away; behold, all things have become new" (2 Corinthians 5:17). It doesn't matter what your circumstances are or how much you have failed; *Yeshua-Elohim* can take your brokenness and make you a new creation. You can leave the past things behind and move forward in life with new or renewed direction and meaning. You can have a deep relationship with the God of order, not the gods of chaos we find all around us.

Order Out of Chaos

When I was a young child, I used to love to watch the TV show *Get Smart*. A fan might best describe the show as James Bond meets a Mel Brooks–style parody. The show's plot centered around Secret Agent 86, Maxwell Smart, and his partner, Agent 99. They worked for a covert counterintelligence agency called Control. The archenemy of Control was Kaos, an international organization of evil that continually conspired to take over the world. Kaos would seemingly succeed if not for the heroics and dumb luck of Maxwell Smart.

The Hebrew phrase that describes the original state of the earth at Creation is *tohu vavohu*. It is best translated as "chaos and empty" (Genesis 1:1–2, my own translation). Just as Kaos was always destructive in *Get Smart*, even more so is true chaos. Life can't exist in a state of darkness and chaos.

Jehovah Elohim, the all-powerful Creator, brought form and life out of that chaos and assigned order to it. This truth is good news because we can understand chaos and overcome it, even in a world becoming increasingly chaotic, with Yeshua (who is God). In fact, as I was writing this, the news reported within a span of a few days about the horrible effects of Hurricane Ida, lava flowing on the Spanish island of La Palma, torrential rain in the northeastern section of the US, and wildfires in California.

Biblically, though, chaos means much more than natural disasters. It represents evil, exile, and death. When chaos pervades the world, it is an uninhabitable, hostile, and dangerous place, unsuitable for life. God must deal with chaos so life can flourish. God's goodness and abundant blessing can't be fully manifested where chaos is pervasive. Jesus, on the other hand, brings order out of chaos. This idea of bringing order out of chaos was true in Creation and is true for our lives and the life of the church. The rabbi and apostle Paul wrote, "God is not a God of disorder but of peace—as in all the congregations of the Lord's people" (1 Corinthians 14:33 NIV).

Chaos kills life and blessing. Chaos creates confusion and clutter that ruin relationships. The TV show *Hoarders* is an example of the destructive nature of chaos. This reality show chronicles the lives of individuals who deal with compulsive hoarding disorder. These people have acquired a vast, incomprehensible amount of seemingly random and often useless objects. Their homes become so cluttered that most of the rooms become unusable and unsafe. Accumulated objects pile up from floor to ceiling, making it nearly impossible to cook, sleep, clean, or entertain. This clutter and lack of space almost always lead to damaged or ruined family relationships. The chaotic state of their outer surroundings and inner emotional lives strains and often ruins even their closest relationships.

The Lord created us for relationships—with Him and with others. But when we live in a place of chaos, there is no room for connection. It's all too easy and common to become a hoarder emotionally, spiritually, or relationally. We can allow insecurities, fears, work, or unhealthy habits to crowd out our most valuable assets—our relationships. Relationship with God and others requires that we make space. He made space for us; we need to make space for Him. It's impossible to be full of ourselves and full of God at the same time. When we decrease, He can increase (John 3:30). To the degree that our lives become filled with the chaos of unhealthy things, we will lack the capacity or the ability to have quality time with God or those important relationships. Proverbs 4:23 says, "Keep [guard] your heart with all diligence, for out of it spring the issues of life" (NKJV). With much diligence, we must guard those most important things in our hearts.

The opposite of chaos, and one of the keys to overcoming it, is order—*seder* in Hebrew. Order is critical to experiencing the fullness of the Lord and His blessing. Order leads to alignment, and alignment leads to God's blessing. This alignment and blessing are seen clearly in the early Creation account.

The first letter of Genesis, and the Bible, is *bet* (ב), which is the second letter of the Hebrew alphabet and has a numeric value of 2. Why is it significant that the first letter in the Bible has a numeric value of 2? This is how I explained this significance in *Mysteries of the Messiah*: "Because God created the world in twos. He created heaven and earth. He created light and dark. He created day and night. He created the sun and the moon. He created the sea and the dry ground. He created man and woman."[9]

Interestingly, only when the two (man and women, day and night, and so forth) work in alignment like those above can blessing (*bracha* in Hebrew) be released. God created the world, and you, for blessing. But for this blessing to come, there needs to be alignment. God created the world to bless it because both Hebrew words (*bereisheet*, or "beginning," and *bracha*, or "blessing") start with the same letter, *bet*.

What does this teach us? That the fullness of God's blessing can only come forth through partnership. When the two function as one in harmonious cooperation and alignment, the fullness of God's blessing bursts forth. When heaven provides rain, the earth brings forth its bounty. The right balance between light and darkness is critical to sustaining biological life. God made man first, but he was not complete until the Lord created Eve, the first woman. The first commandment to be fruitful and multiply can only be accomplished when there is relational alignment. Ultimately God's blessing does not fully manifest until we live in alignment and work in the right relationship and partnership with God and one another.

The Blessing of Order

God created the world for blessing, not cursing. Likewise, He created us to *be* a blessing and to experience the fullness of life (John 10:10). Our relationship with Yeshua releases the fullness of God's blessing in our lives. It is also released in our relationships with other people. God wants to bring order into your life and relationships. He wants to firm up a shaky foundation or establish a new foundation so that alignment and blessing can come in unprecedented ways and give you a divine breakthrough.

Divine breakthrough leads to God's promise to bless us. I've experienced blessing after blessing as I trusted God in faith. His blessing comes in many forms, and sometimes His blessing isn't what I think it should be for my good. But when I look back, I can see how God worked things out—the blessing I thought I wanted wasn't nearly as remarkable as God's blessing. Watchman Nee, Chinese church leader and teacher, commenting on Jesus' miracle of feeding the five thousand, put it this way:

> The miracles are *produced by the Lord's blessing* [not mine]. His blessing changes and multiplies the loaves. *The miracles are based on the Lord's blessing.* . . . When we have blessing, everything goes well and nothing is difficult. Without the Lord's blessing, everything goes wrong and nothing is easy.[10]

Only the Lord's blessing leads to the fulfilled life. What I want doesn't matter. I am blessed when God takes over and works things out.

Order is about relational alignment on a vertical God level and a horizontal people level. In the beginning, the Lord brought order out of chaos, but when Adam and Eve fell in the garden, chaos spread. Adam and Eve experienced disorder in their spiritual lives, in family relationships, and even physically through death and the curse on creation.

Chaos is a reality in our world today, but it's not the finality. God has provided means to minimize and overcome chaos. The ultimate way of overcoming chaos is through Messiah. "Now the earth was chaos and waste, darkness was on the surface of the deep," wrote Moses, "and the *Ruach Elohim* [Spirit of God] was hovering upon the surface of the water" (Genesis 1:2). Commenting on this passage, the third-century writing in the Kol HaTor, a book of Jewish thought and wisdom, Rabbi Hillel Rivlin of Shklov wrote, "'The spirit of God hovered upon the surface of the waters' [Gen. 1:2]—the spirit of the *mashiach* [Messiah]."[11] As it is stated, "The Spirit of the LORD shall rest upon him" (Isaiah 11:2 ESV). Messiah Yeshua is the One who constrained chaos at Creation, and ultimately, because of His death on the cross, He overcame the power of chaos so that order, alignment, and blessing could be restored.

When Jesus was on the cross, darkness occurred from the sixth to the ninth hour (Matthew 27:45). This timing happened because He had to return to the start of Creation—to a time before light when everything was formless and void—to undo the chaos released by the Fall. Through the cross, Jesus conquered the chaos caused by our sin and overcame the forces of darkness. As Rabbi Paul wrote, "After disarming the principalities and powers, He made a public spectacle of them, triumphing over them in the cross" (Colossians 2:15).

But there is so much more to see here. The phrase "chaos and empty" in Hebrew adds up to 430. The number 430, however, also connects to the Messiah. Micah 5:1 says, "You, Bethlehem . . . from you will come out to Me One to be ruler in Israel, One whose goings forth are from of old, from days of eternity." The numeric value in Hebrew of the phrase "from of old, from days of eternity" (*mikedem mimei olam*) is 430. This number alludes to the divinity of Yeshua, since God alone is eternal. It shows that the Messiah is the primary goal of the Torah. (The number of years between the time God made His covenant with Abraham and the giving of the Torah is—you guessed it—430 [see Galatians 3:16–17]. Known as the covenant between the parts, it is one of the most important events in Jewish history.) Only the One who existed from eternity, the Messiah, the eternal, living Word of God, can overcome chaos and restore order, for His existence precedes it, and His power supersedes it.

A Note from Kathie

More than one hundred names for God are mentioned in the Bible. Imagine that!

I love that there are specific names, though, for various aspects of God's nature.

El Roi, for the God Who Sees. *Jehovah Jireh*, for the God Who Provides, and many more.

But *Jehovah Elohim* is one of my favorites. It means God the Creator.

And He's not just the Creator of everything that has come before. He is the God of all creation and is creating new things even this moment.

Isaiah 43:19 says, "Behold, I am doing a new thing; now it springs forth, do you not perceive it?" (ESV).

In other words, "Hey, look around, everybody! I am the God who never changes! I am doing brand-new miracles all over the cosmos—and even in *your life*! Open your eyes! Open your hearts!"

I have a good friend who likes to come over to my home on

beautiful nights and sit with me on my deck under the stars. He inevitably takes out his phone and goes to the app that allows you to point your phone to the sky above you and discover the names of the celestial wonders billions of miles away.

It's not just a restful, enjoyable exercise. Psalm 19:1 tells me, "The heavens declare the glory of God; the skies proclaim the work of his hands" (NIV).

How profound to think of the blanket of tiny lights in the distance as actually being mysterious treasure chests of wisdom and knowledge.

Jehovah Elohim's ways are unfathomable, of course, but He lights our paths with His stars to guide us into understanding His nature.

seven

THE POWER OF THE WORD

Rabbi Jason

The *Torah* of ADONAI is perfect,
   restoring the soul.
The testimony of ADONAI is trustworthy,
   making the simple wise.
The precepts of ADONAI are right,
   giving joy to the heart.
The *mitzvot* of ADONAI are pure,
   giving light to the eyes.
The fear of ADONAI is clean,
   enduring forever.
The judgments of ADONAI are true
   and altogether righteous.
They are more desirable than gold,
   yes, more than much pure gold!
They are sweeter than honey
   and drippings of the honeycomb. (Psalm 19:8–11)

I love God's Word. It encourages, and at times it cuts like a sharp knife. It rebukes Satan, and it calms the churning waters of my soul. A healing, soothing balm, God's Word strengthens my heart and lengthens my days. It gives me the courage to walk in His ways. Filling us with hope, God's Word is the best news we will ever hear! The sixteenth president of the United States, Abraham Lincoln, loved God's Word so much he said the Bible was "the best gift God has given to man" and that "all the good Savior gave to the world was communicated through this book."[1]

Jesus, who is the living Word, and the written Word are both key to overcoming chaos. We need Scripture to overcome chaos because God's Word is woven into the very fabric of Creation. It was through God's words that the world came to be. And in this present moment, He is "upholding all things by His powerful word" (Hebrews 1:3).

The idea of God's Word being part and parcel of the spiritual, immaterial part of Creation is essential to dealing with and defeating chaos in our lives. When God created the world, He spoke 10 times in Genesis 1 (vv. 3, 6, 9, 11, 14, 20, 24, 26, 28, 29). Through these 10 utterances, He spoke the world and the universe into existence and brought order out of chaos.[2]

The 10 utterances of Creation directly connect to the 10 plagues God brought upon Egypt as well as the 10 Commandments. It is no coincidence that Pharaoh and the Egyptians experienced 10 plagues before they set the Children of Israel free. As we have seen, God's Word weaves its way through the fabric of Creation. When Pharaoh chose to disobey God's Word, Egypt went from a state of order to disorder—a reversal of Creation. God desires to bring order out of chaos, but each time Pharaoh disobeyed God's Word, the Egyptians experienced chaos. Instead of light, there was darkness; instead of life, there was death; instead of a blessing, there was cursing. The animals no longer feared man but attacked him. The 10 plagues were an undoing of the 10 utterances of Creation.[3]

Natural and spiritual laws govern the earth. For example, someone might say that they don't believe in gravity. Still, if they jump off a roof, they will experience the painful consequences of their unbelief. Similarly, there are spiritual laws and principles that God has chosen to incorporate into creation. They are as real as gravity, and when we ignore them, like Pharaoh did, we do so to our detriment. This unbelief is what happened in both Egypt and Eden when man disobeyed God's spoken Word. When the spiritual laws and principles of the Word of God are disobeyed or ignored, even out of ignorance, chaos ensues. God's Word makes known these spiritual precepts and principles that bring wisdom, life, and blessing. When we ignore God's Word, we experience chaos and emptiness.

The Egyptians were not the only ones who experienced chaos. So did Israel. God gave 10 Commandments because He desired to bring about a new creation through the Children of Israel. In Jewish thought, if the Children of Israel had not sinned with the incident of the golden calf, the Lord would have brought them into Israel (the Promised Land), sent the Messiah, and established the Kingdom. But they disobeyed God's Word and made an idol, the chaos continued, and all the adults of that generation continued in their disobedience, testing the Lord 10 times (Numbers 14:22). The prophet Jeremiah, describing Israel's disobedience to the Lord and His Word, described the Promised Land as becoming "chaos and empty" (*tohu vavohu* in Hebrew, often translated "formless and void" or "empty"), like it was before God spoke His first creative utterance (Jeremiah 4:23, my own translation). When Israel broke God's Word, the land became uninhabitable, and the people went into exile. One writer said, "There is no sorrow that falls to Israel's lot that is not in part a punishment for their worship of the Golden Calf."[4]

The Hebrew word for "exile" is *golah*, which is a form of chaos. The antidote to exile and chaos is redemption (*geulah*). In Hebrew there is only a one-letter difference between the words "exile" and "redemption"—the letter *aleph* (א), the one most associated with God's names in Jewish thought, since most of them begin with this letter (such as *Adonai* and *Elohim*). When we remove the Lord from our lives—our families, our nation, and the world—we are left in a state of chaos and exile. Just like when the letter *aleph* is removed from *geulah*, there's only chaos and exile (*golah*) remaining. Overcoming exile and chaos in our lives involves choosing to make God's Word central to everything we do, think, and speak.

The Wisdom of the Word

The centrality of Scripture in our lives is fundamental to living a life of abundance and blessing. The reason is that God's Word, which contains His wisdom, is also the blueprint for Creation:

> ADONAI brought me [wisdom] forth,
> the first of His way,
> before His works of old.
> From eternity I was appointed
> from the beginning, before the world began.
> When there were no depths, I was brought forth,
> when there were no fountains abounding with water.
> Before the mountains were shaped,
> before the hills, I was brought forth.
> He had not yet made the land,
> the fields, or the first dust of the earth.
> When He set the heavens in place, I was there.

When He inscribed the horizon on the face of the ocean,

when He established the skies above,

when He securely fixed the fountains of the deep,

when He set the boundaries for the sea,

so that the waters never transgress His command,

when He laid out earth's foundations—

then I was the craftsman beside Him,

I was His daily delight, always rejoicing before Him,

rejoicing in His whole world, and delighting in mankind.

So now, children, listen to me!

Blessed are those who keep my ways.

Heed discipline and be wise,

and do not neglect it.

Blessed is the one who listens to me,

watching daily at my gates,

waiting at my doorposts.

For whoever finds me finds life

and obtains favor from ADONAI.

But whoever fails to find me harms his life—

all who hate me love death. (Proverbs 8:22–36)

God's Word is the blueprint not only for Creation but also for our lives. When we understand and follow the wisdom of God's Word, which contains His divine design, we find life and blessing! Pastor Warren Wiersbe wrote, "When we belong to Jesus Christ and walk in His wisdom, all of creation works for us; if we rebel against His wisdom and will, things start to work against us, as Jonah discovered when he tried to run away from the Lord."[5]

God's Word is powerful. It is how the Lord's promises begin to actualize in our lives. His Word can cut like a surgeon's knife, removing the unhealthy and ungodly thoughts, emotions, and habits. It has the power to renew and restore. "Be transformed by the renewing of your mind," wrote Rabbi Paul, "so that you may discern what is the will of God—what is good and acceptable and perfect" (Romans 12:2). The Word of God is truth, and as Yeshua-Jesus said, "You will know the truth, and the truth will set you free!" (John 8:32).

When delighting "in" and meditating "on" God's Word, we are not only transformed; we also experience great blessing and success. According to the psalmist, we become like trees planted along the riverbank, bearing fruit in our season. Our leaves will never wither, and we will prosper in all we do (Psalm 1:3). After Moses died, the Lord instructed Joshua, "Study this Book of Instruction continually. Meditate on it day and night so you will be sure to obey everything written in it. Only then will you prosper and succeed in all you do" (Joshua 1:8 NLT).

The Light of the Word

Then there was light! The first thing God called out of the darkness of the chaos was the light. But what was this light? It could not have been a natural light since God did not bring the sun, moon, and stars into existence until the fourth day of Creation. This light, according to Jewish tradition, was the supernatural celestial light of God's manifest presence. The rabbis teach that *Elohim* hid this light due to the Fall and set it aside for the righteous in the world to come.[6] But where did He hide His divine light? One place was in the Torah, the Word of God, as Scripture states,

Your word is a lamp to my feet and a light to my path. (Psalm 119:105)

The *mitzvah* is a lamp, *Torah* a light, and corrective discipline the way of life. (Proverbs 6:23)

God's Word provides wise counsel throughout our lives. It is a *lamp*. Like a flashlight, it illuminates our next steps in the darkness. God doesn't always lay out the whole plan, but He shows us the next steps to take in faith. We can trust Him to continue guiding our path.

God's Word also acts as a searchlight. It pierces the darkness and uncovers the shadows—the hidden faults or strongholds in our lives. Searchlights are powerful, just as God's Word is powerful to show us His way and how we can grow in Him.

The connection between light and God's Word is spiritually significant. Life cannot exist without light. Light on a biological level is essential to life, which is analogous to the light of God's Word on a spiritual level. As the psalmist wrote, "With You is the fountain of life—in Your light we see light" (Psalm 36:10). When we delve deeper into, meditate on, and live out God's Word, we draw the divine light of God into our lives. The Enemy often attacks the reliability and integrity of God's Word to cut off the world from a critical source of life and blessing.

The Word Is a Sword

God's Word is compared to light—and also to a sword.

The word of God is living and active and sharper than any two-edged sword—piercing right through to a separation of soul and spirit, joints

and marrow, and able to judge the thoughts and intentions of the heart.
(Hebrews 4:12)

Star Wars was the first movie I ever saw as a child. It's one of my all-time favorites. I'll never forget when I was four years old and very sick. To cheer me up, my dad went out and bought me my first *Star Wars* action figures. Of course, Luke Skywalker, with his blue lightsaber, was my hero. Since God's Word is both a light and a sword, it is the ultimate lightsaber!

As I mentioned above, the Word of God operates like a skilled surgeon. Scripture has the power to cut away the sin and darkness in our lives. It can surgically remove whatever keeps us from Him and the abundant, breakthrough life He has for us. The light of God's Word and the wisdom and the divine promises contained within can empower us to overcome depression, fear, and anxiety. Scripture is a source of joy and light. God's Word is a fantastic weapon that helps defend us against the attacking lies of the world and the devil. The sword of the Word is also a potent offensive weapon that can help us kill the flesh, strengthen our spirits, and bring victory.

The words found in the Bible apply to our lives. Author Jerry Gramckow wrote, "We need it to understand that every part of the Bible has *eternally applicable principles*. Our part is to find those principles, which we then can apply for teaching the truth, convicting of sin, correcting faults, and training in right living."[7]

God's Word brings life, but if misused, it can bring death. As with all weapons, swords can be dangerous when mishandled. God's Word is truth, but truth can hurt and maim a person if used in a harsh and legalistic way. Too many people have been wounded by immature or unhealthy Christians who harshly wielded God's Word against them. Scripture is compared to a "two-edged sword" (Hebrews 4:12). One edge represents truth and the other grace. The truth of God's Word, apart from grace, causes harm and hurts that are, at best, hard to heal or, at worst, spiritually fatal for a person's faith. God's truth must be tempered with grace, compassion, and love to bring life and blessing. We must be cautious with how we use and steward Scripture.

The "two-edged" nature of the Word also points to the design of God's Word, which is old and new. Sharp swords are necessary to overcome the world, the flesh, and even Satan, the tempter—just as Jesus did in the wilderness by quoting Deuteronomy from the Torah. Believers tend to focus on the "new" and don't really know the "old" or value it as much as the New Testament. But we genuinely need to have a strong understanding of both testaments to wield the sword of the Word effectively. The Old Testament is the foundation of the New. Yeshua Himself said, "Every *Torah* scholar discipled for the kingdom of heaven is like the master of a household who brings out of his treasure both new things and old" (Matthew 13:52). Don't settle for half an inheritance or a sword that is sharp on only one side!

Soak in His Word

When we get inside the pages of the Bible, the Word of God gets inside us. It is powerful and creates change. Read it, study it, and learn about God, Yeshua, and the Holy Spirit. Discover how He worked through ordinary, flawed people like you and me. Discover His promises. Reading the Bible is not merely trying to read it in one year and keeping a checklist of accomplishments. It's about soaking in every word and letting the Holy Spirit illuminate how the truth applies to your life. It doesn't matter if you read only one or two verses a day. Sometimes I will camp on one verse for a week, extracting all the truth inside it. Then, a year later, I will read that same verse and get more truth! God's Word is alive. What matters is soaking in His Word every day and using it to His glory. And remember, even the genealogies are essential clues to understanding Messiah. Everything in God's Word is for your benefit.

A Note from Kathie

Ever since I made my first journey to the Holy Land in 1971, I have been troubled by the fact that Jews and Christians divide the Bible into "ours" and "theirs"—the Old Testament for the Jews and the New Testament for the Christians.

This could not be further from the way it's meant to be.

Though Jesus didn't come into the world in physical form until four hundred years after the last book in the Old Testament, Malachi, was written, He was already there in the first book of Genesis!

Jehovah Elohim says in Genesis 1:26, "Let *us* make mankind in *our* image, in *our* likeness, so that they may rule over the fish in the sea and the birds in the sky, over the livestock and all the wild animals, and over all the creatures that move along the ground" (NIV, emphasis added).

Who is this "us" and "our" that Genesis refers to? The New Testament's complementary passage to this, John 1:1, tells us, "In the beginning was the Word, and the Word was with God, and the Word was God" (NIV). And John 1:14 tells us, "The Word became flesh and lived among us" (ISV).

Genesis 1:26 is referring to Jesus! And not only that, but after the Creation that was accomplished by the perfect union of Father, Son, and Holy Spirit, Jesus the Messiah was prophesied 450 times in the Old Testament before He was born in Bethlehem in approximately 4 BC.[8]

The Bible in its entirety is *one story*, not two. It's one magnificent love story about the God who created all things and sustains all things and longs for all He created to return to Him in His house, *bet av*.

eight

YESHUA AND THE WOMAN

Rabbi Jason

As John the apostle wrote, Yeshua is the Word, and He dwelt among us. As He traveled about touching the lives of those around Him, He encountered both critics and followers. There are numerous accounts in the Gospels of how Yeshua changed lives and even raised the dead. One such story stands out as a throng of people surrounded Him. The incident must have had a significant influence to be recorded in three gospels: Matthew 9:20–22; Mark 5:24–34; and Luke 8:42–48.

Jairus, a leader in the synagogue, pushed his way through the crowd and threw himself at Yeshua's feet, begging Him to come heal his little daughter. Yeshua went with him, and the crowd followed. Scripture says the crowd was "pressing upon Him" (Mark 5:24). Watch what happened:

> There was a woman with a blood flow for twelve years, who had suffered much under many doctors. She had spent all that she had without benefit; instead, she grew worse. When she heard about *Yeshua*, she came through

the crowd from behind and touched His garment. For she kept saying, "If I touch even His clothes, I shall be healed."

Right away the blood flow stopped, and she felt in her body that she was healed from her disease. At once *Yeshua*, knowing in Himself that power had gone out from Him, turned around in the crowd and said, "Who touched My clothes?"

His disciples responded, "You see the crowd pressing upon You and you say, 'Who touched Me?'" But He kept looking around to see who had done this.

But the woman, scared and shaking, knowing what had happened to her, came and fell down before Him and told Him the whole truth. And He said to her, "Daughter, your faith has made you well. Go in *shalom* and be healed from your disease." (Mark 5:25–34)

The woman with the flow would have been considered ritually unclean, which meant she could have no physical contact with family or friends. That the woman had lived in this state of ritual impurity, *tumah* in Hebrew law, indicated as well that her husband had not touched her lovingly or intimately for twelve long years. She would have been excluded from the social and spiritual life of Israel. One commentator wrote about this story, "[It] would be a doubtful scenario if Yeshua were not Torah-observant. He would not have been received into a group of Galilean synagogues in the role of a rabbi and a healer if he were not Torah-observant, at least by Galilean standards."[1] Thus, it would have been socially and spiritually scandalous for an unclean woman to reach out and touch Yeshua. Still, this woman was in such a state of desperation that she risked doing the unthinkable.

The woman in this story also knew Scripture and recognized Yeshua as Messiah. Her awareness of Him most likely came from her study of the

Torah and other biblical writings available at the time. Undoubtedly she had tried every possible cure and was suffering both physically and socially. After so many years of continual bleeding, humiliation and shame had become ingrained in her soul. Again, Leviticus 15:25–27 tells us that any such discharge rendered a woman ceremonially unclean. Despite this fact, her touch, incredibly, did not make Yeshua ritually unclean. She was healed the moment she touched His garment—both physically and spiritually. Shame erased, she now knew her Savior personally.

We also can learn from Yeshua's response. In the middle of the pushing and shoving crowd, He stopped and paid attention to one person. He was with a synagogue official and could have easily ignored her. But He didn't. Once Yeshua felt her touch on His garment, He needed to find her. He needed to speak to her.

Yeshua stopped. And He always will when we come to Him.

There's also something special in Yeshua's approach to this woman—and to all women for that matter. His interactions with women, inclusion of women, and treatment of women were a radical departure from the cultural norm of that day. The role of women in Yeshua's day was minimal. Customarily a woman's responsibility was to her family, which meant she primarily lived her life within her home's private sphere. This view is based in part on Psalm 45:13: "The royal daughter is all glorious within the palace" (NKJV). The rabbinic view on this verse holds that a woman's home is the place of her glory and the domain where she holds court as a wife and mother.

The Rambam, Rabbi Moses ben Maimon, commenting on this verse, underscored the traditional view of women's roles within Judaism when he wrote in the twelfth century, "Every women should go out to visit her parents . . . to perform acts of kindness for her friends, a wife is not to be imprisoned in her home, as if it were a dungeon . . . but it is a disgrace for a woman always to go into public places and main streets and a husband should restrain his wife from acting thus. . . . For the essence of a wife's beauty is to be enthroned in the corner of her home, as it says, The complete glory of the princess is within."[2]

Yeshua's perspective on, interaction with, and treatment of women were radical for His day. Unlike other rabbis, He included them in His inner circle, not just as financial supporters but as students and disciples. He welcomed and interacted with respectable Jewish women and with those considered unholy and unclean, like women with the flow, prostitutes, and even Gentiles, like the Samaritan woman. And, as we've discussed earlier, women were among the primary supporters of Yeshua's ministry.

The first followers of Yeshua followed His example by including and empowering women as leaders in the church. Women such as Phoebe served as deacons (Romans 16:1) and others, like Junia, as apostles (Romans 16:7). The four daughters of Philip operated as prophetesses (Acts 21:9) and others, like Priscilla, as teachers and missionaries (Acts 18:26; Romans 16:3–4; 1 Corinthians 16:19).

Too often the church has relegated women to kids' ministry or helps and hospitality types of ministries. While these ministries are greatly needed, women should not be excluded from other kinds of ministry based on gender. This idea of gender separation stands in direct opposition to the teaching and practice of Yeshua and the early church. Instead women should be championed. I believe women have a crucial role to play in the next move of God and the redemption of Israel. As it was at the beginning of the early Yeshua movement, so it will be in the end. Women played a foundational and essential role in New Testament times, and they will once again in our day as we approach the return of the Lord. All followers of the Messiah, especially men, have a responsibility to encourage and support women as they pursue the call of God at this critical time in history.

The Lord washed away the pain and shame of the woman with the blood issue (Mark 5:24–34), of the Samaritan woman (John 4:3–42) who'd had many broken relationships, and of the woman caught in adultery (John 8:1–11). Yeshua did not look down on them but instead met them where they were. He embodied the loving and compassionate heart of the Father and spoke words of healing over them. What Yeshua-Jesus did for them, He wants to do for you.

By the power of the Word, both living and written, you can find tremendous new hope and a future. Through the power of Yeshua-Jesus and the promise of His Word, He can not only heal you but make you whole. The good news is that you don't have to remain stuck. He came to set you free and bring order out of your chaos. When you place your faith in Yeshua-Jesus and order your life around Him and the Word of God, you can experience His living, delivering, glowing, ever overflowing, miraculous healing power. His death on that tree for you and me broke the power of the curse of the Fall so that God might bless you. Don't wait. Believe, receive—just come to Yeshua-Jesus, who is *Jehovah Elohim* in the flesh!

A Note from Kathie

The Bible records thirty-seven of Jesus' miracles. This is certainly a huge part of the reason thousands began to follow Him and listen to Him all over Israel. Many no doubt needed a personal miracle. Others were curious about this remarkable, young, and powerful teacher.

Many of the miracles were physical healings of the body—the ten lepers (Luke 17:11–19), the blind man (Mark 8:22–26), and the woman with the issue of blood (Luke 8:43–48), to name a few.

Others were healings of the mind—the demoniac (Matthew 8:28–34), Mary Magdalene (Luke 8:2), and others who were demon-possessed.

Still other miracles involved the healing of the soul—the woman caught in adultery (John 8:1–11), the late-night meeting with the Pharisee Nicodemus when Jesus told him he needed to be "born of the Spirit" (John 3:1–21), and the Samaritan woman (John 4).

And finally, the spectacular physical miracles—turning the water into wine (John 2:1–11) and feeding the thousands with a few fish and loaves of bread (Matthew 14:13–21).

There were many more, but my point is that Jesus worked miracles because He was *God incarnate*, and, even as He said, "All things are possible with God" (Mark 10:27 NIV).

Part Three

THE GOD WHO SEES

Kathie

In fall 2018 I was staying at a friend's home in a Nashville suburb. My friend had arranged for a "write," which is what those in the music industry call a songwriting session. These are often sessions with complete strangers, and I have grown to love the unpredictable nature of these collaborations. On this particular October day, I was scheduled to write with an amazing singer-songwriter named Nicole C. Mullen. I was familiar with her Grammy-nominated song, "I Know My Redeemer Lives," but I had never met her before.

As always, I prayed before our meeting that the Lord would lead us both and that we'd be sensitive to what He wanted to accomplish in our lives and in our work.

Ephesians 3:20 tells us that God will do "immeasurably more than all we ask or imagine" (NIV). Although I have memorized that Scripture and prayed on it for years, it always surprises me when He actually does it! (Oh, me of little faith!)

God not only shows up in every aspect of our lives; He shows off too!

I had come to the write with two things I had been contemplating for a few weeks before we met. The first was the biblical character Hagar, who has one of the most heart-wrenching stories in the Old Testament. Hagar was the handmaiden of Sarai, Abram's barren wife. Hagar had been given (or sold) to Abram by the Egyptian pharaoh. She was a slave with extremely limited personal freedom and therefore was considered of little value as a human being.

Abram had been promised decades before that God would make him the father of nations, of so many people that they would be "as numerous as the stars in the sky" (Deuteronomy 28:62 NIV). You'll remember from our earlier chapters on Abraham and Sarah that this seemed impossible at the time, as Abram and Sarai were already well into old age and Sarai especially had long since passed her childbearing years.

Sarai became increasingly more frustrated as the time passed. Her faith was tested beyond her patience, and she finally did what we humans so often do: she took matters into her own hands. She literally threw Hagar into her husband's arms so Abram could sleep with her and Hagar could bear a son whom Sarai could call her own and fulfill God's promise.

Hagar's story ended with calamitous results—as any story does when someone chooses a "better" choice than God's. And yet God used even Sarai's terrible decision to bring about His greater purpose.

The other thing I brought to the session with Nicole was what God said in Zechariah 2:5 concerning Jerusalem, which was in peril from enemies: "I . . . will be a wall of fire all around her, and I will be the glory in her midst" (NKJV).

I had read the Bible regularly since I was twelve years old, yet I didn't remember ever noticing this verse before. The poetry took my breath away right before I met Nicole.

I was also taken by Zechariah's use of the pronoun *her* in many translations, which is not very typical of Old Testament verbiage.

The song Nicole and I started writing that day was called "The God Who Sees," because that's the name Hagar attributed to the Almighty when He delivered her from her abandonment in the wilderness.

But we were unable to finish the song because Nicole was leaving for a ministry trip to Africa, and I had to return home to work on the *Today Show* the next day. I assured Nicole that I had the time to complete the song while she was gone, and we made a plan to get together again in Nashville when we both returned.

I've often heard it said, "If you want to make God laugh, tell Him your plans!"

What Nicole and I assumed we would end up with was a three-and-a-half-minute song for Danny Gokey to record. But instead I sat down to finish it, and the Holy Spirit inspired me to continue and add the story of Ruth, another woman in despair many centuries later. Then He prompted me to include the story of David hiding in the Judean wilderness from King Saul and paralyzed with fear.

Lord, I told Him, *this isn't a song per se; it's more of a performance piece.*

And then I had the overwhelming feeling that I was to finish it with Mary Magdalene at the cross and at the tomb of Jesus.

I had become fascinated by how even though these four individuals lived between two and four thousand years ago, their stories felt as though they could have been ripped from today's headlines.

Hagar was a slave who was sexually used, and a single mother. Ruth was a widowed immigrant with seemingly no future. David was an anointed king but terrified and hiding in a cave. Mary Magdalene was mentally ill, having been tormented by seven demons.

But the same God—the God Who Sees—delivered them all from their despair. And this same God who never changes delivers us, too, from ours.

Rabbi Jason

It's true; mothers see and know everything. Part of my spiritual journey involved my friend John and his invitation to me to join him one evening at the messianic congregation led by Rabbi Jonathan Cahn. I had just turned twenty, had grown up Jewish, and had never attended a Christian church, so I did not know what to expect. I was surprised at how moved I was by the music and the message. At one point the lights dimmed in the synagogue, and the congregation began to pray. Because I was searching for spiritual enlightenment and figured I needed all the help I could get, I was more than happy to join in. Following the final "amen," which is one of the few Hebrew words that has hardly changed in 2,500 years, one of the leaders said, "If that was your first time to pray to Yeshua-Jesus, please raise your hand."

It was, so I slipped mine in the air.

"If you raised your hand," he continued, "please stand. You have just been born anew."

After some prodding by a man from Brooklyn sitting next to me, I stood, and Rabbi Jonathan Cahn led me in a prayer to receive Yeshua. Then one of the leaders explained my decision more thoroughly and gave me the first New Testament I had ever seen. I know that may be hard to imagine today, but it's true.

Still unsure of what had just occurred, I took the small Bible home and hid it in my room. It would have been catastrophic if my parents had found out. Of course, my all-seeing mom, who had some sort of inner radar system homed in on her son's affairs, did just that. "What is this?" she confronted me, waving the Bible around like a red flag. "Don't tell me you're a Jew who believes in Jesus!"

The lesson here is, don't try to hide anything from your mother—she sees everything!

I'm poking fun at loving moms, but God does see and know all things concerning us. In this section, we will examine the lives of Hagar, Ruth, David, and Mary of Magdala. Each of their stories reveals a God whose eyes are always on us, who never leaves or forsakes us—a God who gives us the power through the Spirit to do what He has called us to do. He sees in the desert. He sees in the empty spaces. He sees you and me right where we are, whatever the circumstance. In all our pain and joy, we are never out of His sight. He hears our desperate cries and our joyful thanksgivings. Because He loves us so much, when He sees us, He doesn't just leave us. He touches us in ways that bring healing and transformation to our lives and, in many cases, the lives of those around us.

nine

HAGAR

Rabbi Jason

Hagar is one of the most interesting characters in the Bible. "The Midrash tells of Hagar being a daughter of the pharaoh of Egypt when she saw God perform a miracle to save Sarah from the hands of the Egyptian king during her visit with Abraham (Genesis 12:19). Hagar chose not to stay behind in the idolatry, so she went with Abraham and Sarah as a servant in their household."[1] Hagar decided she'd rather be a maid to Sarah than be a princess. Her name, "according to the Midrash, stems from this beginning of her association with Abraham's house. It comes from 'Ha-Agar,' meaning 'this is the reward.'"[2]

Instead of waiting on God and His plan to make Abraham the father of nations, Sarah devised a plan of her own. It was simple—give her handmaid, Hagar, to Abraham. Let her have the child. Hagar was healthy and in her childbearing years. Sarah's suggestion was a logical strategy in keeping with the ancient Near Eastern society's conventional cultural practices. But regardless of how plausible Sarah's idea may have seemed in the natural, it was doomed to fail because it is impossible to achieve God's promises by worldly means or schemes.

Knowing God Sees

From the beginning, God *looked* upon His creation and *saw* that it "was good" (Genesis 1:10). But when God looks, He does not do so as a mere spectator. His gaze is providential, looking to guide us at opportune times and care for His creation with divine intervention. "For the eyes of ADONAI range throughout the earth to strengthen those whose hearts are wholly His" (2 Chronicles 16:9). After God showed up for Hagar when she was pregnant with Ishmael and alone in the wilderness, despairing, with no direction, she called Him *El Roi*, "the God who sees." Scripture says, "She called the name of the LORD who spoke to her, You-Are-the-God-Who-Sees; for she said, 'Have I also here seen Him who sees me?'" (Genesis 16:13 NKJV).

The fact that God sees should be a source of great hope and encouragement for all of us who love Him. No matter what we are going through, He sees and knows it all. Knowing God sees and being seen by Him is life changing. God changed Hagar's destiny and that of her descendants forever because He saw her. But this is true for us too. Being seen by God is particularly evident in the life of Yeshua's disciples. The twelve guys He chose to be His core group were a quirky bunch of ragtag, regular Joes. They were not influencers, intellectuals, or the elites of society. Simon the Zealot was a gangster. Thomas was a doubter. Judas was a traitor. Peter, the rock and ringleader, denied the Lord three times with cursing!

But Yeshua, God in the flesh, saw something in them that they could not see in themselves—promise and potential. He did not see them for who they were but for who they would become. Even when they fell short and blew it, again and again, Yeshua's insight kept pulling the gold out of them. It changed their lives. For example, Peter went from being a wishy-washy denier to a rock-solid dynamo of the faith.

God looks not at the outward appearance but at the heart. He is not affected by time. He is eternal and all knowing, seeing everything that will occur in our lives. He knows our choices before we make them. Yeshua knew Peter would deny Him three times, but He also knew Peter still loved Him and would lay down his life as a martyr one day. Therefore, God does not judge us based on one moment but from the totality of who we will become and what we will do with our lives. He sees us with our end in mind. Although we are a work in progress, God sees us as a masterpiece created by His own hands. He is always watching and willing to help those whose hearts belong to Him.

God sees us, but we must also learn to see Him and trust that He is working on our behalf. Seeing leads to spiritual transformation, success, and blessing. Helen Keller said, "The worst thing in the world is not to be born blind, but to be born with sight, and yet have no vision."[3] How many are blessed with sight yet have no spiritual vision to see that God is present with them in their circumstances?

Yeshua saw everything about His disciples when He picked them. *Adonai* saw Hagar in the wilderness, and He sees you in your situation. We need to see that, because we will never be more than we can see. Seeing leads to being, and being more is based on learning to see as God sees. Unfortunately, though, many people have poor or corrupted sight. Let me explain.

The Two Eyes

The Hebrew word *ayin* means "eye, to see." In Jewish thought, there are two types of eyes. There is the good eye, known in Hebrew as the *ayin tov*, and the bad eye, referred to as the *ayin ra*. Jesus talked about this when He said,

"The eye is the lamp of the body. Therefore if your eye is good, your whole body will be full of light. But if your eye is bad, your body will be full of darkness. If therefore the light that is in you is darkness, how great is the darkness!" (Matthew 6:22–23)

When we see things from the perspective of the good eye, we can perceive the positive, the good, and, most importantly, the hand of God in all things. When we view things through the "bad eye," we see problems, pain, and the bad in everything. The good eye is the optimistic eye of faith and can find good even in seemingly bad situations. The bad eye is the pessimistic eye that sees through the lens of fear and hurt, which creates doubt and negativity. When our bad eye shapes our perception, we live in a state of darkness. But when we learn to see through the good eye, we can see the light even during dark times.

Ayin is also the word for the sixteenth letter of the Hebrew alphabet. This is significant because, as we've mentioned, Hebrew is alphanumeric, which means that letters are written with numbers. The letter *ayin* (ע) has a numeric value of 70. The numeric value of the Hebrew words *sod* (hidden) and *yayin* (wine) also equal 70. The connection between these three words gives us some spiritual insight. It takes grapes to make wine/70. When looking at grapes hanging on the vine, it's hard to imagine that the literal crushing and bottling of them, over time, would produce wine. Each grape has an inner essence, but it is seemingly hidden/70. Yet with a trained eye/70, one can find the hidden/70 potential in the grape and make premium wine/70 as a result!

Cultivating a good eye allows us to see beyond the external. When we view life from the "good eye," we perceive that the crushing and shelving we experience in life are not bad but are just part of the process that transforms us into a fine wine. Instead of focusing on our pain and problems, we see that the process produces something of great blessing in our lives, though not always pleasant. The truly good eye is the eye of faith that sees the blessing, life, and good in all people and situations despite what they may look like on the surface. Like Yeshua, the good eye doesn't see the person we are now but the potential person in ourselves and others.

Revealed and Concealed Good

"God saw that it was good" (Genesis 1:10). Emulating God means learning to see the good. This kind of seeing can be challenging because much of what we go through in life does not appear to be good. Some of you may be thinking, *All that sounds good, Rabbi Jason, but in the world, creation is a brutal place! Where's all this good? I'm hurting. My loved one just died of COVID. I have cancer. I lost my job and can't pay the mortgage. My spouse walked out on me. A hurricane just ripped through my city, leaving devastation everywhere.* You get it. Stories like these abound and hit too close to home. Is it even possible to see good in what seems to be horrific and paralyzingly painful?

Understanding there are two categories of good—revealed and concealed—helps shed some light on this. Revealed good is the apparent good that is visibly beneficial and a blessing to our lives. Revealed good is what we pray for and what we seek to bless others with. Concealed good, on the other hand, is what people most often see as loss and suffering. On the surface, it appears to be bad. It is something we prefer not to experience. Why then is it called "concealed good"? Because Scripture tells us that God is good. If we genuinely believe God is good all the time, what we experience must be good in a way beyond our ability to see it at the time.

It takes little faith to declare that God is good when things are going

THE GOD OF THE WAY

well, but it takes a tremendous amount of faith to trust Him and declare His goodness when life is falling apart—when pain, both physical and emotional, is a present reality. We often correlate the presence of pain with the absence of God. Nothing could be further from the truth. But to embrace the Romans 8:28 promise of Him working "all things" together for the good of those who love Him, we must believe that what seems terrible on the surface has a concealed good that we can't comprehend.

Good does not always mean pleasant. Good means that God will bring benefit and purpose out of every situation for those who love Him and have the faith to see. The issue is not God's goodness but our inability to see. We grow spiritually and experience more peace and comfort as we develop the ability to see from the good eye, through the eyes of faith. This way of looking at life allows us to comprehend that "all" is for good, whether revealed or concealed. Deep-rooted faith teaches us that God's ways are higher than ours, that we see through a glass dimly now, but in the end, when we see Him face-to-face, we will see clearly and understand (Isaiah 55:8–9; 1 Corinthians 13:12). It will all make sense. We need to let the God Who Sees transform our sight as He did for Hagar, Ruth, David, and others whose stories we will explore more in this section, for when we do, we will never be the same.

Did God See Hagar?

Alone in the desert, her future a blur, Hagar felt like an unwanted orphan. She was sure no one cared and that no one was going to be there for her and her son. The good news is Hagar was not alone, although everything around her screamed just the opposite. There is One who always hears and sees—God-Adonai, YHWH, *Elohim*, Yeshua-Jesus! His heart is for the out-cast, the brokenhearted, and those who feel beaten down by life. The words of the psalmist should give us all hope: "ADONAI is close to the broken-hearted, and saves those crushed in spirit" (Psalm 34:19 TLV; Psalm 34:18 in non-Jewish translations).

Adonai is not only the God who sees; He is the God who hears! He's not indifferent to the pain and cries of His children. And more importantly, He doesn't just hear; He responds. For this reason, He told Hagar to name her soon-to-be-born son Ishmael, which means "God hears." God hears the cry of the outcast and the one who, like Hagar, is running away. The name *Ishmael* reveals that God is the One who hears and therefore helps those in need. *Ishmael* as a name is a memorial to God's kindness and faithfulness.

The idea that God hears is a vital lesson further revealed during Israel's slavery in Egypt. Like Hagar, the Children of Israel were being enslaved and treated harshly. For hundreds of years, they suffered, crying out to Adonai for help. For a season, the response from God was silence, and it seemed their pleadings had fallen on deaf ears. Yet that was not the case at all. God had heard, and at the appointed time, He spoke to Moses:

> "I have *surely seen the affliction of My people* who are in Egypt and have heard their cry because of their slave masters, for I know their pains. So I have come down to *deliver them* out of the hand of the Egyptians, to bring them up out of that land into a good and large land." (Exodus 3:7–9, emphasis added)

When the Children of Israel realized that God had indeed heard them and had seen their affliction, "they bowed their heads and worshipped" (Exodus 4:31).

Hearing, Obeying, and Healing

God heard, and so did Hagar. The Lord promised to multiply her seed when He said, "I will increase your descendants so much that they will be too numerous to count" (Genesis 16:10 NIV). But that promise was conditioned on her obedience to His command. He told Hagar to return and submit to Abraham and Sarah, her mistress who had mistreated her (Genesis 16:9). What is interesting is that the name Ishmael comes from the Hebrew word *shema*, which means to "hear" and "obey."

Hagar heard both God's promise and His command. It's one thing to hear God, but it's quite another to obey when what He asks is difficult and unpleasant. Yet, unwaveringly, Hagar went back and submitted to Sarah. Obedience is key to blessing. Too often God's people hear but fail to obey. The Children of Israel saw miracles in Egypt and heard His voice at Sinai but continually failed to obey. As a result, the entire generation that God supernaturally brought out of Egypt died in the desert.

Joshua and Caleb, however, listened and obeyed. Therefore they were the only two adults who were allowed to enter the Promised Land (Numbers 14:30). Unbelief and disobedience always distance us from God's blessing. Believing and obeying, on the other hand, lead to the fullness of His blessing upon us. When the disciples obeyed Yeshua and cast their nets on the other side of the boat after fishing all night and catching nothing, it seemed like a crazy thing to do. After all, they were experienced fishermen. They knew their stuff. Yet when they hauled in the nets, they were so full of fish that they broke (Luke 5:4–11)! The disciples, Joshua, and Caleb obeyed. Likewise, the story of Hagar and Ishmael reminds us that we must learn to hear *and* obey if we desire to walk in God's best for our lives.

No doubt, hearing God's voice can be challenging at times. One reason is that our hurts hinder our ability to hear. The longer we allow our wounded hearts to fester and go unhealed, the more static builds up and obstructs our connection with God. As in any relationship, past scars can create negative filters and walls that block our ability to be intimate. Healing is key to hearing because it opens us up for intimate connections. The Lord wants to heal us and eliminate our fears so we can draw close enough to Him to listen to His whispers to our souls and then trust His directions. "I will instruct you and teach you in the way you should go; I will counsel you with my loving eye on you" (Psalm 32:8 NIV). God's loving eye is on us. He sees and hears. Knowing that He hears our cries and that He cares is foundational to finding healing. Healing and wholeness begin by learning to hear what God has to say and obediently following His Word.

The God of Comfort

The angel of the Lord interacted with Hagar when she fled Sarah's abuse while pregnant and again years later when she and Ishmael were driven out of Abraham's family. The angel did this in a way that demonstrated that God is not only the God who sees and knows but also the God of comfort. Both times Hagar was in extreme distress, and the angel of the Lord came in part to bring her comfort.

There will always be loss in life, but *Adonai*, in His goodness and grace, always wants to bring more comfort than tragedy, more joy than *oy* (Hebrew for "woe"), and more blessing than a curse! *Adonai* always wants to give us double the comfort for the pain: "'Comfort, comfort My people,' says your God. 'Speak kindly to the heart of Jerusalem and proclaim to her that her warfare has ended, that her iniquity has been removed'" (Isaiah 40:1–2).

Comfort, compassion, and consolation are catalysts that help in the healing process. When I was a young rabbi living in Raleigh, North Carolina, I experienced how important and powerful this can be. I once visited congregants in the hospital who had recently lost their newborn child. It was a tragic situation that no one wants to endure. After spending the day with the family, I left the hospital physically and emotionally drained. Walking to my car, I saw a woman standing alone, crying in front of the hospital. She was in obvious distress, yet people were walking right by and ignoring her. Some might have been too rushed to notice her, while others might have thought it was not their responsibility to comfort a stranger. But something moved inside me, and even though I was exhausted, I could not disregard her.

When I asked her what was wrong and if I could do anything to help, she told me that her son was in the hospital dying of terminal cancer. His time was short, and it seemed as if no one cared. Her pastor had not come to visit, nor had the hospital provided the comfort she needed. Alone and grief-stricken, she was in such pain that my heart ached for her.

"May I pray for you and your son?" I asked.

"That would be nice," she replied.

I asked Yeshua to grant peace, comfort, and healing. A tangible wave of peace crossed her face, and it was apparent that the Lord had touched her heart. After profusely thanking me for taking the time to stop, she told me that the care and comfort she experienced at that moment was life-giving.

Concerning comfort, the apostle Paul wrote, "Blessed be the God and Father of our Lord Jesus Christ, the Father of mercies and God of all comfort, who comforts us in all our tribulation, that we may be able to comfort those who are in any trouble, with the comfort with which we ourselves are comforted by God" (2 Corinthians 1:3–4 NKJV).

God is the God of *all* comfort. When we comfort others with the same comfort we have received from Him, we become conduits of His love and grace. Our comforting touch becomes His touch. Our comforting words become His words.

Shortly before His crucifixion, Yeshua told the disciples, "I will not leave you comfortless: I will come to you" (John 14:18 KJV). And how would He comfort the disciples, who would naturally be in deep grief and struggling with feelings of despair after His physical presence was no longer with them? Yeshua's answer was the promised Holy Spirit, who is called Comforter. "The Helper (Comforter, Advocate, Intercessor—Counselor, Strengthener, Standby), the Holy Spirit, whom the Father will send in My name [in My place, to represent Me and act on My behalf], He will teach you all things. And He will help you remember everything that I have told you" (John 14:26 AMP).

For many pastors the word "Comforter" means "one to run to our side and pick us up."[4] The Spirit lives in all followers of Yeshua the Messiah, and part of what it means to be filled with the Spirit is to be full of comfort! Part of operating in the power of the Spirit is to bring comfort to others. The Spirit of Comfort lives in you to comfort others. In Jewish tradition, one of the names of the Messiah is *Menachem*, which means "the comforter/consoler."[5] By bringing comfort and consolation to others as the angel of the Lord brought to Hagar, we model Jesus and continue His ministry.

Happily Ever After

In Jewish tradition, there was a happily ever after for Hagar. Three years after Sarah's death, Abraham was remarried at 140 years of age to Keturah, with whom he had six children. But who is Keturah? And why would he marry and have kids so late in life? And why does the Torah give us so little information about who she was? According to Rabbi Shlomo Yitzchaki, a biblical commentator from the Middle Ages, and a host of other rabbinical scholars, three years after Sarah's passing, Isaac went and brought Hagar back to his father, Abraham, so that the two could be remarried. They believe Keturah is another name for Hagar. She was called Keturah, which means "incense," because her good deeds were as fragrant as incense.[6]

The Torah says, "Now Isaac had come from visiting Beer-lahai-roi and was living in the land of the Negev," and, "After Abraham's death, God blessed Isaac his son, and Isaac lived near Beer-lahai-roi" (Genesis 24:62, 25:11). What was Isaac doing in the place where Hagar and Ishmael were known to live? What was Isaac's motivation for living near Beer-lahai-roi and arranging for Hagar to remarry his father? According to rabbinic tradition, it's possible Isaac knew that his mother, Sarah, whom he loved, had committed a great injustice against Hagar. He wanted to make right what his mother had done wrong. He wanted to see reconciliation in the family.

This reconciliation is evidenced by Ishmael joining Isaac in the burial of their father, Abraham, at Machpelah (Genesis 25:9). The picture presented here gives us a prophetic sneak preview of what will happen in the messianic Kingdom. The descendants of Ishmael and Israel are not meant to be enemies as we see today. There is coming a day when both Jews and Arab nations will return to the Lord to be saved and reconciled with each other in fulfillment of biblical prophecy.

On that day, there will be a highway from Egypt to Assyria. Isaiah 19:23–24 tells us, "In that day there will be a highway from Egypt to Assyria, and the Assyrians will come to Egypt, and the Egyptians to Assyria, and the Egyptians will worship with the Assyrians. In that day Israel will be the third, along with Egypt and Assyria—a blessing in the midst of the earth."

And Rabbi Paul wrote in Romans 11:25–27,

I do not want you, brothers and sisters, to be ignorant of this mystery—lest you be wise in your own eyes—that a partial hardening has come upon Israel until the fullness of the Gentiles has come in; and in this way all Israel will be saved, as it is written,

> "The Deliverer shall come out of Zion.
> He shall turn away ungodliness from Jacob.
> And this is My covenant with them,
> when I take away their sins."

In the messianic Kingdom, Arabs and Jews will both believe in Messiah Yeshua. They also will dwell together in unity like Isaac and Ishmael did for a season. May this day come soon!

Returning to the beginning of our story, the pregnant Hagar named the well where she encountered the angel of the Lord, *Beer Lahai Roi*, translated as "the well of the One who lives and sees." This name commemorates God's intervention in her life that brought comfort and hope. The name of this well is a reminder to us all that God still sees, knows, and acts on our behalf. He will deliver us from death and despair as He did for Hagar, the bondservant of Sarah. All of us are slaves to sin and face death, but God saw and sent His Son, Yeshua, who died for us on the cross and was resurrected that we might have hope and a future!

A Note from Kathie

Hagar's story is at once tragic and triumphant. Scholars debate whether Pharaoh sold this Egyptian woman to Abraham or gifted her. Either way, she was not a free woman but a slave.

Let's think on that fact alone for a moment. Hagar had no rights under the Law. She had no say in her future. And she had no choice but to surrender to Sarah's will when Sarah threw her into Abraham's arms in order to bring about God's promise to make Abraham the father of a great nation.

Abraham had sexual relations with Hagar, and she bore a son, Ishmael, as a result. Hardly a Hallmark love story.

I love that the Bible never whitewashes the truth. People are human, and they have always been capable of both extraordinary good and unspeakable evil, and everything in between.

Abraham was called of God for a divine purpose. God wanted to build a nation in order to ultimately bring about the salvation of all humankind. God chose Abraham, and the Bible calls him a friend of God (James 2:23).

But he was married to a beautiful, barren, and broken woman named Sarah who was tired of waiting for God's will to be done.

She literally took the situation into her own hands: she gave Hagar to Abraham to fulfill God's promise in *her* way, not God's.

I can relate to Sarah. There have been many times in my own life when I have grown weary of waiting on the Lord to give me what He's promised me.

But how desperate she must have been to actually want her husband to have sex with another woman! The depth of her despair was beyond anything I can understand. So, I have compassion for all the individuals involved in this incredible story.

Yet God used them anyway to bring about His eternal plan, which of course was for the only true hero, Yeshua—God incarnate—to walk among us on earth, die a criminal's death, and rise from the dead on the third day. Hallelujah! May we all praise the God Who Sees!

ten

RUTH

Rabbi Jason

Ruth is one of my favorite books in the Bible. Because her story is so important, I dedicated an entire chapter to her in my book *Mysteries of the Messiah*. When considering the God Who Sees and His involvement in our lives, we must consider how He redirects our plans and vision. He did that for Ruth, and He's done that for me.

Years ago I moved across the country to California from New Jersey, pursuing what I thought was my dream job. A multimillion-dollar gift had been given to some friends of mine to start a ministry out here, and they wanted me to play a significant role. It seemed like such a God thing at the time, and I brimmed with excitement for what He was going to do. For a while, life hummed along just fine. My family had joined me, and we even wound up purchasing a home. Then, a year or so later, something happened at a conference on healing that radically disrupted my life.

During the conference, while walking through the parking lot, a friend of mine introduced me to one of the main speakers, Bill Johnson. Right there, the Lord moved on him, and without hesitation, he laid his hands on me and began to pray. As he did, a prophetic word was brought forth through him: "You wear many mantles like Joseph." It was only one sentence, but the power of God was so strong that I was shaking. At that moment, the Lord spoke to my heart that He was about to move in a great way throughout the world and this move would be rooted not in fear but in love accompanied by supernatural wonders and miracles. He impressed on me that if I was going to experience what He had for me, I could not settle for a form of godliness that lacked power. Then the Lord said, *I'm going to take you through a season of Joseph. I'm going to take you through the pits and the prisons. I'm going to strip you, but all the problems and everything that you're going to go through are going to prepare you for My true purposes for your life.*

Not knowing what it all meant, I pondered how literally this word from God might come to pass. But it all started to become clear as I stepped out in faith and obeyed the Holy Spirit's new leading. He prompted me to begin praying for people in the same way Bill Johnson had prayed for me, and the result was incredible healings, miracles, and prophetic words. I was blown away and humbled by what the Lord was doing and how He was using me as a vessel. As this new mantle enlarged, though, other things in my life were reduced. For multiple reasons, I wound up losing my dream job. I was unsure how our mortgage and the rest of the bills were going to be paid; it seemed like an absolute disaster. Yet, even during that stressful time, the Lord kept speaking to me, giving me His supernatural peace. As I simply sought Him, He brought me assurance that all would be taken care of and gave rest to my soul.

During this season God birthed the vision for the ministry we are doing today, which is Fusion Global. We add definition to people's faith in Yeshua by restoring the lost connections to our ancient Hebrew roots. Taking the first steps was scary and stressful, especially when God slammed shut all the doors for finances that I was sure would be open. The rejection was over-whelming, almost crippling. When Joseph was in the pit and the prison, it appeared the Lord had forgotten him. In His perfect timing, however, God brought Joseph out and into his place of divine calling and influence, and He would do so with me.

During this season the Lord also said to me, *You are going to speak before stadiums full of people.* This seemed a bit unrealistic, seeing as I didn't even have a job or ministry position. My friends laughed at me when I told them what God had dropped inside my spirit. But I just kept doing what He moved me to do, praying for people, speaking words of life into them, expecting the Lord to provide and open the doors that only He could open.

He did.

The Lord allowed me to cross paths with Lou Engle, who is well known for his prayer rallies across the globe that commonly had twenty thousand or more in attendance in huge stadiums. Remember, I was an unknown messianic Jew who had moved to California from New Jersey. I didn't know a lot of people, yet the Lord was connecting me with those who would help get me where He was taking me. Lou was one such person. Before one of his big events in Detroit, he had called me on the phone and asked, "How do you break the spirit of anti-Semitism?"

"It's the story of Ruth and Boaz," I said. Then I explained the story to him and how it related to his question.

"Will you come share the story of Ruth and Boaz and what that means for believers today, for Israel and the church, and how important this is for the two to come together?"

Of course I said, "Sure."

I knew something significant was going to happen there. The Lord had made it clear that this would be the beginning of what He was directing me into, the starting point for this new season that He was preparing me for, using everything that I'd gone through. Knowing this, I brought a videographer and crew along at my own expense to film me and the interviews I would do with some of the leaders.

As I was on the platform sharing the message of Ruth and Boaz, a guy unexpectedly rushed up on stage and grabbed the mic. I have no idea how he got past security, but it must have been the Holy Spirit, because he said before the thousands in attendance, "When I came to this event, I hated you. I came to this country as a terrorist, but tonight God opened my eyes, and I realize that Jesus is the Messiah, and He loves the Jewish people. I just want to repent for my hatred toward the Jewish people."

He got down on one knee. I got down on one knee. Then there was a moment of reconciliation of Jew and Gentile, Isaac and Ishmael, coming back together. The power of God fell on that place in an amazing way!

As I was leaving to go home, a woman I had met for the first time at the event felt prompted by the Holy Spirit to give me a $5,000 check. This was the exact amount of money I had spent to go to this event and to bring the film crew. Then she felt led to give me five gold coins and a valuable diamond ring. Placing them in my hand, she said, "This is from the Lord saying that God is always going to guide and provide for you." This was the confirmation I needed, and it sealed for me what the Lord had begun; that what He had promised, He was doing, stadiums and all. That event was the launching pad to where we are now, just as the Lord had told me. I couldn't have made it come to pass if I had tried. Like a chain reaction, that event led to more divine relationships and opportunities that would push us to new levels. At the core, though, our calling has never changed since my encounter with the Lord in the parking lot.

If I had not gone through all those difficulties and had God not removed me from my dream ministry job, I wouldn't be doing what I am today. God used all of it, the problems and the pain, the pits and the prisons, to redirect my path, humble me, mature me, and prepare me for His greater purposes and plan.

God has the ultimate satellite view of our lives. We forget that He is eternal, outside of time. His perspective is different from ours. God sees the big picture from beginning to end and can zoom in on the details at any time to adjust our courses for the best. Because of this, He can take all the different possible scenarios in our lives—choices we make or don't make, mistakes and blunders—and redirect us, working everything together for our good. God is the Master Redeemer of time and the Weaver of circumstances, but obedience is key. Even though He sees us and knows us, our plans and dreams may not be His.

Ruth is a perfect example of this. She experienced hardships and pain. Circumstances crushed her dreams, and she had questions. God stepped in and not only redirected her life but gave us the Messiah through her marriage to Boaz.

Ruth is a prophetic picture of the Gentile bride exalted and delivered from hopelessness (Ruth 1–4).

"Where You Go, I Will Go": Two Paths

A Jewish family living in Bethlehem during the time of the judges (1200–1020 BC) faced severe famine. Naomi, her husband, Elimelech, and their two sons fled for their lives without food and a home. After a short time, they decided to settle in Moab, an interesting choice since the Moabites hated the Jewish people. During their time there, Naomi's husband and two sons died, leaving her alone, save for her two Moabite daughters-in-law, Ruth and Orpah.

Grief-stricken and in survival mode, Naomi heard the famine was over in her hometown of Bethlehem and decided to return. She encouraged Ruth and Orpah both to return to her own "mother's house," feeling that she could not provide any future for them (Ruth 1:8). Orpah decided to return, but Ruth refused, insisting on remaining with her mother-in-law, for whom she had great compassion. Naomi discouraged Ruth and told her to go back "to her people and her gods" (v. 15).

Two paths lay before Ruth. One road was the path of her past—the path of her people, the Moabites. This path was the easier and more logical path. According to Jewish tradition, Ruth and Orpah were sisters and daughters of King Eglon,[1] which meant Ruth was royalty. Incredibly, though, instead of remaining in Moab, she courageously forsook comfort and security for an uncertain future. Choosing to separate from her people, her past, and being a princess, Ruth was drawn to faith in the God of Abraham, Isaac, and Jacob. She was willing to count the cost. She believed Adonai held a promise that was far greater than anything her past could offer. We learn from Ruth's decision that our old ways of being will never lead to the fullness the Lord has for us. She could have chosen the path of royalty by returning to her people, but she knew that was also a path marked by promiscuity and spiritual emptiness. Ruth did not want to "gain the whole world but lose [her] own soul" (Matthew 16:26 NLT). Instead she chose to risk living in perpetual poverty and pursue the path of spiritual riches.

Ruth and Abraham

Ruth chose the way of Abraham, which was completely opposite the way of her people. What the book of Hebrews says in regard to the patriarchs and matriarchs could also be said of Ruth:

Those who say such things make it clear that they are seeking a homeland. If indeed they had been thinking about where they had come from, they would have had opportunity to return. But as it is, they yearn for a better land—that is, a heavenly one. Therefore God is not ashamed to be called their God, for He has prepared a city for them. (Hebrews 11:14–16)

Ruth's actions connect her to Abraham, the only individual in the Old Testament whom God directly called "My friend" (Isaiah 41:8; James 2:23). What made Abraham such a good friend of God was the way he constantly cleaved[2] to Him and followed Him with absolute love and faith, even when things were challenging or testing.

Like Ruth and Abraham, we, too, must be willing to leave all and never stop cleaving to the Lord. Leaving and cleaving are foundational to becoming a friend of God. Abraham modeled this beautifully. He left his country, culture, and relatives to go to a land he did not know. Abraham was always willing to leave all for the sake of the call because cleaving to the Lord was what mattered most to him.

The same can be said for Ruth. The Scripture says that she "clung" to Naomi (Ruth 1:14). Ruth added, "Do not plead with me to abandon you, to turn back from following you. For where you go, I will go, and where you stay, I will stay. Your people will be my people, and your God my God. Where you die, I will die, and there I will be buried. May ADONAI deal with me, and worse, if anything but death comes between me and you!" (vv. 16–17). Ruth embodied genuine friendship and faithfulness, like Abraham, by leaving and cleaving.

This sense of cleaving is an expression of love and devotion that transcends the normal bounds of friendship. Ruth wanted to have this type of relationship with Naomi and her God. We should strive for intimate friendship with Yeshua Adonai and with those closest to us.

Interestingly, Ruth did not remain with Naomi primarily for her own benefit but for her mother-in-law's. Naomi would have been considered an older woman who fled with her family during a time of great crisis among her people. She would not have been welcomed back to Bethlehem with open arms. As they would with a prodigal returning home, people would have looked upon her with disdain. Perhaps this is the reason no one other than Boaz stepped up to help. Boaz's concern and assistance seemed to be solely on account of Ruth, not because of his family ties with Naomi. Ruth's selfless compassion and personal acts of kindness toward her mother-in-law moved Boaz, to whom she had no obligation. Her deep union with the Lord birthed this kindness and love Ruth had for Naomi.

The Ideal Relationship with the Lord

Ruth's complete devotion to Naomi provides a beautiful portrait of how we can achieve an ideal spiritual experience with God. By cleaving to Messiah Yeshua as Ruth cleaved to Naomi, we walk in union with the Eternal One, living in an ever-growing awareness of His presence. This unique union with God brings abundant life now and prepares us for living in His presence in the world to come.

Cleaving is a deep relationship in which one person selflessly and sacrificially joins with another so completely that there is a tangible sense of oneness and shared destiny. To cleave to someone in a biblical sense is the most intimate, intense, and ideal relationship imaginable. This is true on both a spiritual and human level. In this type of relationship, one who cleaves does not act primarily for their own benefit but puts greater priority on the well-being of the one to whom they cleave. One who cleaves relegates self for the sake of the other. It is the ultimate expression of intimate friendship and is the type of relationship the Lord wants to have with us!

In the New Testament, Messiah Yeshua invites us to become His friend: "I am no longer calling you servants, for the servant does not know what his master is doing. Now I have called you friends, because everything I have heard from My Father I have made known to you" (John 15:15).

This statement is radical, especially for the deeply religious culture of that time. Being called a "servant of God" was certainly an honor, but being called a *friend* of God was something else altogether. Being God's *friend* was reserved for those spiritual giants like Abraham and Moses. Yet Messiah Yeshua invites all of us "regular folk" to be not merely servants but His friends! But experiencing this amazing blessing of intimate friendship requires cleaving to Him as Ruth cleaved to Naomi and eventually to Boaz.

First and foremost, we cleave to Jesus to find true life and blessing. To find completion, we also need friendships that we cleave to as Ruth did with Naomi.

While loneliness and isolation are unavoidable realities of living in this fallen world, relationships give richness and growth to our lives. God created us for connection. Fullness comes to us when we have a solid vertical connection with God and strong horizontal connections with others we can pour our love into. Ruth modeled both.

A true friend is the one who runs *in* while everyone else is running *out*. Orpah ran from Naomi, but Ruth ran to her! While surface friendships can happen by chance, rich, deep relationships take intentionality. You will encounter a costly level of commitment as you love the other person like yourself. Yeshua gave the ultimate example of this when He willingly laid down His life for us to receive forgiveness and salvation. Honestly, we can have no more incredible friend than Yeshua-Jesus. He is our Redeemer, that

Friend who sticks closer than a brother, and our model (Proverbs 18:24). "In your relationships with one another," wrote Rabbi Paul, "have the same mindset as Christ Jesus" (Philippians 2:5 NIV). This verse means sacrificially loving and serving others as He did.

The Prophetic Nature of the Kinsman-Redeemer

In addition to the themes of friendship and romance, a powerful word that threads itself throughout the book of Ruth is the Hebrew word *goel*, which means "the one who redeems." The *goel* was a kinsman who was obligated under Torah law to act on behalf of a family member experiencing financial hardship. The kinsman bore the responsibility to sell their family land, home, or even themselves into indentured servitude (Leviticus 25). Ruth and Naomi found themselves in this situation. Ruth desperately needed a "kinsman-redeemer" who would redeem the ancestral property of her late husband and take her as his wife in the process. Without a *goel*, Ruth and Naomi were in dire straits and grave danger from both poverty and physical harm.

With Naomi's encouragement, Ruth approached the wealthy landowner, Boaz, at midnight while he was asleep on the threshing room floor and said to him, "I am Ruth, your servant. Spread your wings over your servant, for you are a redeemer" (Ruth 3:9 ESV). "Ruth was requesting Boaz to become her *goel*."[3] The details of their interaction and the relationship that developed is a type and shadow of the ultimate *goel*, Messiah Yeshua.

The first use of the term *goel* in Scripture is in the description of the supernatural salvation Jacob experienced: "the Angel who redeemed [*hagoel*] me from all evil" (Genesis 48:16). Twice in the book of Exodus, a form of the word *goel* is used to describe the Lord's deliverance of the Hebrews from slavery in Egypt (Exodus 6:6, 15:13).

Ruth's redemption connects to Israel's redemption and points to the Messiah, the ultimate *goel* or Redeemer. It is fitting that the *goel* refers to a human kinsman-redeemer and the Lord God in the Old Testament. Yeshua embodies both the divine and human aspects of the kinsman-redeemer so that we might be saved on both physical and spiritual levels! One reason I believe there were three hours of darkness while Jesus hung on the cross is that the plague of the death of the firstborn in Pharaoh's Egypt happened at midnight (Exodus 11:4). There had to be darkness when Yeshua died as the Passover Lamb so we wouldn't have to experience death like the firstborn of Egypt. The blood of a sacrificial lamb on the Hebrews' doorposts led to Israel's redemption (Exodus 12:13).

Israel's redemption and Ruth's redemption began in the evening and connected to Creation. *Adonai* created out of darkness, and Jewish days start at sunset in the Creation account. The light of redemption and the dawn of a new and better day for Ruth, Israel, and us also begins in darkness. During the darkness, Yeshua's death points to the light of salvation and new creation transformation that we can experience in Him.

The Place of Redemption

The place where Boaz spread his wings over Ruth was a threshing floor. The threshing floor is a symbol of redemption throughout the Scriptures. It was the place where a farmer separated the wheat from the chaff. Just as Ruth went to the threshing floor, all of us must go through seasons of threshing in which *Adonai* refines us by removing the worthless chaff in our lives. Threshing involves beating the stalks of grain with a stick or having oxen walk on them to separate the valuable grain from the worthless chaff. Ruth had been beaten down and stepped on, making her appear worthless as chaff to those who could see only her exterior. Yet Boaz saw below Ruth's surface to her inherent worth and potential. It was when Ruth had reached her lowest point, lying down at Boaz's feet on the threshing floor, that everything changed for her. The same is true for us. Pain and loss are part of the threshing process that God uses to bring out our true beauty and value.

Throughout Scripture, the threshing floor also signifies blessing and judgment. The prophets used the threshing floor and the winnowing process to describe the judgment of God on evildoers, on Israel for committing spiritual adultery, and on the nations who persecute the righteous. For example, Psalm 1:4–5 says, "The wicked are not so. For they are like chaff that the wind blows away. Therefore the wicked will not stand during the judgment, nor sinners in the congregation of the righteous."[4]

John the Baptist described Jesus as the promised Messiah who would ultimately fulfill these prophecies when he said, "His winnowing fork is in His hand to clear His threshing floor and gather the wheat into His barn, but the chaff He will burn up with inextinguishable fire" (Luke 3:17). Matthew depicted Yeshua as a farmer who brings God's plan for humanity to fruition, finalizing the Lord's harvest by gathering in the true believers like wheat into the barn and disposing of the tares like chaff cast into the fire (Matthew 13:36–43). All must pass through the threshing floor of the Lord, but as believers, we do not need to fear, for we are His children and are dear to Him. In your threshing floor season, Yeshua will pray for you just like He prayed for Peter: "Simon, Simon! Indeed, satan has demanded to sift you all like wheat. But I have prayed for you, Simon, that your faith will not fail"

(Luke 22:31–32). Though you may fall momentarily, like Peter, you won't fail, because you are in the prayers of Yeshua, the Great High Priest!

On the flip side, the threshing floor represents the abundance of a plentiful harvest and Adonai's providential provision. The Old Testament prophet Joel wrote,

The threshing floors will be full of grain
and the vats will overflow with new wine and fresh oil.
"I shall restore to you the years
that the locust, the swarming locust,
the canker-worm and the caterpillar have eaten—
My great army that I sent among you."
"You will surely eat and be satisfied,
and praise the Name of ADONAI your God,
who has dealt wondrously with you.
Never again will My people be shamed.
You will know that I am within Israel.
Yes, I am ADONAI your God—there is no other—
Never again will My people be shamed." (Joel 2:24–27)

What Joel speaks of in this passage is what the Lord did for Ruth and longs to do for you. Messiah came that we "might have life, and have it abundantly" (John 10:10). We can have a foretaste now of this, but ultimately we will experience the fullness of God's abundance and blessing in the messianic Kingdom.

The Old Testament prophet Amos wrote,

"In that day
I will restore David's fallen shelter—

> I will repair its broken walls
>
> and restore its ruins—
>
> and will rebuild it as it used to be,
>
> so that they may possess the remnant of Edom
>
> and all the nations that bear my name,"
>
> declares the LORD, who will do these things.
>
> "The days are coming," declares the LORD,
>
> "when the reaper will be overtaken by the plowman
>
> and the planter by the one treading grapes.
>
> New wine will drip from the mountains
>
> and flow from all the hills,
>
> and I will bring my people Israel back from exile.
>
> They will rebuild the ruined cities and live in them.
>
> They will plant vineyards and drink their wine;
>
> they will make gardens and eat their fruit." (Amos
>
> 9:11–14 NIV)

The Messiah Yeshua will bring redemption, abundance, and *shalom* to His people as He did for Ruth and Boaz. May this day, the day of the Lord, come quickly!

The Process of Redemption

Redemption began when Boaz purchased Ruth's late husband's ancestral property and acquired the legal right to become her husband. Boaz's actions and subsequent marriage to Ruth reveal a picture of the redemption that would occur through Messiah. Yeshua-Jesus is our *goel*/Kinsman-Redeemer who must first purchase us through His death on the cross so He might possess us as His bride:

- "You were bought with a price. Therefore glorify God in your body" (1 Corinthians 6:20).
- "The wedding of the Lamb has come, and His bride has made herself ready, She was given fine linen to wear, bright and clean! For the fine linen is the righteous deeds of the *kedoshim* [holy ones]" (Revelation 19:7–8).[5]

Messiah purchased us like Boaz purchased Ruth, but for a much greater price—His own body and blood. He did this so we might become His treasured possession (Exodus 19:5–6). Our lives are no longer our own. We belong to Yeshua and therefore should live to draw near and glorify Him (1 Corinthians 6:20).

This redemption process began when Ruth told Boaz, "Spread your wings over your servant, for you are a redeemer" (Ruth 3:9, my translation). The Hebrew word for "your wings" here is *kenafecha*, which is also an allusion to God's redemptive love for Israel (Ezekiel 16:8).

Like the wings of the Lord under which Ruth took refuge (Ruth 2:12), and like Boaz, who spread the wings of his garment over Ruth to symbolize his willingness to be her kinsman-redeemer, so *Adonai* desires to spread the wings of His garment over you and take you as His beloved bride. All you must do is grab the hem of Jesus' garment, and you will find healing, wholeness, and salvation in Him!

The book of Ruth is a compelling illustration of the ultimate redemption that comes to us through Messiah. To summarize:

- Yeshua, like Boaz, is from the tribe of Judah and from the town of Bethlehem. He is our Redeemer, who gave His life to purchase us out of spiritual poverty and take us to Himself as His bride.
- Yeshua, like Boaz, is generous with the needy. As Boaz did for Ruth, He cares about all people, both Jew and Gentile.
- Just as Boaz embraced Ruth while others rejected her because of her ethnic background, Yeshua drew near to the Gentile outcasts like the Samaritan woman (John 4:1–29) and the Roman centurion (Luke 7:1–10).
- Yeshua, like Boaz, embodies a protector and provider who goes about doing good by feeding the hungry, healing the hurting, and making the broken whole. Yeshua-Jesus is the greater Boaz and the Son of David par excellence!

The personal redemption Ruth experienced through Boaz reflects the love of the Ultimate Bridegroom for His bride, the church. Ruth desperately longed for Boaz to marry her and make a place for her in his home. May we long for Yeshua-Jesus, our Bridegroom, to come, see us, and take us home!

A Note from Kathie

The story of Ruth is one of my all-time favorites in the Bible.

Recently widowed and living with her deceased husband's elderly mother, who was also a widow, she is instantly revealed to us as a sympathetic person.

In the culture of that day, these were two women with very little hope for their future. For this reason, they clung to each other, for they had no one and nothing else to cling to.

Naomi, Ruth's mother-in-law, begged Ruth to leave her because she didn't want to be a burden to her. Ruth, in response, gave one of the most eloquent and profound declarations of love and commitment anywhere to be found in Scripture.

They set out together for the Promised Land—two women traveling alone through the desert with untold dangers before them. And yet they conquered their fears and arrived in Bethlehem, Naomi's ancestral home.

The rest of the story is a classic tale of true love and redemption, resulting in Ruth—a foreigner—actually becoming the great-grandmother of the future king of Israel, David, in the very lineage of the Messiah Jesus around one thousand years later.

You can't make this stuff up! It's too wonderful for words.

It moves me deeply to see through the lens of history how God has used ordinary, broken people to fulfill His grand design for all humankind.

He *sees* us. We are *precious* to Him, and He will *never* give up on us.

He will give us a future and a hope (Jeremiah 29:11).

eleven

DAVID

Rabbi Jason

Have you ever found yourself just going along, doing life the best you can? Things are clicking, you're making progress, and then *boom*! It seems everything begins to backfire. Perhaps you're dependable, you work hard, you display integrity, but for a time nothing goes right. It's like suddenly the cosmos turned against you. I've been there and have a feeling you've been there too. David surely experienced it.

There he was—a faithful shepherd boy, picked by God and anointed to be the future king of Israel. The Holy Spirit was upon him. God brought him out of the sheep fields and supernaturally directed the stone that slew the champion warrior-giant Goliath. David was hailed a hero. He won many battles, and the people danced in the streets, singing his praise. Life was good. He was clearly God's man, which meant smooth sailing ahead, right?

Not even close.

Instead of David being whisked to the throne and praised, Saul's heart burned with jealousy, and he tried to kill David! Suddenly David found himself a fugitive.

First Samuel 21:11 says, "David got up and fled that day from Saul, and went to Achish, king of Gath." Gath was the primary headquarters of the Philistines, where Goliath had lived! To survive living with the enemy, Scripture says that David "changed his demeanor before them and acted like a mad man while in their hands—scribbling on the doors of the gate and letting his saliva run down his beard" (1 Samuel 21:14). Why did David do this? Because his faith in the Lord had been temporarily replaced by a fear of both King Achish and Saul.

David realized living with the enemy was no help, so he departed from there and went to the cave of Adullam.

Reaching the Low Point

It was in the cave, after feigning insanity in front of the Philistines, that David composed Psalm 142. Having hit rock-bottom he wrote,

> Listen to my cry,
>> for I am brought very low.
> Rescue me from my persecutors,
>> for they are too strong for me.
> Bring my soul out of prison,
>> so I may praise Your Name. (Psalm 142:7–8)

David was low. Fear can do that to us. At that moment, David had allowed fear to dominate him, depleting his faith.

Fear gets in the way of our faith. It discourages us, distorting God's purposes and plans for us. Depleting, discouraging, or distorting, no matter how you describe it, fear blocks our breakthrough. "Fear not," said *Adonai* to the prophet Isaiah, "for I am with you, be not dismayed, for I am your God. I will strengthen you. Surely I will help you. I will uphold you with My righteous right hand" (Isaiah 41:10).

David's fear reminds me of another time when fear dominated people's thinking. Numbers 13 recounts the story of the twelve spies. Moses, at the request of the people, sent out twelve spies to investigate the Promised Land. Ten came back with a negative report, and two, Joshua and Caleb, were optimistic about what God had promised. Fear, however, overtook the group, and because of their lack of faith, they spent forty years in the wilderness. That generation didn't get to enter the Promised Land. That's what fear can do. It blocks our breakthrough.

Too many of us are dying in the wilderness, not entering our promised land. Oh, we see the promise far off. We want to enter all that God has for us, but our fear reveals our lack of faith and stops us cold. Our doubt leads to disbelief, and we're caught in a trap. Our disbelief leads to disobedience, and disobedience leads to dismissal from God's blessing and presence.

Faith, however, leads to trust. Trust leads to obedience, and obedience leads to blessing. I don't know about you, but I want all of God's blessing.

When David was alone, his mind wandered, and fear crept in, causing his faith to waver. We must be careful what we allow into our minds. Fear is the currency of the world. Faith is the currency of God's Kingdom. What we spend is up to us. Little faith equals spiritual poverty. Fear is an agreement with a lie and *the* liar. Faith is an agreement with truth and what God says. When we believe the lies the Enemy has spoken over us, we empower the liar. David was listening to a lie that Saul's threat would come to pass—Saul hated him and wanted to kill him. But God had anointed him to be king. For a short time, he believed the lie and not God's promise.

Fear believes for the worst. Fear causes us to die in the desert debilitated. It corrupts and blurs our vision of God and what He can do in any situation. Fear robs us of joy, replacing it with pessimism and cynicism that brings us down low. Faith, however, lifts us and believes Adonai for the best. Fear imprisons. Faith empowers. Fear paralyzes. Faith propels and gives us momentum to overcome mountains. The apostle John wrote, "Everyone born of God overcomes the world. And the victory that has overcome the world is this—our faith" (1 John 5:4).

Fear leads us to dead ends, while faith opens doors for receiving God's promises, presence, and provision. We can trust our future to Adonai because His plans for us are for our good. Instead of seeing the promise, the ten spies saw only the giants. But when Joshua and Caleb saw the Promised Land through the eyes of faith, the giants looked small! Their faith empowered them to know that whatever God promised, He would deliver regardless of the obstacles (Numbers 13–14).

Turning Fear into Faith

Pastor Charles Swindoll wrote, "David was beaten all the way down, until there was no way to look but up. And when he looked up, God was there."[1] He realized that God saw him in his distress. The God Who Sees brought the power of His presence to David.

David wrote several psalms during this period. Psalm 34 is one he wrote concerning his recovery from his fears and anxiety:

I will bless *Adonai* at all times.

His praise is continually in my mouth.

My soul boasts in *Adonai*.

The humble ones hear of it and rejoice.

Magnify *Adonai* with me

and let us exalt His Name together.

I sought *Adonai*, and He answered me,

and delivered me from all my fears. (Psalm 34:2–5)

Fear will seek to create our future using the negative pains of the past. We can choose to project either fear or faith. When we maximize fear, we minimize God. When we maximize God, we minimize fear. David set his fear aside and chose to do these key things:

- **Praise God.** His very soul boasted in the Lord. He exalted God's name. Pastor Charles Stanley wrote in his commentary about Psalm 34, "Even if it's not your practice, pick a day this week and praise God throughout the day. Praise Him when you wake up, praise Him when you eat, praise Him when you leave the house and when you return."[2] David knew the power of breakthrough praise. He didn't praise God one day a week; he worshiped Him every day, forever and ever. David's lineage traces back to Perez, the son of Judah and Tamar. *Perez* means "breakthrough," and his father's name, *Judah*, means "praise." In other words, breakthroughs are born of praise. David and Yeshua-Jesus, the Son of David, lived lives of praise that empowered them to break through seemingly impossible barriers and obstacles. A life of praise gives you the power to defeat your Goliaths.
- **Pray.** David sought the Lord, *Adonai*. He set his fear aside, grabbed

a handful of faith, and cried out to God. In Psalm 118:5 he wrote, "I called on the LORD in distress; the LORD answered me" (NKJV). I like how the NIV puts it: "When hard pressed, I cried to the LORD; he brought me into a spacious place." Biblical scholar Albert Barnes's commentary on this verse says, "I was before pressed on every side; sorrows compassed me around; I could not move; I had no liberty. Now he gave me space and freedom on every side, so that I could move without obstruction or pain."[3]

What do you do when hard pressed? Do you shrink in fear or cry out to the Lord in faith? David freed himself from the negative, enlarged his faith, and chose to trust in God. As a result *Adonai* answered him. Like David in his time of fear and trouble, we should cry out to God, with our hearts open to fellowship and conversation with the Unseen and Most Holy One.

- **Trust.** The writer of Hebrews reminds us, "Faith is the substance of things hoped for, the evidence of realities not seen" (Hebrews 11:1). Faith is knowing, deep in your heart, what is coming your way even though you can't see it. Faith says, "Whether I can see it today, or understand it in my mind, I *know* what God has promised and I know He *will* do it." The foundation of living a life in abundance and overflow begins and ends with faith and trust, not fear.

- **Move forward.** Courage is moving forward in the face of fear. David chose to move forward, and God delivered him. He didn't merely deliver David out of fear and bondage for him to live an ordinary life. The future king of Israel was struggling with fear. The mighty warrior and slayer of Goliath lived in terror with no rest and nowhere to go—except to God. David chose to trust God and have faith in His deliverance. He wrote, "In a day when I am afraid, I will put my trust in You" (Psalm 56:4).

Most of us won't face the types of fears that David did. But we will face fears. It could be unemployment, health, relationship issues, COVID, the explosive society we presently live in, you name it. In Psalm 56, we find David living courageously despite his fears. He took his concerns to God while in the presence of his enemies—in the middle of his challenges. And if we want to live a life in the overflow, it comes down to trusting in God and relying on the reality that He will show up in every circumstance. He's the God Who Sees.

A Note from Kathie

Who doesn't love the story of David? He was the youngest of eight brothers, the runt of the litter, and yet chosen of God to become the anointed king of Israel.

David slew the giant Goliath as a teenager and became the most celebrated soldier in Saul's army. He was a gifted poet and musician, and an equally gifted warrior.

He married the king's daughter and no doubt looked excitedly to a future on the throne of the kingdom of Israel.

But like so many in the Bible, he was forced to wait for many years for God's promise to him to be fulfilled.

During that time, he spent much of his energy running for his life and hiding from King Saul, who was jealous of him and wanted to kill him. Before long, David was forced to flee and hide in the wilderness and the caves of Judea. No longer celebrated. Now a hunted animal.

Many of the psalms he wrote came about as he despaired in the desert.

Waiting . . . waiting . . . for God's deliverance.

Where is God? he must have wondered. *Where are You, Lord?* we know he cried out in abject terror, just as Hagar and Ruth had before him.

David was like so many of us today who are hiding in fear, terrified of our enemies. But just as David's story wasn't over yet, neither is ours.

Did you know that "Fear not" is one of Scripture's most common commandments to us?[4] This is because fear is our most common adversary. But God wants to fight our battles for us. He wants to release us from our covers of darkness into His glorious light.

If only we would "fear not."

twelve

MARY OF MAGDALA

Rabbi Jason

During His travels, Yeshua encountered a demon-possessed woman, Mary of Magdala (Luke 8:2). He set her free from the evil spirits that had tormented her. Yeshua saw her and healed her. Mary's healing led to her becoming one of Yeshua's most faithful followers. She listened to His teaching. She served Him. Mostly, though, Mary loved Him with all her heart.

We can grasp her deep love and devotion to Him at His tomb early Sunday morning. Mary had experienced a life-changing encounter with Yeshua that fueled her love for Him. Despite her deep pain at the loss of her Rabbi and Master, there remained a ray of hope in her heart. Mary had seen and personally experienced the divine power of the Lord in the person of Jesus.

Chasing Away Demons

Before encountering Yeshua-Jesus, Mary suffered severely under the affliction of demon possession. The Bible mentions "certain women who had been healed of evil spirits and infirmities—Miriam [Mary], the one called Magdalene, out of whom seven demons had gone" (Luke 8:2). Just as important as Mary's healing is the power and means by which Jesus healed her.

In the first century, there were three healing methods—medicine, magic, or a miracle. The first two were expensive, and magic also involved an unhealthy superstition. But a miracle was free. Mary's miraculous healing would completely transform her life.

Yeshua cast out of Mary not one but *seven* demons. We must not overlook this essential detail. The number seven in the Bible is the number of completion. There are seven days in a week because God completed the work of Creation in that amount of time. The Torah uses the word "created" (*bara* in Hebrew) seven times in the Creation account (Genesis 1:1, 21, 27 [three times in v. 27]; 2:3, 4). There are seven churches in the book of Revelation and seven angels to these seven churches. Reading further in Revelation, we find seven seals, seven trumpet plagues, seven spirits before the throne, seven thunders, and the seven last plagues.

The use of seven in connection to Mary communicates that she was *completely* possessed. Her affliction was not some minor demonic oppression but full-blown oppression. She most likely dealt with bouts of depression and perhaps temporary insanity before Jesus healed her. The casting out of the seven demons points to Yeshua's absolute power and authority over the demonic forces of darkness.

The number seven is also the number of rest. On the seventh day, God rested from the work of Creation. According to the Torah, every seven years was to be a sabbatical year (*shemitah* in Hebrew; see Leviticus 25). This seven-year cycle gave the land a rest from farming and set free all Hebrew indebted servants. Yeshua's casting out of the seven demons from Mary emphasizes the truth that she experienced complete freedom, rest, and renewal in Him.

A few chapters after Luke mentioned the casting out of Mary's and other women's demons, Yeshua said, "If by the finger of God I drive out demons, then the kingdom of God has come to you" (Luke 11:20). This is interesting because "the finger of God" is associated with God's creative power and care: "When I consider your heavens, the work of your fingers, the moon and the stars, which you have set in place, what is mankind that you are mindful of them, human beings that you care for them?" (Psalm 8:3–4 NIV).

God used His fingers to create the heavens, but He only needed one finger to drive out demons! Casting the demons out of Mary Magdalene and others demonstrates that the God Who Sees has compassion for His creation and that He cares for you too!

The casting out of demons and the multitude of healings Jesus Messiah performed is evidence of God's creative and redemptive power. Understanding and experiencing His power in our lives, as Mary experienced, is critical to transformation, hope, and wholeness. When we don't know God's power in the present, we lose hope for our future. Mary had experienced the power of God in an authentic and personal way. Experiencing Messiah's power in the present gave her new hope for her future.

Helplessness and hopelessness go hand-in-hand. A sense of powerlessness will also lead to the loss of hope. But when we genuinely believe in and know the power of Yeshua Adonai, there is no situation that is helpless or hopeless. Mary's experience with God's healing power led her to generously support Yeshua's ministry, to courageously stand by Him at the foot of the cross, and to be the first and only person the Gospels record who saw the resurrected Yeshua on Easter morning. Her encounter with His power never allowed her to lose heart or hope. Her heart of hope is one of the reasons I believe that God called her to be the first witness to proclaim the good news that He had risen from the dead and was alive.

A New Hope

What a horrible sight it must have been as Mary watched her Messiah suffer and die on the cross. If that was not bad enough, she was also there as they laid Him in the tomb. It was likely at that moment that her hope seemed to die.

The death of Jesus was not the death of hope, however. It just appeared that way. He would rise three days later. And the empty tomb was not the end either; it was a new beginning. The resurrection was the fulfillment of an ancient promise that God meant to birth new hope! And what a tremendous promise it holds. As Mary encountered the risen Yeshua, a new, stronger hope was birthed to life from deep within.

There is no situation beyond hope, just people who have lost hope. The resurrection became a source of hope for Mary and the early followers of Yeshua, and it's still the source of hope for all of us today. Unfortunately many view hope as a vague emotion or desire, almost synonymous with wishful thinking. Usually when people say they are *hoping* for something, it's not what they genuinely believe will come to pass, but what they wish might ideally happen. It can be summarized by the saying, "Let's hope for the best but prepare for the worst."

Wishy-washy (pun intended) hope is the exact opposite of the biblical definition. In Hebrew the word for "hope" is *tikvah*. Every Hebrew word has a root from which it is derived. The root of *tikvah* is *kavah*, which means "to twist, stretch, or strengthen." Hope stretches us. The bigger and greater our hope, the more we will be stretched. But this stretching is for the sake of strengthening. Hope stretches our faith to fortify it.

Tikvah can also be translated as "rope" or "cord," as it is in Joshua 2:17–18 when the spies told Rahab to tie a scarlet cord in her window. The cord would be a sign of promise that no harm would come to her and those in her household.

The unbreakable cord/*tikvah* that Rahab put in her window represented the unbreakable hope/*tikvah* that she had in Adonai's promise. The strength of one's hope is like a rope that becomes stronger when the strands are intertwined and bound together. "A threefold cord," wrote Solomon, "cannot be quickly broken" (Ecclesiastes 4:12). Hope holds us securely in the same way as Rahab's rope held. There is always hope when our faith is intertwined and bound together by confidence in God's character and trust in His promises.

"Hope" in Greek is the word *elpis*. It means a "favorable and confident expectation. . . . It has to do with the unseen and the future. . . . 'Hope' describes . . . the happy anticipation of good."[1] Rabbi Paul wrote, "In this hope we were saved. But hope that is seen is no hope at all. Who hopes for what they already have? But if we hope for what we do not yet have, we wait for it patiently" (Romans 8:24–25 NIV).

Merely wishing for or desiring a particular outcome is like holding on for dear life to a weak rope that snaps under pressure. That's not biblical hope at all. True biblical hope is complete confidence and total trust in Yeshua *Adonai*. "Let us hold fast the confession of our hope without wavering, for He who promised is faithful" (Hebrews 10:23 NKJV).

One's hope is only as strong as the one in whom they hope.

Hope Is Rooted in Promise

Eugene Lang had a huge and memorable impact on a class of sixth graders from Harlem. The school invited Mr. Lang to speak to sixty-one sixth-grade students in the inner city. He knew that most of these students came from homes that struggled financially and that, statistically, most of them would drop out of school.

Mr. Lang wrestled with what he would say to these students to encourage them to pursue higher education and not give up. While standing in front of them, he put down his notes and spoke from his heart. Then he heard the following come out of his mouth, "Stay in school, and I'll help pay the college tuition for every one of you."

Mr. Lang went on to honor that promise, and his words that day forever changed those students' lives. In an instant, they had hope for their future. One student said, "I had something to look forward to, something waiting for me. It was a golden feeling." Close to 90 percent of those students graduated from high school.[2]

Like these kids, Mary's encounter with Jesus at the empty tomb restored her hope in Jesus and His promises for her future!

Hope is rooted in promise—the promise that what God has said, He will do! It's based on the assurance that Yeshua Messiah will keep His word. The resurrection declares that there is hope. Death is not the end! It declares that God cares and will do everything He said He would do. When we interweave God's promises into our hearts and minds, it makes our hope stronger than a three-cord rope.

Evangelist and writer Hal Lindsey said, "Man can live for about forty days without food, and about three days without water, about eight minutes without air . . . but only for one second without hope."[3]

This three-strand cord creates a lifeline that can pull people out of depression, doubt, and disillusionment and into their destiny. This pulling is what Mary Magdalene experienced on that Sunday morning. The empty tomb has become a powerful symbol and reminder of Jesus' resurrection.

I love to take people to Israel. One of my favorite destinations during our Rock, Road, and Rabbi Tour is the Garden Tomb. The Garden Tomb is in East Jerusalem and is one of two possible sites that could have been the location of Joseph of Arimathea's garden tomb where he buried Jesus. They have replaced the original door to this first-century tomb with a more modern one on which there is a sign that reads, "He is not here for He is risen!" The empty tombs remind us that Jesus is not buried but has been resurrected from the dead, which is the foundation of our eternal hope.

The fact that Yeshua rose from the dead validates His message and ministry. The resurrection demonstrates that He was indeed who He claimed to be—the Eternal Word Become Flesh. That's why Resurrection Sunday was such a big deal for Mary and the disciples—because our entire faith hinges not on a teaching or a belief system but an actual historical event.

Rabbi Paul wrote,

If Messiah has not been raised, then our proclaiming is meaningless and your faith also is meaningless. Moreover, we are found to be false witnesses of God, because we testified about God that He raised up Messiah—whom He did not raise up, if in fact the dead are not raised. For if the dead are not raised, not even Messiah has been raised. And if Messiah has not been raised, your faith is futile—you are still in your sins. Then those also who have fallen asleep in Messiah have perished. If we have hoped in Messiah in this life alone, we are to be pitied more than all people.

But now Messiah has been raised from the dead, the firstfruits of those who have fallen asleep. For since death came through a man, the resurrection of the dead also has come through a Man. (1 Corinthians 15:14–21)

According to the Hebrew calendar, Yeshua's resurrection was on no ordinary day but a day of historical hope. Yeshua died on the biblical holiday

167

of Passover as the greater Passover Lamb. But the day He rose from the dead was also a biblical holiday known as Firstfruits, *Yom HaBikkurim* or *Chag HaKatzir* in Hebrew, as we read in Leviticus 23:

> The LORD spoke to Moses, saying, "Speak to the children of Israel, and say to them: 'When you come into the land which I give to you, and reap its harvest, then you shall bring a sheaf of the firstfruits of your harvest to the priest. He shall wave the sheaf before the LORD, to be accepted on your behalf; on the day after the Sabbath the priest shall wave it. And you shall offer on that day, when you wave the sheaf, a male lamb of the first year, without blemish, as a burnt offering to the LORD.'" (Leviticus 23:9–12 NKJV)

On the morning Yeshua rose, the priest would have waved a sheaf (*omer*) of green barley before the Lord as a symbolic gesture of dedicating the coming harvest to Him. If there was an excellent Firstfruits, it created hope in the people's hearts, for it was a sign of the later great harvest coming soon. Rabbi Paul connected Yeshua's death with the holiday of Firstfruits: "Messiah has been raised from the dead, the firstfruits of those who have fallen asleep. For since death came through a man, the resurrection of the dead also has come through a Man. For as in Adam all die, so also in Messiah will all be made alive" (1 Corinthians 15:20–22).

Yeshua rising from the dead on the day of Firstfruits pointed to the blessed hope—the promise that all believers will rise one day as part of the later greater harvest, the resurrection of the dead occurring at His Second Coming.

Not only was the Firstfruits a sign of the greater harvest to come, but it started the forty-nine-day countdown to Pentecost.

Nothing is random with God. Therefore, it is appropriate that Jesus, who died on Passover, would arise from the dead on Firstfruits as "the firstfruits of those who have fallen asleep" (1 Corinthians 15:20). After He arose, Jesus instructed the disciples, "Do not leave Jerusalem, but wait for the gift my Father promised. . . . For John baptized with water, but in a few days you will be baptized with the Holy Spirit" (Acts 1:4–5 NIV). Yeshua's resurrection on Firstfruits started the countdown to Pentecost when His Father gave the gift of His Spirit (Acts 2:1–4).

On this same day, the sixteenth of *Nisan* on the Jewish calendar, the day that the firstfruits were offered (Leviticus 23:9–14) and Jesus rose from the dead (Mark 16), the Children of Israel crossed over the Jordan for the first time to possess the Promised Land in the days of Joshua (Joshua 3). On this same day, Hezekiah completed the rededication and cleansing of the Jerusalem temple that Solomon built (2 Chronicles 29:20–36). Haman, who had tried to destroy the hope of Israel (see the book of Esther), died on the gallows (Esther 7:10). "The odds of just two of these events occurring coincidently on the same day of the Hebrew year are 1 in 129,000."[4]

Hope, in part, is rooted in the belief that God's hand is in the details of our lives and all of history. God sees us in all our circumstances, both good and bad. Mary's tears and fears were wiped away after witnessing the resurrected Jesus, and her hope was restored.

Like Mary, we, too, have a blessed hope! It's an authentic and living hope that has the power to bring real and lasting change in our lives. God sees our needs, and with one finger, He can free us from any demons (depression, helplessness, loneliness, and more) and replace them with His hope. When we allow the rope of our lives to be intertwined and bound to the hope that Yeshua, the Word, and His promises give to us, we create an unbreakable threefold cord.

A Note from Kathie

Though pop culture has immortalized Mary Magdalene in the classic Broadway song "I Don't Know How to Love Him," that sentiment was not true at all. Though she remains a woman of mystery all these years later, as Scripture does not tell us many details about her life, we know she knew exactly how to love Jesus—deeply and profoundly—because He had loved her back to life itself from a lifetime of demonic suffering. He delivered her from the gates of hell, and as a result she dedicated the rest of her life to loving, following, and serving her Savior.

My favorite moment in the Bible is when Mary didn't recognize Jesus in the early light of day and mistook Him for the gardener (John 20:15–16). She asked to be told where her Savior had been taken so she could go and get Him. He replied in one simply astounding word, "Mary," and instantly her eyes were opened.

Her Savior had risen! He was alive—brought back to life just as He had brought her back to life.

I am moved to tears every time at the simple, tender human love between Jesus and Mary. It is exactly the way I believe He feels about me when He says, "Kathie."

It is exactly the same way He feels about *you* when He says your name too.

What grace!

Part Four

THE GOD OF THE OTHER SIDE

Kathie

The genesis for the oratorio *The God of the Way* began several years ago when I was on a rabbinical study trip to Israel led by an extraordinary teacher named Rod VanSolkema and his lovable and gifted wife, Libby. I appreciated being shepherded by a married couple, and I loved watching them synchronize their individual strengths in a way that completely complemented their power as a couple. They both have sharp minds and tender hearts: an irresistible combination!

On one particular day, Rod began by telling us the story from Matthew 14 of when Jesus told His disciples to get into their boat and meet Him on the other side of the lake, before He came walking to them on the water.

I was familiar with the story—I'd been traveling to the Holy Land to take part in intense rabbinical study trips since I was a teenager. I was always hoping to learn more truth about the Scriptures and gain an even deeper understanding of what the Word of God said in its original Hebrew and Greek texts.

I had always assumed that Jesus meant "the other side" to simply mean the other side of the Sea of Galilee. But the fascinating part of studying rabbinically is that you also learn *context*, including customs of the culture when Jesus lived on the earth as well as the geopolitical realities of ancient times.

Once Rod taught us that "the other side" also meant something very different from and more profound than just a physical location, the story took on much deeper meaning.

The area Jesus was telling His disciples to meet Him was the Decapolis— ten ancient villages where the original Canaanites had fled from Joshua's invading army of Hebrews after they'd crossed over the Jordan River to conquer the Holy Land.

These villages were inhabited by people who worshiped many gods and idols. They sacrificed babies to the gods Moloch and Chemosh and others and participated in all manner of sexual perversion. They were the opposite of a devout Jew and were considered unclean.

We can only imagine how the twelve disciples reacted when they heard Jesus basically tell them to go to the ancient-day equivalent of Sin City!

What would we do today if Jesus asked us to do the same? Would we be as confused and terrified as the disciples were two thousand years ago? Would we decide to say, "No, Jesus. I mean, You're cool and You do amazing miracles and I like all Your stories, but what You're asking defies everything I've ever been taught. I'll catch up with You when You get back and hear all about it"?

Or would we trust that He had a purpose for everything He said and did, and maybe if we followed Him He'd lead us on the adventure of a lifetime?

Rabbi Jason will guide us as we get in the boat and experience it for ourselves.

Rabbi Jason

It was drilled into our heads when I was growing up to "always look both ways before crossing the street." This warning was especially true for a boy in eastern New Jersey, where the sidewalks and streets were often our playgrounds. Whether we were throwing a ball, riding our Sting-Rays, or doing anything else kids do, maneuvering around vehicles was an everyday occurrence. Though our parents taught us well, we sometimes made some not-so-thought-out dashes to the other side of the street. Fortunately my friends and I survived. But there were times when I went into bustling downtown Manhattan with my parents when merely walking along the crowded sidewalks, or at the subway station, or crossing the street, was overwhelming—especially to a waist-high six-year-old. Yet, because my dad or mom had a firm grip on my hand, I knew I was safe. We would make it to the other side. I kept a clenched hold on their hands, never wanting to drift from their sides, not taking any chances.

My parents guiding me was a shadow of *Adonai* guiding us. All loving, all knowing, and all seeing, He takes us by the hand and goes to the other side with us. It might be a dangerous journey or through a dark storm, but as we clench our hands in His with trust, He will faithfully lead us. And not wanting to drift from His side, we gain a deeper intimacy with Him.

In another way, Yeshua went to the other side for us, and He calls His followers to meet Him where all the broken, lost, and desperate souls are and to serve them with His love. This calling is bigger than us. We can't do it on our own. Yet, while Yeshua calls us, He also takes our hands and guides us.

That's what this section is all about. Through several biblical characters—Peter, the demoniac, the Samaritan woman, the prodigal son, and Cornelius—we will discover that Yeshua is the God of the Other Side. He is the One who never passes by but crosses over to meet us where we are. As we mature in Him and decide to go with His plan and not our own, He always goes with us to the other side.

PETER WALKS ON WATER

Rabbi Jason

The wind whipped with intense fury, pushing the water into massive waves that swirled and sucked and smashed down upon the man who was fighting for his life. Raindrops slashed across his face, and he gulped large amounts of water as he kicked and gasped in his frantic struggle against nature's cruel turbulence—but to no avail. The man was drowning. And to think, mere moments ago, he had been full of courage, stepping out in faith, obeying his Master's call—but that was then. Circumstances had abruptly changed. Distracted by the water's threatening force, his confidence had vanished. The sea, along with his fear, was engulfing him, dragging him down deeper into despair.

Maybe he had misunderstood. Yet he was almost certain he had heard his Master say, "Come." Yes, he was positive. Could he completely trust the Master? Surely, He wouldn't call him out of the boat only to let him drown? He had never let him down in the past.

Then, with one final surge of energy—one last leap of faith—the man lurched up in a desperate attempt to grasp the arm that was reaching down for him. If he could but cling to his Master's hand, the man knew he would be safe. Immediately Jesus reached out His hand and caught him.

Of course, the man in the above passage is the apostle Peter, and the Master is Jesus. This story is key to discovering the God of the Other Side. We find the account of Jesus walking on water in three gospels (Matthew 14:22–33; Mark 6:45–51; John 6:16–21). In it Yeshua's manipulation of the elements is on full display as even the water is subject to Him. It's an incredible lesson for Peter and the disciples—and the fulfillment of messianic prophecy that points to Yeshua as the Messiah.

Earlier we learned about Yeshua's power over creation. Rabbi Paul wrote that He is the firstborn over everything that exists, seen and unseen, having created it all (Colossians 1:15–20). Yeshua walking on water demonstrated this.

Peter's Lesson

Yeshua had just morphed five loaves of bread and two fish into a feast for five thousand, with twelve full baskets left over! Some scholars say the Bible only counted the men, so it was probably more like ten to fifteen thousand with women and children. Everyone was in awe and patting their satisfied bellies when Yeshua told the disciples to hop in the boat and head on over to the other side of the sea while He stayed behind to pray.[1] These were experienced fishermen. It was only about eight miles across the sea. After just witnessing such an incredible miracle, they were like, "Sure. Whatever you say! No problemo. We got this." They jumped into the boat with no clue what was about to come down.

While Yeshua was alone on the mountain fellowshipping with His Father, a major storm driven by strong winds abruptly materialized seemingly out of nowhere, turning life-threatening. A quick, violent storm is common on the Sea of Galilee. One writer described the storms this way:

> These tempests are caused by the situation of the lake in the Jordan Rift
> with steep hills on all sides. The cooler air masses from the surrounding
> mountains collide with the warm air in the lake's basin. Winds sometimes
> funnel through the east-west-oriented valleys in the Galilean hill country
> and rush down the western hillsides of the lake. The most violent storms,
> however, are caused by the fierce winds which blow off the Golan Heights
> from the east. One such storm in March 1992 sent waves ten feet (3 meters)
> high crashing into downtown Tiberias and caused significant damage to
> the city.[2]

Recently a boat was discovered in a nearby site of Migdal that gives us an idea of what a first-century fishing vessel might have looked like. The boat discovered was roughly twenty-seven feet long, seven and one-half feet wide, and four feet tall with a cutwater bow and a recurving side. It had a single square sail but also oars for rowing.[3] In other words, it didn't give much protection from sudden tempests, and ropes were the only seat belts!

As the disciples wrestled with nature, they must have been wondering, *Yeshua knows all things. Why did He tell us to go to the other side if He knew a storm was coming?* Now, fearing for their lives as the wind and waves beat on them, their faith began to waver.

Interestingly, Yeshua was aware of what was going on, but He didn't jump up and run to their rescue. He continued to pray and allow His disciples to struggle (the NIV translation of Mark 6:48 tells us the disciples were "straining at the oars"). During a previous violent storm, Yeshua had been with the disciples catching some z's in the boat while they were freaking out. After they had shaken Him awake, Jesus had calmly rebuked the winds, and the sea became like glass (Matthew 8:26). Not on this trip. This time their Messiah was miles away.

Just as He'd done with Lazarus, Yeshua let them wait until it appeared all hope was lost. With control over all creation, He didn't need to rush to be "on time." He knew exactly what to do and when. The disciples were in His hands.

Faith or Fear?

After Yeshua sent out the disciples, He went into the hills to pray. Mark 6:48 tells us, "Around the fourth watch in the night, *Yeshua* comes to them." That's about three in the morning. He looked from the mountainside and saw His men struggling in the sea. Immediately He stopped praying and went into action. He walked out to them on the water. Because Yeshua's walking on water was so miraculous and defied the laws of physics, it must be seen in the context of the monumental parting of the Red Sea. Often, our first response when experiencing the pounding storms of life is fear and panic. Even though we want to believe God is in control, our circumstances scream that we are going under.

This was Israel's feeling when they were being pursued by Pharaoh, up against the Red Sea. God raised up Moses to lead them out of the bondage of Egyptian slavery. Through his hands, God wrought ten miraculous signs in the form of plagues. After the tenth, Pharaoh finally relented and let Israel go. Yet his decision was short-lived. Pharaoh's heart soon hardened again, and he unleashed Egypt's full military might to pursue enslaving the Israelites once more.

While the *Bnei-Yisrael* (Children of Israel) were encamped at the Red Sea, Pharaoh's troops pressed in. With water as far as the eye could see on one side and the innumerable enemy on the other, panic set in. According to Jewish and rabbinical tradition, the leaders of the twelve tribes began to argue among themselves. The heads of the tribes of Reuben, Simeon, and Issachar[4] wanted to drown themselves in the Red Sea. They preferred martyrdom to returning to Egypt as slaves. Likewise, today one can quickly develop a martyr complex when feeling trapped and unfairly abused. It's the belief that one must endure suffering out of a deep sense of duty, love, or spiritual commitment. Moses responded by saying, "Stand still, and see the salvation of the LORD" (Exodus 14:13 KJV).

The leaders of the tribes of Dan, Gad, and Asher wanted to wildly charge the camp of the Egyptians in hopes that it might confuse or scare them. It would be a kind of Hail Mary action borne out of a sense of fear and desperation. Moses responded by essentially saying, "Stay put and forsake this plan."

The tribal leaders of Judah, Ephraim, and Manasseh wanted to go to war. They sought to take matters into their own hands by taking up arms against the Egyptians. They believed it was better to die fighting for their freedom than to surrender.

Zebulun's, Benjamin's, and Naphtali's leaders wanted to surrender and return to Egypt as slaves. They thought all the other options were futile. From their perspective, it was best to give up peacefully so that they and their children could survive. But *Adonai* said through Moses, "You will never return to Egypt" (Exodus 14:13, my paraphrase).

The tribes' responses were wrong. *Adonai* did not want the Children of Israel to give up, lie down, or surrender. He did not want them to go forward fighting in their own strength or act according to their self-devised plans. Nor did He want them to return to slavery in Egypt. God does not begin a good work and fail to finish it!

If we are not careful, we'll make the same mistakes the leaders of the twelve tribes did, leaning on human logic and reasoning or emotion. In those situations where we feel trapped and fearful, it's God's solution we need, not our own. Listening for His instructions and moving forward in faith keeps us from being paralyzed by fear! Listening and moving in faith are difficult, but it's exactly what God asked of Moses and the Children of Israel and exactly what He asks of us: "*ADONAI* said to Moses, 'Why are you crying to Me? Tell *Bnei-Yisrael* [Children of Israel] to go forward'" (Exodus 14:15).

It's important to note that *Adonai* did not part the Red Sea before telling Israel to go through it. Taking those first steps of faith into the water was required before the parting began. God often expects the same from us before He moves on our behalf. Don't wait for a miracle when God says, "Go." Instead step out in faith and watch your personal Red Sea part!

While the wrath of nature battered the disciples' boat, Yeshua did not part the sea. Instead He did something equally grand, proving Him to be the "prophet like [Moses]" described in Deuteronomy 18:15–18. Yeshua *walked to them on the water*, demonstrating His power and authority over creation as well as over the unique storms we face in life.

As Peter saw his Master walking on water, he shouted out, "Command me to come to You on the water."

"Come," Yeshua said (Matthew 14:28–29).

Notice, while there were twelve disciples in the boat, only one had enough faith to step into the fury and attempt to walk on water.

Sure, Peter doubted when the waves thrashed around him, and he began to sink, but we must give him credit for trusting enough to try. Like the faith of Moses, who led the people into the sea before it parted, and the faith of Peter, who stepped out of the boat, miracle-working faith involves taking risks for God. Willing to overcome our fears and doubts, we step into the unknown, trusting that Yeshua will either make a way for us or keep us from drowning as He did for Peter. We can't forget: Peter did walk on water by himself for a while, and then with Yeshua—something none inside the boat experienced. The person who always stays in the boat and plays it safe will never see God do great and mighty things on their behalf. Don't be afraid to put your feet in the water! Step out of the boat. When you take that step of faith, you have the potential to step into amazing things by God's grace!

Any opportunity requires a risk. But often, fear paralyzes us and leads us to a place of apathy, procrastination, and complacency. We would instead settle for the status quo rather than going after all God has for us. Settling is such a tragedy. Fear can rob us of God's best.

"Faith" Is Also Spelled R-I-S-K

When we look at Kingdom greatness and God's inheritance, we can see that we're required to take risks. But, candidly, risk can be scary.

What if Peter would have shrunk back in fear? What if he had never left his seat on the boat? Fear is what makes us settle and keeps us locked in mundane and unfulfilling patterns of life. Sometimes being knocked out of our comfort zones is the best thing that could happen, but God prefers we move in faith. Look what God was able to accomplish through Peter's life once he stepped out of the boat.

Sadly, too many of us would like to settle rather than pioneer into our inheritance. What about you? Do you hear Yeshua beckoning, *Come. There's more. I have something better for you. Won't you step out into your destiny with Me?* If we are to fulfill our God-called purpose, we must be willing to trust Him enough to risk all. It is time to follow in the footsteps of Peter and step out into the water. Though our faith may falter at times, Yeshua is patient and faithful. He won't let us drown.

The Man Who Made the First Move

Peter wasn't the only one who took a step of faith and jumped into the sea. Nachshon, the son of Aminadav, was a fifth-generation descendant of Judah. His sister, Elisheba, was married to Aaron (Exodus 6:23). When God commanded Moses to get the people moving, at that moment, Nachshon took a step of faith. Both the *Midrash*[5] and Talmud[6] tell us,

> When Israel stood facing the Sea of Reeds, and the command was given to move forward, each of the tribes hesitated, saying, "We do not want to be the first to jump into the sea."
>
> Nachshon saw what was happening—and jumped into the sea.
>
> At that moment Moses was standing and praying. God said to him, "My beloved ones are drowning in the stormy seas, and you are standing and praying?"
>
> Moses replied, "Master of the world, what am I to do?"
>
> Said God, "You lift your staff and spread your hand over the seas, which will split, and Israel will come into the sea upon dry land."

And so it was. Following Nachshon's lead, the Israelites entered the sea, and God did the rest.

Afterward God rewarded Nachshon. When Moses completed the tabernacle, the princes of the twelve tribes of Israel offered special inaugural sacrifices and gifts. While Judah was not the most senior of the tribes, had flipped it up and propped it against the wall. Oscar and Lorenzo hunched over the electronics on the carpet. Sixty-four wires the size of a single hair needed to be meticulously fitted into individual, small holes and then topped with a dash of solder.

Lorenzo positioned the wires in the holes, while Oscar melted the solder with the soldering iron. With each drop of solder, a small puff of gray smoke trellised into the air. They barely talked during the delicate, nerve-racking work. If Oscar hit the wire with the soldering iron, the wire would instantly melt and disappear, forcing them to pull out everything they'd done, restrip all the wires, and start over.

By the time they had done fifty wires, it was roughly two in the morning. Their eyes hurt after hours of staring at tiny wires. The stakes were higher now too. A mistake now would mean ripping out the completed connections. If that happened, they wouldn't have enough time to resolder everything before the competition. Every connection needed to be perfect now.

"Let's take a break for a second," Oscar said.

They sat back and rubbed their eyes. The room was filled with an acrid, burnt smell. Everybody else was asleep.

"Thanks for staying up with me," Oscar said.

"You think I'm going let you do this by yourself?" Lorenzo said. Oscar thought Lorenzo meant that they were all in this together until Lorenzo added, "You'd probably screw it up if I wasn't watching you."

Lorenzo grinned at him with a big, crooked-tooth goofy smile. Oscar chuckled. He never would have been friends with a kid like Lorenzo, but now he was glad they were teammates.

"Shut up," Oscar said, picking up the solder gun. "Let's get this done." They had fourteen left. Oscar moved carefully and slowly while Lorenzo positioned the fifty-first wire.

Lorenzo said a silent prayer to the Virgin Mary, and they worked through the final batch of wires, connecting the last one around 2:30 a.m. They turned the power on and tested the joysticks. The machine worked.

THE BANNER ABOVE the pool declared WELCOME TO THE 2004 NATIONAL ROV COMPETITION. A set of high-powered fans blew across the surface, obscuring the view below. Teams could make out the vague outline of a large black structure but nothing more. A loudspeaker blared Hawaiian music. This was the main event: the underwater portion of the Explorer-class competition had begun.

Monterey Peninsula College was called to the pool. Their fifteen-person team deployed three vehicles: two ROVs—dubbed Romulus and Remus—and a third craft, the Sea Wolf, which served as their eyes in the sky. It floated on the surface with a camera system to guide the operation. Romulus was a heavy-lift submersible and ran off three car batteries in the command tent. Remus was a smaller, more agile bot designed to explore the interior of the mocked-up submarine. Even with all that robotic firepower, Monterey only picked up 30 out of 110 points. The mission tasks were proving to be even more difficult than anticipated.

Cape Fear Community College managed a slightly more successful run. Their robot had a beautiful extruded-aluminum frame with a shiny blue fiberglass-covered foam top. They called it the Sea Devil 3. Its shell gleamed so nicely in the morning sun that Allan took to calling the bot a piece of "underwater jewelry." One of its most impressive features was a chamber at the top that was connected to a scuba tank in the command tent. It allowed the operators to add to or remove air from the chamber to fine-tune buoyancy on the fly. When the robot picked up a heavy object and had trouble surfacing, they sent a blast of air down a tube and the ROV came right up. It was a good idea with solid engineering behind it, and yet they managed to post only 40 points by the end of their thirty-minute run.

There were eleven teams in the Explorer division, and all of them had chosen to measure themselves against a higher standard. As a result, most of the teams were more confident and accomplished, and all of them posted at least 5 points. Nonetheless, some experienced catastrophic failures early in their missions. Their robots simply sank to the bottom of the pool and sat there, unresponsive. After a few minutes of fruitless troubleshooting, the teams had to ignominiously haul their robots out of the water by the tether. One stranded robot emitted a giant air bubble from the depths.

Lorenzo watched from the side of the pool and laughed. "It farted."

Lorenzo's joking didn't lighten the mood. If these other teams were struggling, it meant that Carl Hayden should expect to have an even tougher time. The Explorer division was clearly punishingly difficult, but it also gave them a sliver of hope. If they could just get their robot to work and complete a single task, they'd be ahead of the teams whose robots shorted out. That meant they wouldn't finish last.

The judges called MIT to the pool, and the college students lowered their compact, welded-aluminum ROV into the water. They quickly piled up points. They sped around the pool, locating objects and confidently investigating the interior of the mocked-up submarine. Locating the underwater pinger was one of the most challenging tasks. The event organizers had scattered four dummy pingers around the pool so that teams wouldn't luck into picking the right one. MIT located it using their Knowles Acoustics MR-8406 underwater microphone.

They weren't perfect though. They found the barrel with the leaking fluid and maneuvered up to it. This task was worth

15 points—more than any other. Since 3 points were subtracted for diluting the red sample fluid with pool water, the MIT team built a dual bladder system. When their pump was activated, it would fill one bladder and then a second. In theory, the pool water already in their sampling tube would flow into the first bladder, before the second bladder filled with unadulterated red fluid. The only problem: they couldn't get their sampling tube into the barrel. The opening was too narrow. MIT gave up and sped away, confirming what Oscar had suspected: the task was impossible. Still, MIT had amassed 48 points, putting them in first place.

On the edge of the pool, Lorenzo was cramming tampons around Stinky's circuit board, lining the edges with clumps of the cottony things. He and Oscar were operating on a few hours of sleep, but they were amped up.

"Put one over there," Oscar ordered, pointing to a corner of the briefcase.

"I know what I'm doing," Lorenzo said, ignoring Oscar. He felt that the tampons were his domain. He'd earned the right to put them wherever he wanted.

"We need Carl Hayden High School on deck," one of the judges said over the PA system.

Their time had come.

"Okay, guys," Allan told the kids. "You probably won't have more than ten minutes before the leak shorts the controls, so go as fast as you can for the easy stuff."

"Just get some points," Fredi said. "That'll put you ahead of a lot of teams."

"We will," Oscar said confidently.

The teachers watched the boys roll their equipment toward the "command shack," a somewhat flimsy aluminum structure draped with a large, blue plastic tarp. It created a tented shelter that was enclosed on three sides.

"Boy, I hope this works," Allan said.

"Me too," Fredi responded.

The judges started a timer. Like the other contestants, Carl Hayden had five minutes to set up inside the shack and complete a safety check. Everybody burst into action. Oscar and Lorenzo rolled their monitor cart into position inside the darkened structure. Cristian carried a piece of particleboard that held the joysticks and topside electronics. Luis off-loaded Stinky onto the edge of the pool and handed the tether to Cristian, who connected it to the control system. Lorenzo fitted a purple balloon onto Stinky's bilge pump. Oscar flipped the power switch.

Stinky was operational.

Leah Herbert checked a box on the score sheet beside the words *Team is ready for the mission.* Herbert was an ROV specialist at Oceaneering International, a company that builds and operates ROVs primarily for the oil and gas industry. She was flanked by judges Bryan Schaefer and William Kirkwood, two ROV specialists from the Monterey Bay Aquarium Research Institute. Together, they would determine which tasks had been completed and award points accordingly.

"You guys are clear to get wet," Herbert told them. "You've got thirty minutes."

"Okay, Luis, let's go," Oscar said.

Luis lowered Stinky into the water, and Lorenzo prayed again to the Virgin Mary. He prayed that the tampons would work, but then wondered if the Virgin got her period and whether it was appropriate for him to be praying to her about tampons. He tried to think of a different saint to pray to but couldn't come up with a good one. The whir of propellers brought him back to the competition.

Stinky careened wildly as it dived toward the bottom. Luis stood at the pool's edge, paying out the tether cable. From the control tent, Cristian, Oscar, and Lorenzo monitored Stinky's descent on their videoscreens. Via the robot's front-facing camera, they could see the bright, sparkling poolscape that Stinky was moving through.

"There's something there." Cristian pointed. Down below, they could see a black object on an elevated tarp. It was the towfish, a mock-up of an underwater sonar device. Just seeing it was worth 5 points. The judges standing behind them in the command shack made a notation. With 5 points, they were tied for last place.

"*Vámonos*, Cristian, this is it!" Oscar said, pushing his controls too far forward. They were nervous and overcompensated for each other's joystick movements, causing Stinky to veer off course. The towfish and tarp disappeared off their screens.

"Go back!" Cristian said.

"I got it." Oscar corrected course and they sped down toward the object.

"You're going too fast," Cristian said.

Oscar hit reverse, and the propeller blast pushed the towfish off the tarp. They circled the tarp but could no longer reach the towfish.

"Let's do the next thing," Oscar said hurriedly. He didn't want to waste any time.

"What's that?" Lorenzo asked, pointing to an object on the screen. It looked like a barrel.

"It's the fluid-sampling thing," Cristian said.

"That's last," Oscar said. "Let's keep moving."

They rotated and saw the looming mass of the mocked-up submarine in the distance. So far, Stinky was holding up. The joysticks were functioning and the robot responded to all their commands. Oscar pushed forward and Stinky motored toward the structure. Cristian pulled back, and Stinky moved toward the surface.

"Let's try to do the measuring," Oscar said.

They managed to hook the loop of their tape measure onto the end of the submarine and reversed, spooling the tape out. When they reached the end of the sub, Lorenzo flicked on the black-and-white camera that was pointed at the tape measure. The screen was pure white.

"I can't see anything," Oscar said.

The camera exposure had been set when they were indoors at Scuba Sciences. During their practice run the previous day, it had been hazy in Santa Barbara. Now the sun was shining strongly, and the light overwhelmed the iris. The measurement was there—they just couldn't see it.

Still, they got 5 points for deploying the tape measure. They motored over to the sub's "periscope"—a tall plastic tube—and aimed their laser range finder at the bottom. Again, it gave a reading, but the image coming from the camera was blown out and they couldn't see it. They got 5 points for being able to hover beside the periscope while gauging the depth even if they couldn't actually report the measurement.

Most of the remaining tasks involved entering the submarine structure, a hazardous endeavor. Oscar was worried that Stinky could get snagged, ending their mission.

He checked the time: they had fifteen minutes left. "Let's go back to the barrel.".

"I thought we were going to do that last," Cristian said.

"Let's just try it." Oscar spun the robot and headed back toward the barrel.

At Scuba Sciences, they usually couldn't place Stinky's bent copper proboscis into a half-inch pipe. The few times they did, it took dozens of tries over hours. Now the minutes were counting down on their mission. Cristian wasn't sure it was worth trying, but Oscar was in charge.

The teens readjusted their grips on the joysticks and leaned into the monitors as Stinky approached the barrel that had frustrated the MIT team. The "barrel" was a one-gallon paint can painted with red and green camouflage. A half-inch tube protruded five and a half inches out the top. The control tent was silent. Now that they were focused on the mission, both Oscar and Cristian relaxed and made almost imperceptibly small movements with their joysticks. Oscar tapped his control forward, while Cristian gave a short backward blast on the vertical propellers. As Stinky floated forward a half inch, its rear raised up and the sampling pipe sank perfectly into the drum.

"*Dios mío*," Oscar whispered, not fully believing what he saw.

"Hit the switches," Cristian shrieked.

Lorenzo had already activated the pump and was counting out twenty seconds in a decidedly unscientific way.

"*Uno, dos, tres, cuatro* . . . ," he mumbled, until he got to twenty. He turned the pump off. They couldn't see if the balloon had filled, so there was no telling if it had worked.

"Let's get it to Luis," Oscar said.

Oscar backed Stinky out of the barrel. They spun the robot around and piloted it back to Luis at the edge of the pool. He hauled Stinky out of the water, and Oscar, Cristian, and Lorenzo poured out of the command shack. The purple balloon sat plumply inside Lorenzo's hacked-open milk container.

Oscar carefully removed the balloon. Cristian grabbed a plastic graduated cylinder to measure the fluid inside. Finding the barrel was worth 5 points. Collecting a sample and returning it to the control shack was worth another 5. They'd get 1 additional point for every hundred milliliters they collected—up to five hundred milliliters, for a total of 5 possible extra points. Oscar began to pour the liquid into the cylinder.

"*Ciento, doscientos, trescientos*," Cristian said with mounting excitement as Oscar poured the fluid in. Finally: *quinientos*—five hundred milliliters. They had collected a complete, though slightly diluted, sample and would receive a wholloping 12 points. That brought them to 27 points so far, more than most of the other teams.

"Can we make a little noise?" Cristian asked Pat Barrow, a NASA lab operations manager supervising the contest.

"Go on ahead," he replied.

Cristian started yelling. Luis stood there with a silly grin on his face, while his friends danced around him. They had done something that some of the best engineering students in the country had failed to accomplish.

"Let's go, let's go," Oscar said, cutting the celebration short. They still had ten minutes left and he didn't want to waste any more time. They were now in contention for a top spot. Luis quickly lowered the ROV back into the water.

Oscar piloted Stinky toward the submarine. They hadn't yet explored the interior and there were a lot more points to be won. Cristian kept Stinky level as Oscar motored gingerly forward. The robot inched into the structure, trailing its tether. The walls were black and the passageway was treacherously narrow. The tether began to grind against the structure, pulling them back. Seconds ticked away and they weren't getting anywhere.

"We've got to do something different," Oscar said.

With a minute left, Oscar tried to make a tight turn, and the prop wash blew open a compartment, revealing a golden bell.

"That's the captain's bell," Cristian shouted.

As the time ran out on their mission, the judges marked them down for another 5 points. That meant they had amassed 32 points. Not only had they not finished last, their mission score placed them in third place behind MIT and Cape Fear Community College. Everything would be determined now by the scores they received on their engineering review.

Fredi and Allan couldn't believe it. They rushed to the command shack. Fredi snapped pictures as if the kids were celebrities. Allan grabbed Cristian and shook him like a tree.

"Congratulations," Allan said. "You officially don't suck."

"Can we go to Hooters if we win?" Lorenzo asked.

"Sure," Fredi said with a laugh. "And Dr. Cameron and I will retire too."

THE AWARDS CEREMONY took place over dinner, and the Carl Hayden team was glad for that. Oscar felt as if he had run twenty miles with a fifty-pound rucksack, and even flavorless iceberg lettuce looked good to him. Their nerves had calmed. Fredi and Allan tried to temper their expectations. The teens felt that they had done great during the engineering review but, in reality, they probably hadn't. The teachers told them that they had probably placed somewhere in the middle of the pack. They'd be lucky to get fourth or fifth overall. Privately, each of them was hoping they'd hold on to third. No matter what, they agreed, they were proud of what they had accomplished.

The first award was a surprise: a Special Prize that wasn't listed in the program. Bryce Merrill, the bearded, middle-aged recruiting manager for Oceaneering International, an industrial ROV design firm, was the announcer. He explained that the judges had created this spontaneously to honor special achievement. He stood behind a podium on the temporary stage and glanced down at his notes. The contestants sat crowded around a dozen tables. Carl Hayden High School, he said, was that special team.

The guys trotted up to the stage, forcing smiles. It seemed obvious that this was a condescending pat on the back, as if to say, "You did well, considering where you came from." They didn't want to be "special"—they wanted third. It signaled to them that they'd missed it.

They returned to their seats, and Fredi and Allan shook their hands.

"Good job, guys," Fredi said, trying to sound pleased. "You did well. They probably gave you that for the tampon."

"Hey, you got an award," Allan pointed out. "Everybody back home is going to be really proud of you."

Allan and Fredi tried to look on the bright side. Nobody had expected them to get *any* award. It was actually pretty amazing.

Oscar nodded. Allan was right. The whole team had come farther than even they had expected. Maybe they hadn't placed at the top of the rankings, but everybody now knew that they were talented engineers. That was a pretty remarkable accomplishment on its own.

"Come on, guys," Oscar said encouragingly. "This is great. For the rest of our lives, we can say we won an award here."

Lorenzo decided it was fun just to have gotten up onstage and have everyone clap for him. He'd remember that forever.

THE CEREMONY WAS coming to an end. A few small prizes were handed out (Terrific Tether Management, Perfect Pickup Tool), and then Merrill moved on to the final awards: Design Elegance, Technical Report, and Overall Winner. The MIT students shifted in their seats and stretched their legs. While they had been forced to skip the fluid sampling, they had completed more underwater tasks overall than any other team. The Cape Fear team had posted the second-highest number of points during the underwater mission. They sat across the room, fidgeted with their napkins, and tried not to look nervous. The students from Monterey Peninsula College looked straight ahead. They'd placed fourth behind Carl Hayden in the underwater trials. They were the most likely third-place finishers. It would all come down to how the judges graded the teams' oral and written presentations. The guys from Phoenix glanced back at the buffet table and wondered if they could get more cake before the ceremony wrapped up.

Then Merrill leaned into the microphone and said that the ROV named Stinky had captured the design award.

"What did he just say?" Lorenzo asked.

"Oh my God!" Fredi shouted. "Stand up!"

It didn't make any sense to Lorenzo. There was nothing pretty or elegant about their robot. Compared to the gleaming machines other teams had constructed, Stinky was a study in simplicity. The PVC, the balloon, the tape measure—in each case they had chosen the most straightforward solution to a problem. It was an approach that grew naturally out of watching family

members fix cars, manufacture mattresses, and lay irrigation piping. To a large swath of the population, driveway mechanics,
box-frame builders, and gardeners did not represent the cutting
edge of engineering know-how. They were low-skilled laborers
who didn't have access to real technology. Stinky represented
this low-tech approach to engineering.

But that was exactly what had impressed the judges. Lisa
Spence, the NASA judge, believed that there was no reason to
come up with a complex solution when an elementary one would
suffice. She felt that Carl Hayden's robot was "conceptually
similar" to the machines she encountered at NASA.

The guys were in shock. They marched back up to the stage
and looked out at the audience with dazed smiles. Lorenzo felt
a rush of emotion. The judges' Special Prize wasn't a consolation award. These people were giving them real recognition. He
thanked Merrill and headed back to his seat with the others.
Now they'd really have something to talk about in Phoenix.

Before they could get off the stage, Merrill announced that
they had won another prize: the Technical Writing Award.

Lorenzo didn't know what was happening. It seemed impossible that they would win three awards, particularly one for writing. *Us illiterate people from the desert?* Lorenzo thought. He
looked at Cristian, who had been responsible for a large part of
the writing. Even Cristian was amazed. To his analytical mind,
there was no possibility that his team—a bunch of ESL students—
could have produced a better written report than kids from one
of the country's top engineering schools.

Merrill congratulated them. They had just won two of the
most important awards. It was astonishing, but now the room
was ready for the announcement of the top three overall finishers. The Carl Hayden kids returned to their seats. They were now
a highly decorated underwater-robotics team. It had been an
amazing run, something they'd never forget.

Merrill began the countdown. "Third place goes to Cape Fear

Community College," he said. There was a round of applause. Sea Devil 3, their ROV, was a work of art with robust capabilities and had amassed the second-highest number of mission points. The Carl Hayden kids were surprised. They had assumed that Cape Fear would grab second place. It was a given that MIT would win the championship, so they figured that Monterey Peninsula College had slid into second place. They were a solid team that had performed well underwater and likely aced the engineering review. Carl Hayden figured they might have gotten as high as fourth place. That was pretty exciting.

After the applause for Cape Fear died down, Merrill cleared his throat for the next announcement. "And second place goes to MIT," he said into the microphone.

There was a feeling of shock in the room. Cristian looked at Fredi.

"MIT got second?" Cristian blurted.

"So who won first place?" Lorenzo asked the table.

Fredi realized that something extraordinary was about to occur. He leaned across the table and grabbed Lorenzo's shirt. "Lorenzo, if what I think is about to happen does happen, I do not, under any circumstances, want to hear you say the word *Hooters* onstage."

"And the winner of the Marine Advanced Technology Education ROV Explorer-class championship goes to . . ."

Merrill started drumming on the podium. A deep rumble rose up around the room as others joined in. Only nine months earlier, the Carl Hayden students hadn't known what an ROV was. There was no way they could win.

Merrill stopped drumming.

The room fell silent, and Merrill leaned into the microphone. "Carl Hayden!" he shouted.

The 2004 Marine Advanced Technology and Education Explorer class ROV championship was not going to a big-league university, or a team of seasoned competitors. It was going to four high school students who had simply hoped not to finish last.

"Oh my God," Allan said. He felt tears welling up. He grabbed Fredi and shook him. "Oh my God!"

Lorenzo threw his arms into the air, looked at Fredi, and silently mouthed, *Hooters.*

The students from MIT stood up and began to clap. Other competitors stood as well, and by the time the Carl Hayden team made it to the stage, most of the room was on its feet. The teenagers from Phoenix were getting a standing ovation. The audience roared their support.

The kids from the desert had won.

"WE BEAT MIT!" Cristian screamed out to the ocean.

They had hiked a mile down the darkened beach. They couldn't contain themselves inside the awards hall and had gotten out as quickly as they could. They didn't want to be rude, but it was too much to handle without a little yelling.

"We wo-o-o-o-o-on!" Oscar hollered into the night sky.

"*AHHHRGH!*" Luis roared.

He was so loud, everyone fell silent. The night was quiet—just the sound of the waves crashing softly.

"I want you guys to know how proud I am of you," Allan said.

"From now on, you guys are the team that beat MIT," Fredi told them. "You know what that makes you?"

"What?" Cristian asked.

"Badasses," Fredi said, smiling.

"Damn," Lorenzo said, getting used to the idea. "I'm a badass."

Oscar couldn't remember being happier, but his eighteenth birthday was only days away. It brought a significant decision for him. Once he turned eighteen and became an adult in the eyes of the law, his legal status in the United States would change. He was always at risk of deportation, but as a youth, he couldn't be banned from reentering the country. However, if he was caught and deported after he turned eighteen and a half, he would be barred from returning to the United States for three years. If he was nineteen and a half or older and caught, the ban would increase to ten years. The law was meant to incentivize immigrant teens to return to the country where they were born.

But, for Oscar, there was little to go back to. He remembered

Mexico—he'd left when he was twelve—but there was nothing there for him anymore. His parents were in Arizona, as were his friends and mentors. It was hard to imagine walking across the border to Mexico in a week's time when his entire life was in the United States. And fundamentally, he viewed himself as an American. He figured that he would eventually be able to convince the government that he was worthy of citizenship.

Fredi took a picture of the kids standing by the shore that night. Oscar, Cristian, and Lorenzo threw their fists in the air. Oscar held up his index finger to signal that they were number one. Luis looked confused. On the beach around them, piles of shrimp had been washed ashore. There were hundreds that had been overpowered by forces beyond their control. Fredi took pictures of everything that night so nobody would ever forget.

FOUR

ON DECEMBER 16, 2004—five months after the Carl Hayden triumph in Santa Barbara—Russell Pearce took the stage at the Brookings Institution's Falk Auditorium in Washington, D.C. The Arizona state representative had been invited to talk about policies affecting children in immigrant families. The session was titled "The Future of Children," and Pearce expressed his strong belief that being too nice to immigrants wasn't good for the country or even the immigrants themselves.

"You don't have a right to have compassion," Pearce insisted. "None of us would do anything to harm children. But sometimes our policies, well intended, do much damage."

To Pearce, Arizona and the United States had become too hospitable to immigrants. They were flooding the country, illegally receiving welfare, and getting a free education at taxpayers' expense. Many voters in Arizona seemed to believe that immigrants had come to the country to leech off the government. From this perspective, immigrants weren't here looking for work, they were poor, lazy families that would contribute less than they received to the country. Pearce felt that policies needed to be put in place to discourage them from entering the United States.

Pearce championed a solution. Just a month before his speech in D.C., voters in Arizona had passed Proposition 200, a bill that barred illegal immigrants from receiving public benefits, from welfare to education. The text of the proposition summarized the motivation succinctly: "This state finds that illegal immigration is

184 • JOSHUA DAVIS

causing economic hardship to this state and that illegal immigration is encouraged by public agencies within this state that provide public benefits without verifying immigration status." Fifty-six percent of voters voted in favor of the proposition and it passed.

Sheriff Joe Arpaio responded to the rising tide of anti-immigrant sentiment among voters in Phoenix by forming civilian posses to hunt for illegal immigrants. Starting in 2006, the posses were made up of more than three hundred civilians who were encouraged to track down illegal migrants. They were told to identify cars that appeared to be carrying illegal immigrants, as well as houses where they lived. Though they were only supposed to turn the information over to sheriff's deputies, many of the volunteers were armed. Both opponents and supporters of the posses saw them as a way of scaring migrants out of the country.

Far from cooling down, the debate over immigration was only getting more heated. On May 15, 2006, President Bush ordered six thousand members of the National Guard to begin patrols of the U.S.-Mexican border. The intent was to buttress the Border Patrol's efforts to capture immigrants and prevent migrants from crossing. "The reason why I think this strategy is important is because deploying the six thousand troops to complement the work of the Border Patrol will get immediate results," Bush said. "And it's time to get immediate results."

The question was: Would militarizing the border achieve the desired results? "It's as if we expect border control agents to do what a century of communism could not: defeat the natural market forces of supply and demand and defeat the natural human desire for freedom and opportunity," noted New York mayor Michael Bloomberg told Congress. "You might as well sit in your beach chair and tell the tide not to come in."

OSCAR WIPED the white gypsum dust from his face. It was a hot Tuesday afternoon in Phoenix eight months after the success in Santa Barbara. The half-built apartment complex in front of him was teeming with workers. He was wearing a leather carpenter's belt slung with a hammer, and he lifted a four-foot-by-twelve-foot section of Sheetrock from a pile. He may have proven himself to be one of the most innovative underwater engineers in the country, but now he was just another day laborer.

He had chosen to stay in the United States past his eighteenth birthday and now felt stuck: there was nothing for him in Mexico, and he was like a ghost in the United States. He was running the risk of being banned from the country for years. Still, Oscar maintained a sense of optimism. As he trudged through the half-built units hauling hundred-pound sections of drywall, he studied the plumbing and electrical wiring. He wanted to make sure he was learning something.

In the heat, when he let his thoughts wander, he thought about college. He dreamed that he would major in mechanical engineering, serve in the military, and go on to have a career as an engineer. It all seemed like a mirage, since he couldn't afford the first step. He was making between five and eight dollars an hour, and a degree from Arizona State University would cost approximately fifty thousand dollars. There was no way he could raise that kind of money by sheetrocking.

Cristian had a similar problem. He also dreamed of going to college, but his hopes flagged when the air-conditioning unit in his family's trailer broke. Without AC, the trailer turned into an unlivable aluminum oven in the desert heat. His parents had to spend three thousand dollars of savings to buy a new unit—money that Cristian had hoped could be used to at least start college.

After graduation, Luis started working two jobs. During the day, he filed papers at a Social Security office. In the evenings, he continued to work as a short-order cook for Harold Brunet at Doc's Dining & Bar in Youngtown. It seemed unrealistic to expect that his life would change that much. He assumed that Santa Barbara had been nothing more than a blip, a brief glimpse into the opportunities that other people had. He tried not to think too much about it.

In April 2005, I published an article in *Wired* detailing the 2004 MATE championship in Santa Barbara. It was the first national coverage of the event, and the story provoked a variety of responses. Hooters called to invite the entire robotics team to a free dinner. ("That was hella cool," Lorenzo recalls.) Many readers wrote to express their support for the Carl Hayden robotics program.

"If the really long list of immigrant inventors who have made this country and the world a much better place is to stop here and now, we will also likely become the newest declining nation," one reader commented.

The *Wired* office was soon flooded by e-mails offering to help the four young roboticists continue their education. Individual readers eventually contributed more than $120,000 to a scholarship fund set up by the school district for these kids. This generosity opened up a world of opportunity for them. It now looked like college was within their grasp.

The article also made the four Carl Hayden teens the faces of a generation of kids who were born elsewhere and had grown up without residency papers in the United States. In 2004, there were an estimated 1.4 million kids who fit this description. Despite their numbers, these children were largely invisible. Their families avoided publicity. After all, nobody wanted to invite scrutiny if it meant deportation.

At first, the Carl Hayden team didn't realize that their story would attract much notice. Nobody had paid attention when they first won the MATE competition, so they figured the *Wired* article wouldn't change anything. But in the weeks following publication, additional media requests poured in. When ABC's *Nightline* asked to broadcast their story, the teammates had a meeting in the robotics closet. Fredi and Allan explained that the show wanted to focus on their immigration status. They were being asked to talk about living illegally in the country on national television. It could lead to trouble for all of them.

"If you were my own kids, I would tell you not to do it," Allan said. "It's too risky."

After discussing with their families overnight, the teens reconvened the next day. They agreed that if any one of them didn't want to do it, they would say no to ABC. Cristian's family was very concerned and didn't want him to participate. He wasn't convinced though. Cristian thought that it was important to speak out. Lorenzo and Luis agreed. They needed to talk about their experience. Otherwise, traditional stereotypes about immigrants would persist. Voters naturally fell back on their assumptions about what low-income Mexican migrants were like. Stories of migrants stealing or fighting made the news, but when Carl Hayden won the national underwater-robotics championship, no prominent news outlet covered the story initially.

"We got a chance to say something," Lorenzo said.

"I agree," Oscar said. "This is a Rosa Parks moment. It's about more than us now."

They decided to do the broadcast.

THE MEDIA ATTENTION prompted some to wonder if Santa Barbara had just been a fluke, a one-time accident of fate. Cristian and Lorenzo—who hadn't yet graduated—proved them wrong. In 2005 and 2006, the Carl Hayden robotics team won the top prize at Dean Kamen's Arizona FIRST competition in Arizona. They went on to the national championships both years and were a top competitor. They placed third at the 2005 MATE event and second at the 2006 event, beating MIT (again) both times. In 2007, MATE organizers held the event in Canada, in effect preventing the undocumented students at Carl Hayden from attending. To compensate, Fredi and Allan formed their own underwater-robotics competition, an event that continues to this day.

More than anything, the 2004 underwater-robotics team inspired the kids that came after them. The robotics team swelled to more than fifty members, all of whom heard the tale of how Oscar, Luis, Lorenzo, and Cristian had succeeded with little more than their ingenuity and some spare parts. Now, when the team competed, the cheerleaders showed up. In 2008, the team won the national Chairman's Award, the most prestigious prize at Kamen's FIRST competition. Year after year, they consistently performed at or near the top of every division they entered.

They also tried to get other kids excited about robotics. During the fall, before the year's serious robot building got underway, team members fanned out to local elementary schools in West Phoenix. They brought old robots with them and gave demonstrations to the younger kids. In 2004, the Carl Hayden robotics team hosted a junior robotics competition in their gym. Within a few years, the event grew to include hundreds of young students and had to be relocated to Arizona State University.

The team's rising profile brought new supporters. In 2005, a group of businessmen in Oregon and Washington read the *Wired* article and decided to help. They formed a foundation that provided college scholarships for members of Allan and Fredi's robotics team. Between 2005 and 2010, the foundation spent $720,000 and sent twenty-three kids to college. "Our country cannot afford to squander the talents of these kids," says Peter Gaskins, one of the businessmen. "I'm just not willing to accept that this is the way it has to be."

The robotics program became a pathway to college. Robotics students won more scholarships than all of Carl Hayden's athletic programs combined. "This team has transformed so deeply that expectations, dreams, and possibilities have expanded beyond what was previously unimaginable," said John Abele, the billionaire cofounder of Boston Scientific, in announcing the top award at Dean Kamen's 2008 robotics competition. "What was once a struggling school is now a soaring inspiration that demonstrates a passionate partnership . . . can unlock the dreams hidden within."

Fredi and Allan may have succeeded in giving their immigrant students new dreams, but often the reality was that those dreams were impractical. Many Carl Hayden students didn't have Social Security numbers or green cards and couldn't get normal jobs even if they did graduate from college. It kept Fredi up at night. He worried that his kids would drop out of the program if they felt that it wasn't going to lead to better lives. In his mind, that led to a ripple effect of catastrophic proportions. Kids would drop out of school entirely if they didn't see the point, crime would increase, society would lose great minds, and the next generation wouldn't be prepared to take over the country. At least that's what went through his mind late at night. He might be able to inspire and train extraordinary engineers, but the world didn't seem to want them.

ALLAN AND FREDI urged Cristian to apply to MIT; it seemed like a natural fit. But to Cristian and his family, Boston seemed too far away, too foreign. His parents wanted to keep him close given his residency status. They felt better having him nearby. A private university also seemed forbiddingly expensive.

Arizona State University was a safer choice. Cristian would qualify for in-state tuition and would be able to cover the costs with the scholarship windfall. Still, ASU was a difficult departure from Carl Hayden. Cristian found himself in lectures with almost four hundred students. His chemistry teacher stood in front of the lecture hall and read the slides he projected onto a screen. It was mind-numbing and infuriating, particularly because 10 percent of the chemistry grade was tied to attendance. It felt like the antithesis to four years of building robots at Carl Hayden.

Since his parents hadn't gone to college, he found it hard to share his feelings with them. Instead, he regularly stopped by Carl Hayden to talk to Allan and Fredi. "I'm not learning anything, but I have to show up anyway," he fumed on one occasion. "It's a huge waste of time."

"You have to jump through the hoops," Allan told him. "It'll be worth it."

Cristian stuck with it, but statewide sentiment was turning against him. When ABC's *Nightline* aired their segment on the Carl Hayden kids, Arizona State Representative Russell Pearce explained to viewers that it was inappropriate to focus on a small group of students: "You can't paint this picture of this sweet child over here that we all probably know. And all of us know somebody that's here probably illegally that is a wonderful, wonderful person. You can't take it to that emotional element and, and let that play. Because, look at the damage to America overall."

Midway through Cristian's freshman year, Dean Martin, an Arizona state senator, sponsored Proposition 300, an effort to extend Proposition 200's ban on public services for undocumented immigrants to education. The referendum sought to prevent state colleges and universities from offering reduced in-state tuition to undocumented residents who'd grown up in Arizona. "Arizona is currently giving away millions of your tax dollars as subsidies to illegals," Martin wrote in a ballot argument sent to voters. "U.S. citizens from other states attending Arizona schools have to pay the full cost of tuition. However, citizens of foreign countries, who break the law to enter Arizona illegally, are given taxpayer subsidized tuition . . . It's not fair; it's not right."

Russell Pearce was an outspoken proponent of the new measure. "Free state services for all takes away the incentive for illegal aliens to become full citizens and legitimate members of American society," Pearce wrote in support of Proposition 300. "It is vital that we spend our tax dollars on helping Arizonans and not aid and abet illegal aliens."

On November 7, 2006, Proposition 300 passed with 71 percent support. Cristian's tuition quadrupled as a result. Normally, one year of residency in Arizona would qualify a student for in-state tuition. Cristian had lived in the state since the age of five but was now deemed to be an out-of-state student. His first-semester tuition was about $2,000, but the next semester was now going to cost roughly $8,000. To get through the remaining three and a half years of college, he would need $56,000. His share of the scholarship money would get him only halfway through to a degree. If he took only two classes, he wouldn't trigger the tuition increase, but the mechanical-engineering department required students to take a full load of classes to remain in the program. It seemed hopeless. He decided to drop out.

Technically, he should have returned to Mexico. Once there, he could apply for a visa, though if he admitted that he had stayed in the United States beyond his eighteenth birthday, he would be banned from reentering the country for years. He hadn't been in Mexico since he was a young child: it was a foreign country to him. He couldn't bring himself to leave the United States.

For the next five years, Cristian took intermittent courses at Gateway Community College. He found work at Home Depot and was assigned to the floor-and-wall department, where he helped customers order carpets and blinds. When someone bought a particularly large order of tile, he would walk in front of the forklift waving a flag to clear a path down the aisles.

At home, he set up a small laboratory in the corner of his room. He bought a soldering iron for thirty dollars and kept his eye out for deals at Home Depot. When two hundred feet of doorbell wire went on sale for three dollars, he bought himself a spool and brought it home. Most nights, he stayed up late, inventing new machines from scavenged parts. He found a broken guitar on the street, repaired it, and made a sound-effects pedal for it. He designed a new wheel that could rotate in any direction. He kept a gallon of muriatic acid beside his bed to etch circuit boards. At night, amid the smell of solder and machine oil, he felt most happy.

IN MAY 2006, Lorenzo walked up to the stage in the auditorium at Carl Hayden to receive his diploma. He was the first member of his family to graduate from high school. It should have been a happy day. At one time, Principal Ybarra was on the verge of expelling him. Now he was a nationally recognized robotics star. But as Lorenzo shook hands with Ybarra onstage and accepted the diploma, he scanned the crowd. His father hadn't shown up.

Lorenzo tamped down his feelings and tried to focus on his future. With his share of the scholarship money, he enrolled full-time in Phoenix College's Culinary Studies program and went on to receive an associate's degree after two years. Luis also went to cooking school, attending the Cordon Bleu College of Culinary Arts in nearby Scottsdale. Together, the two friends formed Neither Here, Nor There, a catering company that specialized in Mexican-fusion dining. They started with their mothers' recipes but revamped them, turning a traditional green mole sauce into a mole pesto by adding basil, pine nuts, and cream. They catered weddings, church retreats, baby showers, and quinceañeras. It was fun but intermittent, and both had to get steadier jobs. Luis found work as a night-shift janitor at the federal courthouse in downtown Phoenix. From nine at night until five in the morning, he wandered the halls of justice with a trash cart and buffed the marble floors. Lorenzo got a job as a dishwasher at St. Francis, an upscale restaurant in central Phoenix.

Lorenzo's added income wasn't enough to save his family's home and, in 2009, Lorenzo handed the keys over to the Realtor

194 • JOSHUA DAVIS

who had bought the property. The guy walked through the house and was astounded by the state of poverty the family had been living in. The building was poorly built to begin with, but now the walls were discolored from years of use. The Realtor got the distinct impression that bugs were crawling on him and hurriedly left. On his way home, he bought a bottle of rubbing alcohol and doused his legs and feet. He couldn't imagine how anyone would live there. But to Lorenzo, it was his home.

While the kids from Carl Hayden struggled to get by, the second-place winners of the 2004 MATE competition excelled. Thaddeus Stefanov-Wagner, the student who had rebuilt MIT's electronics in a week, landed a job as a mechanical engineer at Bluefin Robotics. The company was founded by MIT alumni and built self-piloting ROVs for commercial, military, and scientific customers. Jordan Stanway, the team leader in 2004, got a Ph.D. in oceanography from MIT and the Woods Hole Oceanographic Institution and builds underwater robots for the Monterey Bay Aquarium Research Institute. Other team members went on to work at NASA and ExxonMobil. They were all exceptionally talented students and deserved to do well.

Meanwhile, in Phoenix, Lorenzo's dishwashing abilities impressed his superiors, who promoted him to prep cook and then line cook. On a typical Friday night at the restaurant, the airy dining room fills with well-dressed patrons. There are exposed roof beams, rough-hewn brick and concrete walls, and a roll-up, see-through garage door. Like many hip restaurants, it feels as if someone spent a lot of time and money to make it look rustic and down-trodden.

The patrons tend to ignore the cooks, who are clearly visible in the open kitchen. Lorenzo stands there for hours every day roasting salmon and pork chops. He's also responsible for the prosciutto-fig-and-goat flatbread and the Moroccan meatballs. He sends out dozens of plates every day for customers who appreciate the pleasant tang in the chile verde sauce and the crunch of the stuffed peppers. They eat the food never knowing the history of the twenty-five-year-old robotics expert who cooked it.

us holy and pure. He wants to do a dry cleaning for our souls—remove the dirt and make us clean.

Yeshua told this parable to reorient us to the truth and put things back into perspective. Physical pleasure is good when it's connected to a spiritual source and divine inner essence. God wants to pull us back into balance from our overindulgence in the physical and material to an equilibrium that includes a deeper focus on the spiritual.

What's Up with the Pigs?

As you will remember from the story of Yeshua and the demoniac, pigs are not kosher even though they have cloven feet. They don't chew their cud, which is also a determiner of whether an animal is kosher. In this story, the pig could represent that which seems to be desirable and pleasurable but is unclean. This is an aspect of how the pig tricks us. It appears kosher on the outside but is unclean on the inside.

The younger brother became like the pigs. His physical and sensual desires drove his actions. He lived solely to meet his physical needs and urges. In the end, he became lower than the pigs because they ate better than he did (Luke 15:16).

The Hebrew word for "pig" is *hazir*, which has the Hebrew root word spelled *chet-zayin-resh* (ריזח). The Hebrew verb meaning "return" uses the same consonants. This suggests that someday the pig will return and become kosher. The pig will become on the inside what it appears to be on the outside. This doesn't mean that the Torah is incorrect. It means that the pig will be transformed. It will chew its cud and become a new creation (2 Corinthians 5:17).

As Rabbi Paul has reminded us in Romans 6:19, breakthrough begins with repentance and return. To fully experience a transformation, the younger son had to go through barrenness to obtain a breakthrough.

Once again we can see ourselves in the story. Sometimes a person must hit bottom before reality sets in. Trying to do things on our own, we fail. The younger son took a job forbidden for any Jewish person to perform, and he even tried to eat the pigs' food. Being on the bottom isn't fun. Sometimes, however, we need to go to the absolute end so we see more clearly. There's only one place to look when we're on the bottom, and that's up.

But Luke 15:17 tells us, "He came to his senses." The prodigal realized that his father's hired hands were better off than he was because his father gave them *more* than what they needed. Rabbi Russell Resnik wrote, "The son displays regret for his sin and is ready to make restitution by returning to his father, confessing his sins, and offering to live with him like a hired servant. Finally, he resolves to return, changing his whole life direction from a journey away from home to a journey back."[5] The younger son came to his senses and realized everything he needed was in his father's house.

How many of us have come to our senses and realized that all we need is with our Father? Sure, we may have a scarred past; we may have even given in to our basic instincts at our lowest point. We thank God for certain aspects of our past, good things and achievements. At some point, however, we need to come to our senses and begin trusting Him for His daily presence and provision in the here and now. He is steadfast. Adonai never ceases; His mercies never end; great is His faithfulness, for they are new every morning; His blessings are new every day (paraphrasing Lamentations 3:22–23). We cannot just look to the past—what we have done and had or where we have been. Living in the present and looking expectantly to the future is what's important. Ask, "What does God want me to do *today*?"

The Compassionate Father

I heard a story told by an Iranian pastor that is similar to this parable. There was a father who was a physician in good health. One day his son asked his father for his inheritance. The physician went to his pastor and said, "My son wants me to die! He has asked for his inheritance." Three months later, the father died. The boy's mother later said that her husband died the night his son asked for his inheritance. He died of a broken heart.

According to Jewish laws of inheritance, a father could divide his inheritance while living. But he had to split it between both sons. He could not give the inheritance to one son and not the other. Here's the hang-up: The sons could not take possession until after their father died. The father could legally live off his estate until his death—anything he produced was his until he died. The sons had ownership but not possession. They could sell the property, but the new owner could not possess it until the father died. The younger son took one-third of the family's wealth and sold it cheaply so he could run away from his family and his father. His father sold the land at a reduced rate because the buyer would have to wait until the father's death to possess it.

Yet look at the father's response. Even though his son took advantage of him, he wasn't offended or angry. He didn't act like a victim.

How a story ends is key to understanding its meaning. We tend to focus on the judgmental, hard-hearted older brother, contrasting him with the compassionate father. But the radical nature of this parable is rooted in the extreme compassion the father showed toward his wayward son!

How would you feel if your son or daughter asked for one-third of your wealth, went to a far-off place, left you like you were dead, and wasted everything you worked so hard for?

How could the father be so kind and compassionate toward his son?

The Cantor and the Klansman: A Story of Redemption

Larry Trapp was once the Grand Dragon of the KKK for the Realm of Nebraska. But then he completely changed his life, denouncing a life once filled with racial hatred and violence. What was the catalyst for Trapp's change? The kindness of a cantor, Michael Weisser, and his wife, Julie.

Trapp's former life was replete with hate literature, neo-Nazi meetings, and threats to African American and Jewish leaders. Rumors tell us he was involved in bombings and arson threats.

But after Trapp gave a threatening call to the Weissers, they didn't respond with hate. Instead they responded with a message of love. They offered to take Trapp, who was then blind and wheelchair bound, to the grocery store. After speaking to this kind couple, Trapp renounced the KKK, moved into their home, and converted to Judaism. What a change a little love and kindness can make.[6]

The cantor did not see merely a Klansman. He saw something more. He saw a hurting and broken man whom God loved, which moved him to have radical compassion.

This kind of compassion is about sight. It's about finding the good in someone. The father saw not only his son's flaws but also his full potential. He did not see his son only as a sinner. He also saw him as a saint. The father did not see his son as a loser who lost everything because of stupid decisions. Instead he saw his son as a winner who was transformed because he was willing to learn from his disastrous choices. In other words, he did not judge him just by his actions but by his essence!

The father stood on the promise of Proverbs 22:6: "Train up a child in the way he should go, when he is old he will not turn from it." I remember a time when one of my boys became terribly upset with our family and me.

He said some harsh things. I told him, "Your words are not okay, but they don't hurt me because this is not really you speaking. It's your anger and it's self-centered, sinful, and not true." I reminded him that he was better than these words and that I loved him at that moment and always. I didn't become angry, because I understand another proverb that says, "Foolishness is bound up in the heart of a child" (Proverbs 22:15). This kind of unlikely outburst is possible with any child. But that shouldn't change our love for them.

As children of God, we are in the process of not just growing old but of growing up spiritually, emotionally, and relationally. Compassion allows us to see people not as they currently are but for who they are called and created to be.

Yeshua did this better than anyone else. He saw people whom others viewed as worthless and sinful through the eyes of compassion! As we learned with the woman at the well, He saw people differently, so He treated people differently. He saw infinite value and worth in her, and it changed her. Think about the choice of His disciples:

- Thomas was a doubter.
- Peter was a denier.
- Simon the Zealot was a gangster.
- Levi the tax collector was a sellout.
- Judas was a hater and traitor.

But Messiah saw something in them that no one else did.

I had some prodigal-type trouble as a teen. But thankfully my dad and mom never gave up their faith in me despite what I did or said. They knew me and saw the real me; they stood by me and loved me. Ultimately it was God's love and compassion, along with theirs, that changed me.

Focusing on the good we see in people allows those bits of goodness to grow slowly over time and, hopefully, with God's help, negates the negative and the bad.

Yeshua chose to view the Samaritan woman through the eyes of compassion, not harsh judgment like the older brother in this parable. By so doing, He tipped the scales of judgment toward mercy and grace. When we evaluate someone, it's like we have a scale in our hands—we can judge favorably or unfavorably. When we judge favorably, we choose compassion by intentionally looking into the soul and spirit of the person for their holiest potential. Living from the place of judgment rather than compassion causes us to focus on the negative. Our lives then become defined by the disappointments we experience instead of the *shem*, the essence of who God wants us to become. Like the father in this parable, a compassionate person sees a person's true essence as a masterpiece created by *Adonai*'s own hands in His image and not based solely on their actions.

The Hebrew word for "compassion" is *rachamim*. The root word is *rechem*, or "womb." As Rabbi David Fohrman pointed out, "The womb's sole purpose is to nourish the 'potential' of a fetus. The womb has no agenda for itself. It focuses on the ever-changing needs of the fetus, enabling the growing baby to increasingly function on its own. Finally, the womb relinquishes the baby, launching it onto the long journey toward maturity and independence."[7]

Compassion nurtures both love and life. This duality of compassion is why God chose Moses. Moses handled his sheep with compassion, and he loved the Children of Israel even more than he loved the sheep. His loving compassion was so incredible that he treated the people with grace and compassion instead of a harsh critical spirit and judgment. Even when they criticized his leadership and wanted to stone him so they could return to Egypt, Moses remained compassionate.

Instead of "The Prodigal Son," the name of this parable could very well be "The Compassionate Father." Not only is it a vivid example of *Adonai*'s overwhelming love for us, but it's also a story that demonstrates how we should show compassion toward others. We can choose how we want to view people—from a critical perspective or a compassionate one. The choice is ours.

Strict judgment rarely brings lasting transformation to the individual being judged. Instead it often kills the person from within. Choosing to exercise love and compassion releases the potential for healing and transformation to take place. It was the father's compassion that healed his son. There is no greater power than compassion rooted in love!

Despite what would have been social ridicule, the father's mercy, love, and forgiveness reconciled him with his wayward son. Our heavenly Father does the same with us. When we seek Him, He openly welcomes us into His loving arms regardless of our condition. Such good news is difficult for the legalistic, older-brother types to comprehend.

The Older Brother

The older son was angry and didn't want to go in. So his father came outside and pleaded with him. But he answered and said to his father, "Look, so many years I've slaved away for you—not once did I ignore your order. Yet you've never given me a young goat so I could celebrate with my friends. But when this son of yours came—the one who has squandered your wealth with prostitutes—for him you killed the fattened calf!" (Luke 15:28–30)

Yeshua gave the audience an exciting twist in the parable with the older son. Here we have the dutiful, hardworking brother. Yet his response isn't what we might expect from a person who seemingly did everything his father wanted him to do. Instead of welcoming his little brother back into the family, he was furious. He forced his father to come outside to talk with him. Even after speaking with his father, he refused to join the celebration.

Why did the older brother have this attitude?

- He thought he was more deserving than the younger brother.
- He thought he was the faithful one.
- He thought he was the dutiful, hardworking son.
- He thought he was the responsible one.
- He thought he was the righteous one.
- He was a legend in his own mind!

The older son was living in denial. He did not see his authentic self, but only an illusion of who he was. As the big brother, firstborn, he should have embodied his father's heart because he was destined to become the head of the family. Unfortunately he was not like his father, and, tragically, he did not understand his father.

God's original intent for the firstborn was to be the family's priests. It was the firstborn who would serve in the tabernacle and temple and be the spiritual leaders. This intent changed when the Children of Israel made and worshiped a golden calf (Exodus 32). Moses and Aaron's tribe of Levi were the only ones who did not participate in this ritual. At that time the firstborn lost their special status, and the honor transferred to the Levites (Numbers 18:20–30).

Hillel, a first-century Jewish sage and the foremost master of biblical commentary and interpreter of Jewish tradition in his time, said, "Be of the disciples of Aaron, love peace and pursue peace, love your fellows and bring them close to the Torah."[8] The older brother should have been the peacemaker. He should have had the priestly role in his home, but he didn't.

The audience of religious leaders was shocked by this teaching. How could Yeshua choose to freely associate and eat with such notoriously sinful people? His teaching was powerful, but they had a difficult time seeing past their judgmental attitudes.

For us, the older brother is symbolic of those who judge harshly. He had no mercy or compassion for his younger brother; for him, there was only strict justice.

Justice and Mercy

"God [Elohim] saw that the light was good. So God [Elohim] distinguished the light from the darkness" (Genesis 1:4). The Hebrew word Elohim is the name of God exercising justice. But He saw that the world could not endure with only justice, so He brought mercy to the world and joined it to justice. Hence, when God created the world, He did so both with His attributes of justice and mercy. Ultimately God decreed that mercy should overcome strict justice. This idea is supported by Psalm 89:3: "The world was built with compassion [chesed]."[9] The older brother did not understand the heart of the father, so he focused his life on justice without compassion.

There is a real danger in being like the older son. How can we expect to be judged favorably if we judge others harshly? Yeshua said, "With the judgment you judge, you will be judged; and with the measure you use, it will be measured to you" (Matthew 7:2). The older brother's measure was strict justice, and he was unable to change his perspective.

Author Stephen Covey wrote about being on a subway one Sunday morning when a man and his children boarded the train. Immediately the kids started running up and down the train car annoying riders, yelling, screaming, and knocking papers out of readers' hands. Finally, Covey could no longer stand the apparent disregard and discipline this parent was showing. "Mister," he said to the man, "you need to correct your children. They're bothering the passengers." The man looked up from his daze and took notice. "Oh, I'm sorry. We just left the hospital where their mother died about one hour ago. I guess they don't know how to handle it and frankly I don't either."[10]

Covey said there was a shift in his paradigm from being critical to being empathic at that moment. This new information changed how he saw the situation, caused different behavior, and got a different result. We must continually challenge our assumptions about ourselves, others, situations, and things. Judging without knowing the facts is presumptuous. It's wrong to hold others to a stricter standard than we do for ourselves. This tendency is the older brother's way. He only responded with anger, offense, and judgment. When we live with bitterness and judgment, we become just like him. "The law was given through Moses, but grace and truth came through Jesus Christ" (John 1:17 NKJV). Justice with mercy is the compassionate way. It's Jesus' way.

As Messiah, Yeshua came to free us from harsh judgment. There is no condemnation in Him (Romans 8:1). Leadership Ministries wrote, "The person who is *in* Christ is safe and secure from condemnation now and forever. He will not be judged as a sinner; he will not face condemnation. He is beyond condemnation; he shall never be condemned for sin; he shall never be separated from the love of God which is *in* Christ Jesus our Lord."[11] Since we're not under condemnation as believers in Yeshua, why do we judge people so strictly? One reason is that we are hurt because we feel wronged and insecure in ourselves or our positions. We easily and quickly pick up offenses for real and imagined slights, or we compare ourselves with others and set compassion aside for judgment.

The older brother was more lost than his younger sibling. He did not truly love his father or his brother. He was, in essence, a servant serving his master for the sake of reward. He didn't understand his father's heart and chose to live in anger and with a judgmental spirit rooted in egotism. While the younger brother was stuck in selfishness, the older brother was stuck in pride. Like the rich young ruler, he thought that if he followed the rules, he'd be fine and blessed (Mark 10:17–27). Experiencing God's fullness in our own lives and becoming a bridge of compassion to others requires a paradigm shift from judgmentalism and the egotism of "I" and "me" to "we."

The Prodigal Prophet

The last two chapters of the book of Jonah parallel amazingly the parable of the prodigal son. God had sent the prophet to warn the people of Nineveh that they needed to repent from their sins or face His wrath. Surprisingly, the Ninevites listened to Jonah's words. Like the younger son of Yeshua's parable, they repented and received God's forgiveness. But like the older son, Jonah did not rejoice in their newfound redemption.

Jonah 4:1–3 says,

It greatly displeased Jonah and he resented it. So he prayed to ADONAI and said, "Please, Lord, was not this what I said when I was still in my own country? That's what I anticipated, fleeing to Tarshish—for I knew that you are a gracious and compassionate God, slow to anger and full of kindness, and relenting over calamity. So please, ADONAI, take my soul from me—because better is my death than my life."

Like the older brother, Jonah was angry. God tried to soften his heart, first with kindness, by growing a large plant to shield him from the sun. Yet Jonah did not relent, so God killed the plant and exposed Jonah to the sun and wind. Jonah's attitude and anger remained unchanged. The book of Jonah ends much like the parable, with the Father's voice explaining, "You have pity on the plant for which you did no labor or make it grow, that appeared overnight and perished overnight. So shouldn't I have pity on Nineveh—the great city that has in it more than 120,000 people who don't know their right hand from their left—as well as many animals?" (Jonah 4:10).

Interestingly, Jonah was grateful for the compassion he experienced in the belly of the fish. Still, he did not want to extend that same compassion to other people. Like the older brother, he wasn't thankful that the Ninevites repented.

God wanted to partner with Jonah in the work of redemption and transformation. Still, for that to happen, compassion needed to be at the root of his motivations. The people God calls us to reach might repent, but if we don't extend compassion, we won't be part of the healing process.

Both the older son and Jonah were bitter and angry people. They refused to celebrate finding a lost soul. Sometimes we can fall into the same trap when our self-righteousness leads us to forget all Yeshua has done for us.

How can we be transformed and be more open to God's will in our lives? We start by recognizing that we need help. The younger son "came to his senses" (Luke 15:17). He realized that his father had more for him than the world did. The older son and Jonah walked away; their pride kept them from recognizing that they needed help.

Pastor Robert Morris outlined several more things we can do when we're stuck in pride. Here are three of his points:

1. *"Repent to God and others. . . .* Repentance and confession are not the same thing. . . . You can confess your sins and not repent. . . . Repentance means that you change your mind. . . . It's not just that you change your mind about your sin; it's that you change your mind about yourself. You change your mind about who God created you to be."[12] Both the older son and Jonah had false self-images. They trusted more in themselves than in the Lord.

2. *"Renounce the lies of Satan. . . .* Every bondage begins with a lie." The elder brother believed lies about his father. He doubted the goodness of his father and chose to believe that his father was withholding from him what he rightfully deserved. That's exactly what Adam and Eve did in the garden. They believed Satan and felt God was withholding the best fruit from them. Friends, when we trust and obey God, He never withholds. "The older son never left home, but . . . he was in bondage to bitterness, unforgiveness, resentment, hate, jealousy, envy."[13]

3. *"Receive the gifts of the Father. . . .* The [father's] robe represents the robe of righteousness [Isaiah 61:10]. . . . Your righteousness comes from God and what Jesus did on the cross, not from your own works. . . . [The father's] ring represents authority. . . . Jesus gave us authority in Luke 10:19. . . . We have to receive God's authority over the enemy. . . . The shoes of power, and the gift of power from the Lord is not something, it's someone. Acts 1:8 [says], 'You shall receive power when the Holy Spirit has come upon you.'"[14]

The God of the Other Side runs to receive people who wish to turn from their past and have a new beginning and a transformed life.

A Note from Kathie

The parable of the prodigal son is one of the most endearing and enduring stories in the Bible. Although it is an ancient tale, it seems more relevant than ever in our modern, broken world. Today, more than at any time in my memory, the nuclear family has been torn asunder and happy endings are increasingly hard to find.

When Jesus told this parable at the synagogue in Capernaum, His audience very well may have pictured the "distant country" he was describing as the Decapolis, the ten pagan cities we discussed earlier that were on the other side of the Sea of Galilee. The people there worshiped numerous gods and practiced unspeakable sexual and violent acts in the course of their "worship." So, when the lost son set out for such a place, you can only imagine how shocked Jesus' audience was.

"Oh, God, no! Not the other side—he'll be lost forever!"

But that's not the end of the story. The son suffered deeply and finally realized that the life he had before with his father and his brother was far superior to the one he had set out to find. The grass is always greener on the other side? Hardly ever. And *never* if you're leaving the love and security and protection of your loving father to find it.

I love the moment when the heartbroken father, who had never stopped praying for his lost son, saw him from a distance and dropped all pretense of decorum, modesty, and pride to hitch up his cloak and run to embrace and kiss his grimy, pig-smelling son.

"He's home! He's home!" is all he could cry as he lost himself in their embrace. It is truly the quintessential expression of our heavenly Father's love for each of His sin-soaked, broken, and lost children. You and me.

A timeless tale.

seventeen

CORNELIUS AND PETER

Rabbi Jason

The God of the Other Side also reaches across borders and boundaries to restore people and bring unity. Rabbi Paul wrote, "There is neither Jew nor Greek [Gentile] . . . for you are all one in Messiah *Yeshua*" (Galatians 3:28). The revelation of our unity in Yeshua has produced a hunger in me for this full inheritance, this abundant blessing, offered by God. We don't have to compromise and settle for half of the story. The Bible is a treasure map that points to all the riches and inheritance that are ours in Yeshua. When believers connect to the roots of their faith, more abundant fruit and revelation are the results.

Do you remember what Jesus prayed for in His final prayer for the disciples? "Holy Father, keep them in Your name that You have given Me, so that they may be one just as We are" (John 17:11). This prayer discloses the Messiah's heart toward unity. God's presence, power, and provision are closely linked to the unity of His people.

The story of Cornelius's and Peter's visions opens the door for us to grab hold of our full inheritance and unity.

Cornelius's Vision

Before we look closely at this man named Cornelius, let's backtrack a bit so we can fully understand the context of Cornelius's vision, Peter's vision, and the God who wants to take the Gospel message to the other side.

A Brief History

Yeshua told His disciples, "You will receive power when the Holy Spirit comes on you; and you will be my witnesses in Jerusalem, and in all Judea and Samaria, and to the ends of the earth" (Acts 1:8 NIV). He didn't ask or try to persuade gently; He commanded His disciples to go and preach the Gospel to the world. The Gospel doesn't discriminate. It is for every person regardless of nationality, ethnic background, economic standing, and color. The universality of the Gospel is demonstrated early in the book of Acts and how the movement began in Jerusalem.

A bit later, we read about Philip going down to a city in Samaria where he "proclaimed the Messiah there" (Acts 8:5 NIV). A revival began as people accepted the Gospel when Philip preached. Many were baptized, and things were going so well that the apostles in Jerusalem sent Peter and John to Samaria!

The Gospel continued to travel as believers from Samaria and other villages traveled freely in the Roman Empire. As the years passed and persecution began to occur, believers were scattered, and the Gospel spread "into the world." Thirty years later, Rabbi Paul wrote, "You heard before about this hope in the true message of the Good News that has come to you. In all the world this Good News is bearing fruit and growing, just as it has in you since you first heard it and came to truly know God's grace" (Colossians 1:5–6).

While the Gospel message went from Jerusalem to Samaria to the world, it was a gradual progress.

Who Was Cornelius?

Beginning in Acts 10, we read about the next significant wave in spreading the Gospel as it was being proclaimed to the Gentiles. And this good news came to them most unusually, marking one of the most significant turning points in the history of Christianity.

Scripture tells us,

> In Caesarea there was a man named Cornelius, a centurion of what was called the Italian Cohort. He was a devout man, revering God with all his household. He gave *tzedakah* [charitable giving] generously to the people and prayed to God continually. About the ninth hour of the day, he saw clearly in a vision an angel of God coming and saying to him, "Cornelius!" (Acts 10:1–3)

Herod the Great had named this city Caesarea in honor of the emperor of Rome. A major seaport, sixty-six miles northwest of Jerusalem, it became the residence of the Roman governor of Judea, containing a regular military garrison (Acts 23:23–24).

A centurion had command over one hundred men (in Latin a *centuria*). They were soldiers who worked their way up the ranks. A cohort was one-tenth of a legion, "made up of six thousand men. Five cohorts were stationed in Caesarea and another in Jerusalem."[1] Centurions were the backbone of the Roman army. *The Acts of the Apostles* tells us, "An ancient historian describes the qualifications of the centurion like this, 'Centurions are desired not to be overbold and reckless so much as good leaders, of steady and prudent mind, not prone to take the offensive to start fighting wantonly, but able when over-whelmed and hard-pressed to stand fast and die at their posts.' Cornelius therefore was a man who first and foremost knew what courage and loyalty were."[2]

It's interesting that a man such as Cornelius, who was steeped in Roman army culture, would be called a devout man of God (Acts 10:2). He was likely a Gentile who had tossed aside the idols and culture of Rome. He was not a Jew, although he may have attended synagogue, believed in the One True God, and taught his family the ways of God.

Cornelius was a man of prayer. Praying at the ninth hour was important, as we'll see below. In addition, he had a heart of charity (*tzedakah* in Hebrew). The Bible paints a picture of a courageous, loyal soldier who believed in God, prayed to Him, and expressed charity and kindness. There's another centurion who may have been a role model for Cornelius. In Matthew 8:1–13 Yeshua contacted a centurion whose servant needed healing. He told the centurion, "Amen, I tell you, I have not found anyone in Israel with such great faith!" (Matthew 8:10). It was also a centurion in Matthew 27, who as a witness to Yeshua's crucifixion declared, "This really was the Son of God!" (v. 54).

Living in the important city of Caesarea that headquartered the governor, Cornelius probably served Pontius Pilate. Caesarea was also significant for Jesus and the disciples. Several gospel accounts took place there (for example, Matthew 16:17–18; Mark 8:27). After Philip baptized the Ethiopian eunuch, he was taken to Ashkelon, then to Caesarea. In Acts 9, when the believers felt Paul's life was in danger from the religious leaders in Jerusalem, they whisked him off to Caesarea for his safety. Later in this chapter we'll find God calling Peter to Caesarea. Rabbi Paul stopped there during his second missionary journey. The Romans would eventually send him there for his trial, where he remained for two years.

Acts 10:3–8 then tells us about an encounter Cornelius had with an angel. Although frightened, his response was, "What is it, Lord?" The angel told Cornelius to send men to Joppa and find the apostle Peter. Verse 3 tells us Cornelius was praying "about the ninth hour of the day [3:00 p.m.]." Acts 3:1 gives reference to this time of the day being the most important time of prayer in a Jewish person's day. "Jewish Law makes it our duty to pray three times daily: in the morning, in the afternoon and at nightfall. These prayers are called morning prayer (*shacharit*), afternoon prayer (*minchah*) and evening prayer (*arvith* or *maariv*)."[3] Cornelius was praying with Israel as he prayed on the ninth hour. Perhaps Christians today should pray along with the Jewish people by learning certain prayers like the Shema (Deuteronomy 6:4–9).

The root word for the number nine, *tisha* in Hebrew, is *shah*, which means "to turn toward." In Genesis 4:4 God "looked favorably upon Abel and his offering." God respected or looked with favor upon Abel's offering. Cornelius's vision at the ninth hour demonstrates that the Lord was turning toward and looking favorably on the Gentiles.

Matthew 27:46 reminds us that Yeshua, at the ninth hour, cried out to God, "Why have You abandoned Me?" It was at the ninth hour that Elijah prayed to God against the prophets of Baal on Mount Carmel, and God answered by sending fire from heaven (1 Kings 18:36–39).

Peter's Vision

The story moves from Cornelius's home to Joppa and Peter. Peter was visiting a friend in Joppa, some forty miles south along the Mediterranean coast. He was there at the request of the other disciples because Dorcas, a devout woman, had died. God, through Peter, brought her back to life. This miracle showed the power of the Holy Spirit in the early church. While Cornelius's representatives neared where Peter was staying, the apostle "fell into a trance" (Acts 10:10).

Scripture tells us,

> [Peter] became very hungry and wanted to eat; but while they were preparing something, he fell into a trance. He saw the heavens opened, and something like a great sheet coming down, lowered by its four corners to the earth. In it were all sorts of four-footed animals and reptiles and birds of the air.
>
> A voice came to him, "Get up, Peter. Kill and eat."
>
> But Peter said, "Certainly not, Lord! For never have I eaten anything unholy or unclean."
>
> Again a voice came to him, a second time: "What God has made clean, you must not consider unholy." This happened three times, and the sheet was immediately taken up to heaven. (Acts 10:10–16)

This trance was a game-changing revelation for Peter that would have been radical to the first Jewish followers of Jesus. All the apostles and first believers were Jews who honored the Torah and kept its commandments. Because of Peter's initial reaction, the Lord spoke to him again and gave another supernatural vision. The fact that this encounter happened while he was in a "trance" is an important detail that has deep spiritual and theological meaning.

The Greek word translated as "trance" is *ekstasis*. This word is the same word in the Greek Septuagint that is often translated as "deep sleep" in

Genesis. Remember, no suitable partner was found for Adam. So the Lord caused "a deep sleep to fall on the man and he slept; and He took one of his ribs and closed up the flesh in its place. *ADONAI Elohim* built the rib, which He had taken from the man, into a woman" (Genesis 2:21–22).

This connection is subtle but has incredible implications. In the New Testament, Jesus was called "the King of the Jews" and the Second Adam, as Rabbi Paul wrote, "'The first man, Adam, became a living soul.' The last Adam [Yeshua] became a life-giving spirit" (1 Corinthians 15:45). As we discussed earlier in this book, the Second Adam died on the cross because sin entered the world when the first Adam ate from the tree. He died on the cross, which is a tree, to make atonement for the first sin of the first man and woman that caused the Fall. But Yeshua must make atonement not just for Adam but also for Eve, who was the one taken from "the side" of Adam. This is one of the reasons they pierced Yeshua's side at the crucifixion.

But there is something more here. Yeshua represents the new Adam, but Adam *needs Eve.* When Yeshua's side was pierced, He was birthing the new Eve, the church who would become His bride. In the first days after the crucifixion and resurrection of Christ, the church who is the bride of Messiah was only Jewish. But this was never God's intent. As a result of the Yeshua's death, something amazing happened:

> In Messiah *Yeshua*, you who once were far off have been brought near by the blood of the Messiah. For He is our *shalom*, the One who made the two into one and broke down the middle wall of separation. Within His flesh He made powerless the hostility—the law code of *mitzvot* contained in regulations. He did this in order to create within Himself one new man from the two groups, making *shalom*, and to reconcile both to God in one body through the cross—by which He put the hostility to death. (Ephesians 2:13–16)

Peter's vision was the start of this radical new revelation! The Great
Commission to "make disciples of all nations" (Matthew 28:19) is, in reality,
an extension of the first commandment: "God blessed them and God said
to them, 'Be fruitful and multiply, fill the land, and conquer it'" (Genesis
1:28). In the same way children are born through the intimate union of man
and woman, it takes Jews and Gentiles partnering together to raise up sons
and daughters for the Kingdom. As man is incomplete without woman, so
the people of God (the church) are incomplete and can't be entirely fruitful
without the union of Jew and Gentile.

Joppa, Jonah, Peter, and Second Chances

Peter had this vision while he was in the city of Joppa, which was an
ancient and vital port city located in Israel. Again, details are essential. Of
all the places where Peter could have this vision, why Joppa? Interestingly,
it was the place where Jonah fled from the Lord. Jonah is the only Hebrew
prophet whom God called to bring the message of salvation to Gentiles.
Jonah did not want to go and call the people of Nineveh to repentance, so
he disobeyed and tried to flee to Tarsus from Joppa.

Peter received the vision in Joppa because he is the New Testament
Jonah. Let's look at some of the similarities. Jonah and the Children of
Israel would have thought of Ninevites in much the same way Jews thought
about Romans in Peter's time. God told Jonah to arise and go. Instead Jonah
disobeyed by going in the opposite direction of Nineveh. Due to his disobedience, Jonah camped out in the belly of a fish for three days and nights.
After he was coughed up on shore, Jonah finally got the message and did
what God told him to do, albeit reluctantly (Jonah 1 and 3:1). Why do many

of us choose the difficult path when simply obeying God and relying on Him can give us an easier one?

The Lord told Peter to arise and eat in Acts 10, which meant he was to speak the message of salvation to Gentiles. Like Jonah, he was reluctant and didn't want to do it. After God spoke to him three times, he was faithful to proclaim the good news to the Gentiles.

God gave Jonah and Peter a second chance. Peter was the one chosen to be the "rock" (Matthew 16:18). He was the pillar and the foundational leader of this new and developing community, the church. Peter was not a weak, wimpy, or fearful guy. He was a man's man, a rugged, gritty fisherman. He had lots of *chutzpah* and was not afraid of a good fight. The night they arrested Yeshua, Peter took out his sword and cut off the ear of the high priest's servant, Malchus (Luke 22:50–51).

Peter was the apostle who boldly declared to Yeshua, "I'll never deny You!" (Mark 14:29–31). Yet just the opposite happened. After Yeshua's arrest Peter denied Him three times . . . and then the cock crowed just as his Master had prophesied. After the death of Yeshua on Good Friday, Peter lost hope, and fear and despair overcame him. But on the third day, he found the empty tomb and hope began to arise. Still unsure about his future, probably feeling more like a pebble than a rock, Peter decided to go fishing. Maybe he went fishing because he figured he should return to his old job. After all, he'd been such a failure at his new one. Do you ever feel like you've blown it in a big way—like it's unfixable and you're lower than scum? That was Peter. But thankfully *Adonai* is a God of second chances.

You may remember that sometime after the resurrection, before He ascended, Yeshua was calmly walking on the beach. At the same time, Peter and the disciples were out fishing. He called out to them to drop their nets on the other side of the boat. The nets overflowed with fish, and Peter jumped into the water again and swam to shore. The Bible says after they all had eaten breakfast, Yeshua turned to Peter and asked, "Simon, son of Jonah, do you love Me more than these?" (John 21:15 NKJV).

Can you imagine how Peter must have felt at that moment? Did Peter think to himself, *Boy, I am a real Jonah! I can't believe that I denied the Lord like Jonah did and spent three days in the belly of the fish, fishing!* When Yeshua addressed him as Simon, son of Jonah, instead of the familiar Simon Peter, it wasn't to make Peter feel guilty and small. Instead He was restoring Peter and giving him a second chance.

To understand this we must look at the only other time that Yeshua called Peter "the son of Jonah." In Matthew 16 Yeshua asked the disciples, "But who do you say I am?" Simon Peter answered, "You are the Messiah, the Son of the living God." Yeshua then said to him,

> Blessed are you, Simon son of Jonah, because flesh and blood did not reveal this to you, but My Father who is in heaven! And I also tell you that you are Peter, and upon this rock I will build My community; and the gates of *Sheol* will not overpower it. I will give you the keys of the kingdom of heaven. Whatever you forbid on earth will have been forbidden in heaven and what you permit on earth will have been permitted in heaven. (Matthew 16:15–19)

By calling Peter the son of Jonah after his denial in John 21, Yeshua was saying to Peter, "Don't forget who I called you to be and what you are called to do. You are still My rock! I am going to use you to build My church. You blew it, but I am the God of second chances!"

Peter was to be the New Testament's "greater than Jonah"—in the best sense of the word "greater." Peter would be the one who would start revival among the Jewish people and use the keys of the Kingdom to open the door to salvation among the Gentiles, beginning with Cornelius. God is good! He forgives, restores, and is always willing to go to the other side and give us a second chance, as He did with Jonah and Peter, when we blow it.

Up on the Roof

Every detail in Scripture is there for a reason, so we must take notice that Peter went to the roof to pray. A roof is a place where a person can get away from others, their influences, and their opinions. The psalmist wrote, "I lie awake, like a lonely bird on a roof" (Psalm 102:8). The roof is also the highest point of a home. It symbolizes a higher vantage point that leads to a new and elevated perspective. It makes perfect sense that Peter had this vision on the roof. Peter needed to rise above the common view held by his Jewish friends and family—that Gentiles are unclean and unholy and therefore should be avoided. Peter needed a new vantage point. He needed a fresh perspective that allowed him to see that God was elevating the position of believing Gentiles to a position of equality with Jewish believers in the Kingdom.

A Note from Kathie

I love the story of Cornelius for so many reasons. Here was a man of incredible professional accomplishment—a Roman centurion, meaning he commanded one hundred soldiers beneath him. And, although he technically ruled over the Jews in Palestine, he loved them and respected their faith and went out of his way to bless them.

Cornelius knew innately what was not obvious to the naked eye: he was a sinner, and something deep and mysterious was missing from his life. He knew he needed a Savior.

So Jehovah God sent an angel to tell Cornelius how to find this Savior, and he immediately did what the angel told him to do: *Send for a man named Peter, a disciple of the risen Jesus, and he will bring you the message of salvation.*

By now the incredible tale of Jesus' resurrection had no doubt spread like wildfire throughout the land, only continuing the amazing stories from the last three years of Jesus' miraculous ministry.

Cornelius had to be fascinated beyond measure by what he had heard of this young Jewish rabbi who healed the sick, the lame, the afflicted, the lepers, and the demon-possessed. He even raised the dead back to life. Who was this man? Was he for real? Was he the long-awaited Messiah the Jews had believed for centuries would finally come to save them from not only their sins but also their enemies?

Cornelius must have been confused about that last part. He didn't feel like an enemy to those people he had come to admire so much. I'm convinced something in Cornelius's soul was broken when he received the news in Caesarea that this humble rabbi had been crucified during Passover for crimes against God and crimes against the Roman Empire.

Cornelius likely believed that a great injustice had been perpetrated against this Jesus. Perhaps he even sensed the story wasn't over.

But not in Cornelius's wildest dreams could he have imagined the role he would play in the history of humankind unfolding before his very eyes. He sent some of his workers and some of his soldiers to Joppa to find Peter and bring him to Caesarea, more than thirty miles away![4]

Peter, of course, had been experiencing his own divine intervention. An angel had visited him as well and directed him through a dream to go to Caesarea—to go to the home of Cornelius and bring him the message of salvation. Cornelius, a faithful soldier, did exactly what the angel commanded; and Peter, a Jew, watched as Cornelius, a Gentile, and his entire family kneeled and asked Jesus into their hearts. He saw them fall to their knees and raise their hands in holy praise to the Almighty.

He heard them speak in tongues and glorify Jehovah God in the highest heavens. And he finally understood in the deepest part of his soul that salvation was *not just for the Jews* as he had been taught his entire life.

He realized that *Jehovah Elohim* loved *everyone* He had ever created, and He longed for them to know Him and worship Him in spirit and truth. In that one moment, the whole world changed forever and would never be the same.

Both men obeyed the angel. Both men realized that Jesus was the way, the truth, and the life, and that no one could come before the Father of heaven except through Him (John 14:6).

eighteen

THE POWER OF UNITY

Rabbi Jason

What happened at Cornelius's house connects to Acts 2. Acts 2 is a reenactment of Mount Sinai (Exodus 19). It happened on Pentecost—the Jewish biblical holiday that celebrates the events of Mount Sinai (the first Pentecost). The booming of the wind in Acts was like the thundering at Sinai. The tongues of fire over the disciples' heads parallel the cleft tongue that came out of God's mouth when He uttered the Commandments. According to the *Targum*, an ancient Aramaic paraphrase or interpretation of the Hebrew Bible, the split tongue looked like a fiery bird, which is said to have inscribed the tablets of the covenant. The text reads, "Like torches of fire, a torch of fire to the right and a torch of fire to the left. It flew and winged swiftly in the air of the heavens and came back . . . and returning it became engraved on the tablets of the covenant and all Israel beheld it."[1]

In Acts 2, on the second Pentecost, God imprinted His Word just as He did on Mount Sinai—but not on stone tablets. Instead He wrote it *within* His people, on the tablets of their hearts. This was what He had promised long before: "I will make a new covenant with the house of Israel. . . . I will put My *Torah* [Law] within them [in their minds]. Yes, I will write it on their heart" (Jeremiah 31:30, 32).

It was radical for these Jewish followers of Yeshua to have a Sinai experience. It was even more radical for the Gentiles in Caesarea to have the same experience.

In traditional Jewish thought the soul of every Gentile convert was supernaturally at Sinai. They felt that every Gentile who went through full conversion had a private Mount Sinai experience. This idea is what makes Acts 10 so significant. These Gentiles were having a personal Sinai experience without being required to go through a full conversion to Judaism. They didn't need to be circumcised or follow the six-hundred-plus laws. The Gentiles received the same Holy Spirit as the Jews. That's radical! Gentiles are not full members of the Jewish community today. They can't participate in many things unless they convert. Cornelius's experience flew in the face of what Judaism taught, but it served to bring unity—Jew and Gentile together as followers of Yeshua. This leads to a radical unity of God's people.

This unity of God's people, first on Sinai, then many years later in Jerusalem, sparked the fire and wind of the Spirit, which then created a wildfire of transformation. I hold firmly to the fact that God's *presence*, *power*, and *provision* are in direct proportion to the unity of His people.

Yeshua's followers could be described as unified on the day of Pentecost (*Shavuot*). The book of Acts records incredible unity (emphasis added, apart from Hebrew words):

All these with *one mind* were continuing together in prayer—along with the women and Miriam, *Yeshua's* mother, and His brothers. (Acts 1:14)

When the day of *Shavuot* [Pentecost] had come, they were *all together* in one place. (Acts 2:1)

Through the hands of the apostles many signs and wonders were done among the people. And they *were all with one accord* in Solomon's Porch. (Acts 5:12 NKJV)

I believe one of the reasons we don't see the kind of revival we desire is because Adam and Eve, Jew and Gentile, are not partnering together. They are not unified. We cannot be genuinely fruitful without each other.

Jesus gave us the Great Commission. He said, "Go therefore and *make disciples of all the nations*, baptizing them in the name of the Father and of the Son and of the Holy Spirit, teaching them to observe all things that I have commanded you; and lo, I am with you always, even to the end of the age" (Matthew 28:19–20 NKJV, emphasis added). This commission to His disciples, and us, is rooted in the call to Adam and Abraham to be fruitful. We can't fulfill Yeshua's command if we are apart from each other.

Harmony Produces Blessing

If Jew and Gentile don't function in alignment or unity, there will be *tohu vavohu*, "chaos." We find this phrase in Genesis 1:2 as it described the earth's condition immediately before God created light (Genesis 1:3). When God brought order out of the chaos, there was light. When we bring unity and alignment to people or situations, there are blessings. When Jew and Gentile unite, there is order and alignment that lead to restored blessing and *shalom*.

Unity is the foundation and fruit of redemption. Unity began in

Jerusalem, and then, over time, the Gospel went to all nations (Acts 1:14, 2:1, 5:12). There was unity. The new believers (both Jew and Gentile) were in one accord, and then God moved.

One Accord and One Mind

William Seymour, the African American holiness preacher who initiated the Azusa Street Revival, wrote, "I can say, through the power of the Holy Spirit, that whenever God can get a people that will come together in one accord and one mind in the Word of God, the baptism of the Holy Ghost will fall upon them, like as at Cornelius' house (Acts 10:45, 46)."[2]

At Mount Sinai we find healing as the people connected with God. In the book of Acts, we find oneness and miracles happened. How? Oneness leads to wholeness and blessing. Unity and oneness align heaven and earth, as we often pray in the Lord's Prayer, "Your kingdom come, Your will be done on earth as it is in heaven." Wholeness and blessing come when God's family love one another and sacrificially unite to advance the Kingdom. The Kingdom we're all waiting for won't come if we, Jew and Gentile, are not united! Unity, therefore, is not an elective—it is a requirement.

Unity isn't easy. We can't merely sit by a campfire and sing "Kumbaya" to achieve unity. Unity strikes at our ego. We want to do things *our* way. For the Kingdom to come, we must surrender part of ourselves—our likes and desires—for the sake of the other person. We must be willing to humble ourselves and receive the other person or group. We must be willing to listen to the other person and seek to understand them before we react.

Joni Eareckson Tada wrote, "Believers are never told to become one— we're already one, and we're expected to act like it."[3] A house divided cannot stand, but a united house can't be defeated. We need to act as one body of

Messiah that doesn't take offense and that is defined by His love. Yeshua prayed, "Now I am no longer in the world, but these are in the world, and I come to You. Holy Father, keep through Your name those whom You have given Me, *that they may be one as We are*" (John 17:11 NKJV, emphasis added).

As we realize that the God of the Other Side reaches across boundaries to come to us, we must also reach across boundaries to reach each other. Charles H. Brent (1862–1929), Episcopal bishop of the Philippines and of Western New York, wrote, "The unity of Christendom is not a luxury but a necessity. The world will go limping until Christ's prayer that all may be one is answered. We must have unity, not at all costs, but at all risks. A unified church is the only offering we dare present to the coming Christ [Messiah], for in it alone will He find room to dwell."[4]

Let's give the God of the Other Side room to dwell. Let's answer Yeshua's prayer and strive to be one—Jew and Gentile together reaching the world for Him.

A Note from Kathie

As we've discussed, when Jesus told His disciples "Meet Me on the other side" after feeding the five thousand, He had in mind a specific place on the eastern shore of the Sea of Galilee known as the Decapolis.

It's beyond my imagination to visualize what the Decapolis must have been like in the time of Jesus with all its sexual perversion, idol worship, and child sacrifice. Though today the area lies in ruins, destroyed by earthquake, the bones of thousands of infants have been discovered.

It's heartbreaking, but the truth is that children are being trafficked all over this world in record numbers even today—"sacrificed" to the lust and depravity of people hell-bent on satiating their passions regardless of who it destroys.

So we have to ask ourselves: Does Jesus still want us to go to places that are so foreign to our civilized sensibilities?

I believe that when He said to His disciples "Follow Me," He envisioned our world today. He envisioned His followers—you and me—leaving the *shalom* of our comfortable lives and bravely stepping into the chaos of the lives of the broken, the unloved, the unwashed, and the unsaved.

I have met thousands of these people in the world of entertainment where God called me to serve Him decades ago.

Let's be honest. It's easy to hurry by the homeless sleeping in the streets, cast judgment on the addicted shoving needles into their bodies or the hookers on the street corners selling themselves to strangers to survive. We don't want to look. We want to sit in our pews week after week, happy to pray for them and maybe send them some money, but certainly never venture into their stench to actually ask them their names and love them the way Jesus did.

Billions of taxpayer dollars have been wasted on government programs to alleviate suffering and poverty, and many well-meaning people have served tirelessly. So why isn't it working?

In general I think it's because we've left God out of the solution. We've fed a body but ignored the soul. We've provided a bed but not shared the hope that only God can provide.

Some organizations I've worked with through the years have had phenomenal success—the Dream Center in Los Angeles, Samaritan's Purse, Childhelp, the International Justice Mission, and Agape Awakening, to name a few.

They all serve differently, but their common denominator is that they serve in the name of Jesus and rely on His power and His Holy Spirit to strengthen and guide them. I am in awe of the depths of their devotion. I want to be more like them today than I was yesterday.

I don't want to be lukewarm. I want to be on fire to share God's love with the people who need it most. I want to meet Jesus at the "other side" and watch Him transform their lives, deliver them from their fears and their diseases and their hopelessness.

If we had the cure for cancer, would we share it? I think any decent person would. Well, we as believers have the cure for the malignancy of the soul. His name is Jesus, Yeshua, and people all over the world are dying because they don't know He loves them.

We are supposed to tell them. Then we're supposed to show them by the way we live.

Jesus said, "Love one another as I have loved you" (John 15:12 NKJV). May our answer forever be, "Yes, Yeshua, yes."

CONCLUSION

Kathie

The Hebrew language contains no word for "coincidence" because Jews believe that God is either sovereign in all things or He is not God at all.

It was no coincidence that my dear friend Angie Clawson set up a writing session for me with Nicole C. Mullen in Franklin, Tennessee, in October 2019. It is no coincidence that both Nicole and I, who had never met beforehand, came to that session with Hagar on our hearts and began to write the song "The God Who Sees."

From that day forward the Holy Spirit moved in countless, methodical, and often miraculous ways to bring about the production of *The Way*.

The fact that it was all accomplished during the COVID-19 pandemic is testimony to the unfailing faithfulness of *Jehovah Elohim*, Creator God.

I have felt His presence and His Holy Spirit power from that very first note Nicole and I wrote, and I marvel these three years later at all He has brought forth—almost like streams of living water.

Psalm 18:30 says, "His way is perfect; the word of the LORD is flawless" (BSB).

I have prayed every moment to be faithful and stay true to the calling to remain on this journey until the last word was written and the last note was sung.

But in the end, as always, it was God's faithfulness that brought it to fruition. Blessed be His name!

It took hundreds of individuals to complete the task, and I'm so grateful to everyone. But as I close out this extraordinary season in my life, I'm left with the same breathless wonder that I felt as a child when I looked up at the starlit nighttime sky and exclaimed, "Look what my God has made!"

It is my fervent prayer that Jehovah Adonai will anoint *The Way* and this companion book, *The God of the Way*, to change millions of broken, hungry, seeking hearts all over the world.

Only His Word can accomplish this. And only His way can lead us home.

SHALOM,

KATHIE LEE

ACKNOWLEDGMENTS

Kathie Lee

It is always important to pause and thank all the individuals who are so crucial to the success of any project you work on. I'm grateful to so many people who helped me bring *The God of the Way* into being:

My literary agents, Albert Lee and Pilar Queen. My UTA agent, Nick Barnes, and my editor, Stephanie Newton.

My coauthor and friend, Rabbi Jason Sobel. His depth of understanding Scripture is always invaluable to everything we do together, and I thank God for him.

Christine Gardner, who keeps all the wheels turning.

Matt Baugher, who always sees the promise and importance of my passion.

And finally, above all, my Messiah, Yeshua, for divinely inspiriting His Holy Spirit to use me for His Kingdom. All honor and glory and praise be unto Him.

Rabbi Jason

This book is the accomplishment of a team effort. First, I want to thank my wife and forever love, Miriam. Your continued love, support, and encouragement have meant so much. You embody the joy, grace, and kindness of Messiah so well. Your gift as a worshiper, singer, and songwriter has been transformational in countless lives, including my own. I count myself blessed to be your husband. Thank you for who you are and all you do for God and our family.

Thanks to my boys, Avi and Judah. Being your dad has been one of the greatest blessings and joys in my life. Avi, I love your entrepreneurial spirit and your zeal to pursue your dreams. It challenges and inspires me to do the same. Judah, your passion for life, commitment to excellence, kindness toward others, and constant words of encouragement are true inspirations. You will always be my LG. I love you both so much and know you will do great things in life and for God.

To my parents, Robert and Jean Sobel. Thank you for always being there for me and believing in me. You have sacrificed so that I could pursue my dreams. I could not be more blessed or grateful for having you for my parents. My boys also share in that blessing, having you as their Zeyde and Bubbe.

To my wonderful aunt Carol and aunt Wendy. Thank you for all the ways you have been there for me throughout the years. Aunt Wendy, thanks for encouraging me to pursue the spiritual path, and Aunt Carol, for being like a second mom! I love you both so much!

A big thank-you to my cowriter and friend, Kathie Lee Gifford. Your love for God and passion for His Word are infectious and a real inspiration. Co-laboring with you to help people see Scripture in its original Hebraic context has been a joy and blessing. Who could have guessed that people would be so hungry to go deeper into their Jewish roots? God is so good! I value your friendship, insights, and commitment to make Messiah Yeshua and the message of the good news known.

Next, I want to offer my sincerest appreciation and thanks to the entire

Fusion Global team. Each one of you has played an incredibly important role in the creation of this book.

Ted Squires, you have been a wonderful mentor and coach. Your wealth of business knowledge and publishing experience have been invaluable. You have worked with the most amazing authors and some of the most influential books for over four decades, and I am humbled that you would work with me. You are the best. But even more than all that, I value how you have become more than a friend—like family. I love you and your tremendously gifted wife, Terry, so much.

A huge thank-you to Wayne Hastings. Your partnership in this endeavor has been such a blessing. I can't thank you enough for all the effort you have put into helping make this book what it has become. Your years of experience as a writer, researcher, and Bible teacher, and your work in publishing have made such a difference. I could not imagine having someone more gifted than you as a team member. On top of all that, you are one of the humblest servant-leaders I know. Thank you.

I also want to thank Max Davis. Max, you are an incredible writer. I appreciate how you used your unbelievable talent for storytelling to help make this book even better. You are so gifted and full of the Spirit, which makes you wonderful to work with and a gift for the body of Messiah.

To Alicia Barmore, thank you for all you have done throughout the years to help build the administrative infrastructure for Fusion. Your tireless effort and commitment to serve have been a huge blessing. I know the best is yet to come for you and Favour Consulting.

Thank you, Drew Nicolello. What would Fusion do without you? I have met few people who are as gifted creatively in filming and photography and so many aspects of social media and tech. Thank you for always being there and willing to fill in the gaps. I value you as a friend, leader, and team member. You have done many great things, but your future is even brighter.

To the Fusion board—Wendy Miller DeGolia, Lesley Burbridge, Helena Hwang, Kevin Malone, Don Fitzgibbons, and Dane Welch—your wisdom, counsel, service, and friendship have been invaluable throughout the years. Your support has been a continual source of encouragement and has enabled us to affect the lives of many people. Thank you!

I want to give a special thank-you to the entire Thomas Nelson team. Thank you, Damon Reiss, Stephanie Newton, and Carrie Marrs. Thanks as well to Debbie Wickwire. You might be retired, but you are not forgotten. Working with you has been a joy and blessing.

Finally and most importantly, I want to thank God. I give all thanks to You. Every blessing and good thing in my life is a gift from You. I gratefully acknowledge that I would not be who I am or be doing what I love without You, Yeshua! Todah L'El and Baruch HaShem!

NOTES

Chapter 1: Abraham

1. Martyn Lloyd-Jones, *Magnify the Lord: Luke 1:46–55* (1998; repr., Fearn, Ross-shire, UK: Christian Focus with Bryntirion Press, 2011), 74–75.

2. "How Long Did It Take for God to Call Abraham?" IDSWATER.com, May 27, 2021, https://idswater.com/2021/05/27/what-time-period-was-abraham-president/.

3. Charles F. Stanley, *The Charles F. Stanley Life Principles Bible: New King James Version* (Nashville: Nelson Bibles, 2005), Genesis 15:6.

4. Babylonian Talmud, Yevamot 64b, https://talmud-bavli.com/talmud-seder/seder-nashim/yevamot/64b.

5. Russell Resnik, *Creation to Completion: A Guide to Life's Journey from the Five Books of Moses* (Clarksville, MD: Messianic Jewish Publishers, 2006), 11.

6. Rabbi Menahem Posner summarizes Abraham's ten tests as follows: "G-d tells him to leave his homeland to be a stranger in the land of Canaan (Genesis 12:1). Immediately after his arrival in the Promised Land, he encounters a famine (12:10). The Egyptians seize his beloved wife, Sarah, and bring her to Pharaoh (12:15). Abraham faces incredible odds in the battle of the four and five kings (14:14). He marries Hagar after not being able to have children with Sarah (16:3). G-d tells him to circumcise himself at an advanced age (17:24). The king of Gerar captures Sarah, intending to take her for himself (20:2). G-d tells him to send Hagar away after having a child with her (21:12). His son Ishmael becomes estranged (21). G-d tells him to sacrifice his dear son Isaac upon an altar (22:2)." Menachem Posner, "What Were Abraham's Ten Tests?," Chabad.org, https://www.chabad.org/library/article_cdo/aid/1324268/jewish/What-Were-Abrahams-10-Tests.htm.

7. Nathan Hyman, "Sleeping Through the Night—Parshat Vayeira," MarehKohen

.com, November 15, 2019, https://marehkohen.com/2019/11/15/sleeping-through
-the-night-parshat-vayeira/.

8. Rabbi Abraham Twerski, "Weekly Parsha: Vayeira," Anshe Emes, October 12,
2013, https://anshe.org/weekly-parsha-vayeira/.

9. David M. Edwards, *Worship 365: The Power of a Worshipping Life* (Nashville:
B&H, 2006), 13.

Chapter 2: Sarah

1. Andrew Murray, *Waiting on God! Daily Messages for a Month* (New York;
Chicago; Toronto: Revell, 1896), 74.

2. Rashi on Genesis 23:1:1, trans. Sefaria community, Sefaria.org., https://www
.sefaria.org/Rashi_on_Genesis.23.1.1?ven=Sefaria_Community_Translation
&lang=bi.

3. Michah Gottlieb, *The Jewish Reformation: Bible Translation and Middle-Class
German Judaism as Spiritual Enterprise* (London: Oxford University Press,
2021), 187.

4. Sara Esther Crispe, "Esther: Hidden Beauty," Chabad.org, https://www.chabad
.org/theJewishWoman/article_cdo/aid/367185/jewish/Esther-Hidden-Beauty.htm.

5. Babylonian Talmud, Megillah 14a, cited in Menachem Posner, "The 7
Prophetesses of Judaism," Chabad.org, https://www.chabad.org/library/article
_cdo/aid/4257802/jewish/The-7-Prophetesses-of-Judaism.htm.

6. Babylonian Talmud, Megillah 14a, in Posner, "7 Prophetesses."

7. John Keats, *Hyperion* (Amsterdam: M. W. W. Van Lennep, 1879), 3.

8. Yeshivat Maharat, "When Will My Life Begin?," Sefaria.org, November 13, 2020,
https://www.sefaria.org/sheets/334013?lang=bi.

Chapter 3: Moses

1. Rabbi Jason Sobel, *Mysteries of the Messiah: Unveiling Divine Connections
from Genesis to Today* (Nashville: W Publishing, 2021), 69.

2. Russell Resnik, *Creation to Completion: A Guide to Life's Journey from the Five
Books of Moses* (Clarksville, MD: Messianic Jewish Publishers, 2006), 151.

3. The mountain is not identified. It may be near and to the south of Caesarea
Philippi, on the route to Capernaum and eventually Jerusalem (Matthew
16:13, 21; 17:24).

4. Sid Buzzell, Kenneth Boa, and Bill Perkins, eds., *The Leadership Bible:
Leadership Principles from God's Word* (Grand Rapids: Zondervan, 1998), 73.

5. Collin Hansen, comp., "What I Would Have Done Differently: Billy Graham's Regrets, in His Own Words," *Christianity Today*, https://www.christianitytoday.com/ct/2018/billy-graham/what-i-would-have-done-differently.html.

6. *Standard Lesson Commentary* (Cincinnati: Standard Publishing, 1990), 64.

Chapter 4: Joshua

1. Merriam-Webster, s.v. "zeal," https://www.merriam-webster.com/dictionary/zeal.

2. Hayim Nahman Bialik and Yehoshua Hana Ravnitzky, eds., *The Book of Legends Sefer Ha-Aggadah*, trans. William G. Braude (New York: Schocken, 1992), 522.

3. Throughout Jewish history several rabbis were also called "sages." The rabbis were not your normal, everyday rabbis of old. They were the rabbis who truly understood our oral and written traditions. Many created the writings of the Talmud and Mishna.

4. Bamidbar Rabbah 21:3, trans. Sefaria community, Sefaria.org, accessed February 10, 2022, https://www.sefaria.org/Bamidbar_Rabbah.21.3?lang=bi.

5. David H. Stern, ed., *The Complete Jewish Study Bible* (Peabody, MA: Hendrickson, 2016), 276. Commentary material supplied by Messianic Jewish Publishers and edited by Rabbi Barry A. Rubin.

6. A *midrash* is a unique Jewish literary form that includes stories and interpretations of the Torah. The ancient rabbis searched the Torah and, in effect, read between the lines to give the text a fuller meaning.

7. Bamidbar Rabbah 21:3, Sefaria.org, https://www.sefaria.org/Bamidbar_Rabbah.21.3?lang=bi.

8. "Joshua (1355–1245 BCE)," Chabad.org, accessed February 14, 2022, https://www.chabad.org/library/article_cdo/aid/129625/jewish/Joshua.htm. Menachem Posner, "Moses," Chabad.org, accessed February 14, 2022, https://www.chabad.org/library/article_cdo/aid/73398/jewish/Moses.htm.

Chapter 5: Mary

1. Omar C. Garcia, Bible Teaching Notes, s.v. Matthew 1:18, https://bibleteachingnotes.blog/2018/09/15/matthew-1/.

2. Truth2Freedom, s.v. Matthew 1:18, https://truth4freedom.wordpress.com/.

3. Warren W. Wiersbe, *The Bible Exposition Commentary*, vol. 1 (Wheaton, IL: Victor Books, 1996), 172.

4. Nicky Cruz, *Soul Obsession* (Colorado Springs, CO: WaterBrook, 2005), 149.

5. R. Kent Hughes, *Luke: That You May Know the Truth*, Preaching the Word (Wheaton, IL: Crossway Books, 1998), 49.

6. C. H. Spurgeon, *The Metropolitan Tabernacle Pulpit*, vol. 14 (Pasadena, TX: Pilgrim, 1970), 202.

7. Lyun Ya'akov on Ta'anit 9a; Kli Yakar, in Rabbi Yirmiyahu Ullman, "Ask the Rabbi," Ohr Somayach, https://ohr.edu/explore_judaism/ask_the_rabbi/ask _the_rabbi/7033.

8. William Barclay, *The Gospel of Luke*, The New Daily Study Bible (Louisville, KY; London: Westminster John Knox, 2001), 16.

9. Janet Bly, *Managing Your Restless Search* (Colorado Springs, CO: Victor Books, 1992), 134.

10. Rabbi Ted Riter, "April–Savlanut / Patience," Jewish Values for Everyday Living, March 29, 2011, https://jewishvalueseveryday.blogspot.com/2011/03 /april-savlanut-patience.html.

11. Riter, "April–Savlanut / Patience."

12. Barney Kasdan, *God's Appointed Customs: A Messianic Jewish Guide to the Biblical Lifecycle and Lifestyle* (Baltimore, MD: Messianic Jewish Publishers, 1996), 32–33.

13. Dasee Berkowitz, "Through Women of the Haggadah, Deepening the Seder Experience," Jewish Telegraphic Agency, April 2, 2011, https://www.jta.org /2011/04/02/lifestyle/through-women-of-the-haggadah-deepening-the -seder-experience.

14. Cora Jakes-Coleman in her introduction to Sarah Jakes, *Dear Mary: Lessons from the Mother of Jesus for the Modern Mom* (Bloomington, MN: Bethany House, 2015), 7–8.

Chapter 6: *Jehovah Elohim*: Creator God of Everything We See

1. Arnold Cheyney, *Legends of the Arts: 50 Inspiring Stories of Creative People* (Culver City, CA: Good Year Books, 2007), 16.

2. Gerard Van Groningen, "God, Names of," *Baker Encyclopedia of the Bible* (Grand Rapids: Baker, 1988), 880.

3. "Here's how the Hebrew numeric system works: the first ten Hebrew letters increase in value by a factor of one (*aleph* is 1, *bet* is 2, and so on). The next ten Hebrew letters increase in value by a factor of ten (*kaf* is 20, *lamed* is 30, and so on). The final Hebrew letters increase in value by a factor of one hundred (*kof* is 100, *reish* is 200, and so on) through the final letter, *tav*, with

a value of 400." Rabbi Jason Sobel, *Mysteries of the Messiah: Unveiling Divine Connections from Genesis to Today* (Nashville: W Publishing, 2021), 195.

4. Van Groningen, "God, Names of," 881–82.

5. Akiva Mattenson, "Rosh HaShanah and God's Battle for Compassion," Lehrhaus, September 3, 2018, https://www.thelehrhaus.com/timely-thoughts /rosh-hashanah-and-gods-battle-for-compassion/.

6. Rashi, in Sari Laufer, "Angels Among Us," Sefaria.org, accessed February 10, 2022, https://www.sefaria.org/sheets/17809?lang=bi.

7. William Davidson Talmud, Sanhedrin 6a, Sefaria.org, accessed February 10, 2022, https://www.sefaria.org/Sanhedrin.6b.10?lang=bi.

8. Timothy Keller, *Walking with God Through Pain and Suffering* (New York: Dutton, 2013), 45.

9. Sobel, *Mysteries of the Messiah*, xiii.

10. Watchman Nee, *Expecting the Lord's Blessing* (Anaheim, CA: Living Stream Ministry, 1993), 4, emphasis added.

11. Rabbi Hillel Rivlin, Kol HaTor 2, Sefaria.org, accessed February 10, 2022, https://www.sefaria.org/Kol_HaTor.2.147?ven=Kol_HaTor&lang=bi.

Chapter 7: The Power of the Word

1. Roy P. Basler, ed., *Collected Works of Abraham Lincoln* (New Brunswick, NJ: Rutgers University Press, 1953) 7:542. "Abraham Lincoln and the Bible," Abraham Lincoln's Classroom, https://www.abrahamlincolnsclassroom.org /Abraham-lincoln-in-depth/abraham-lincoln-and-the-bible/.

2. Dr. Joshua Kulp, *Mishnah Yomit*, Pirkei Avot 5, Sefaria.org, accessed February 10, 2022, https://www.sefaria.org/Pirkei_Avot.5.1?ven=Mishnah_Yomit_by _Dr._Joshua_Kulp&vhe=Torat_Emet_357&lang=bi&with=all&lang2=en.

3. "With ten utterances: Nine [times in the creation story does it state] 'and He said'; and 'In the beginning' is also an utterance, as it is written (Psalm 33:6), 'With the word of the Lord were the heavens made.'" Bartenura on Pirkei Avot 5:1:1–3, Sefaria.org, https://www.sefaria.org/sheets/46693.13?lang=bi&p2 =Bartenura_on_Pirkei_Avot.5.1.1–3&lang2=bi.

4. Louis Ginzberg, *The Legends of the Jews*, vol. 3 (1911), "The Installation of Elders," Internet Sacred Text Archive, https://www.sacred-texts.com/jud/loj /loj304.htm.

5. Warren W. Wiersbe, *Be Skillful*, "Be" Commentary Series (Wheaton, IL: Victor Books, 1996), 30.

6. William Davidson Talmud, Chagigah 11b:23, Sefaria.org, accessed February 10, 2022, https://www.sefaria.org/Chagigah.12a.14?lang=bi.

7. Jerry Gramckow, *In Search of the Silver Lining: Where Is God in the Midst of Life's Storms?* (Baltimore, MD: Messianic Jewish Publishers, 2000), 134.

8. Alfred Edersheim, in Walter C. Kaiser, "Jesus in the Old Testament," Gordon Conwell Theological Seminary, August 9, 2011, https://www.gordonconwell.edu /blog/jesus-in-the-old-testament/.

Chapter 8: Yeshua and the Woman

1. David Friedman, *They Loved the Torah: What Yeshua's First Followers Really Thought About the Law* (Baltimore, MD: Messianic Jewish Publishers, 2001), 33.

2. *Tehillim Psalms* (Brooklyn, NY: Artscroll Mesorah, 2005), 572.

Chapter 9: Hagar

1. Christine Graef, *The Rock from Which You Were Hewn* (Eugene, OR: Wipf & Stock, 2020), 14.

2. Nissan Mindel, "Hagar," Chabad.org, accessed February 13, 2022, https://www .chabad.org/library/article_cdo/aid/112053/jewish/Hagar.htm.

3. Helen Keller, quoted in Marcus A. Roberts, *Thoughts for Your Day: Meditations Food for Contemplation* (Bloomington, IN: AuthorHouse, 2019), e-book.

4. Jack Hyles, "Meet the Holy Spirit," Faith Bible Baptist Church, accessed March 29, 2022, http://www.fbbc.com/messages/hyles_meet_holy_spirit.htm.

5. William Davidson Talmud, Sanhedrin 98b, Sefaria.org, accessed February 10, 2022, https://www.sefaria.org/Sanhedrin.98b.14?lang=bi.

6. Bereishit Rabbah 60–61, trans. Sefaria community, Sefaria.org, accessed February 10, 2022, https://www.sefaria.org/Bereishit_Rabbah.61.7?lang=bi.

Chapter 10: Ruth

1. Ruth Rabbah 2:9, trans. Sefaria community, Sefaria.org, accessed February 10, 2022, https://www.sefaria.org/Ruth_Rabbah.2.9?ven=Sefaria_Community _Translation&lang=bi.

2. For more on what it means to cleave, see the section titled "The God of the Other Side," and specifically the story of Peter.

3. Richard L. Strauss, "Two to Get Ready—the Story of Boaz and Ruth," Bible.org, https://bible.org/seriespage/5-two-get-ready-story-boaz-and-ruth.

4. For other scriptures on this topic, read Hosea 13:3 and Micah 4:11–12.

5. For other scriptures on this topic, read 2 Corinthians 11:2 and Revelation 1:5.

Chapter 11: David

1. Charles R. Swindoll, *David: A Man of Passion and Destiny* (Nashville: W Publishing, 1997), 75.

2. Charles F. Stanley, *The Charles F. Stanley Life Principles Bible: New King James Version* (Nashville: Nelson Bibles, 2005), Psalm 34:1.

3. Albert Barnes, *Notes, Critical, Explanatory, and Practical, on the Book of Psalms* (Ann Arbor: University of Michigan, 1868), 169.

4. For example, see Genesis 15:1; Joshua 10:8; Judges 6:23; 1 Samuel 22:23; 2 Kings 6:16; Psalm 27:3; 46:3; 56:5.

Chapter 12: Mary of Magdala

1. W. E. Vine, *An Expository Dictionary of New Testament Words* (Nashville: Thomas Nelson, 1985), 311.

2. "Eugene Lang, Investor Who Made College Dreams a Reality, Dies at 98," *New York Times*, April 8, 2017, https://www.nytimes.com/2017/04/08/nyregion /eugene-lang-dead-harlem-college.html.

3. Jack Canfield and Mark Victor Hansen, *Chicken Soup for the Soul: Celebrating People Who Make a Difference* (New York: Simon & Schuster, 2012), e-book.

4. Jonathan Nicholson, "From Death to Harvest: Finding Jesus in Firstfruits and Pentecost," Hilltop House of Prayer, accessed March 29, 2022, https://hilltoptlh.org /blog/2020/05/from-death-to-harvest-finding-jesus-in-firstfruits-and-pentecost/.

Chapter 13: Peter Walks on Water

1. John identified "the other side" as Capernaum (John 6:24) and Mark as Gennesaret (Mark 6:53).

2. Todd Bolen, "The Sea of Galilee," Jerusalem Perspective, October 31, 1989, https://www.jerusalemperspective.com/1476/.

3. "Research," JesusBoat.com, accessed March 29, 2022, https://www.jesusboat.com /the-jesus-boat-research/.

4. Mekhilta d'Rabbi Yishmael 14:13, Rabbi Shraga Silverstein, trans., Sefaria.org, accessed February 10, 2022, https://www.sefaria.org/Mekhilta_d'Rabbi_Yishmael .14.13.2?ven=Mechilta,_translated_by_Rabbi_Shraga_Silverstein&vhe =Mekhilta_--_Wikisource&lang=bi.

5. Mekhilta, Beshalach 5; Pirkei d'Rabbi Eliezer 42, Gerald Friedlander, trans., Sefaria.org, https://www.sefaria.org/Pirkei_DeRabbi_Eliezer.42?ven=Pirke _de_Rabbi_Eliezer,_trans._Rabbi_Gerald_Friedlander,_London,_1916&vhe =Pirkei_Derabi_Eliezer&lang=bi; Exodus Rabbah 13 (Shemot Rabbah), trans. Sefaria community, Sefaria.org, accessed February 10, 2022, https://www .sefaria.org/Shemot_Rabbah.13?ven=Sefaria_Community_Translation &vhe=Midrash_Rabbah_—_TE&lang=bi; and others.

6. Sotah 37a, in Mendy Kaminker, "Nachshon ben Aminadav: The Man Who Jumped into the Sea," Chabad.org, accessed February 10, 2022, https://www .chabad.org/library/article_cdo/aid/2199147/jewish/Nachshon-ben-Aminadav -The-Man-Who-Jumped-Into-the-Sea.htm.

7. Tony Evans, *The Tony Evans Bible Commentary* (Nashville: Holman Bible Publishers, 2019), 1 Peter 1:6–7.

8. Terho Kanervikkoaho, "Messiah Walks on Water," Caspari Center, May 8, 2017, https://www.caspari.com/2017/05/08/messiah-walks-on-water/.

Chapter 14: The Demoniac

1. David L. McKenna and Lloyd J. Ogilvie, *Mark*, The Preacher's Commentary Series, vol. 25 (Nashville: Thomas Nelson, 1982), 108.

2. Charles R. Swindoll, *Mark,* Swindoll's Living Insights New Testament Commentary (Carol Stream, IL: Tyndale House, 2018), 129.

3. Amy-Jill Levine and Ben Witherington III, *The Gospel of Luke* (New York: Cambridge University Press, 2018), 238.

Chapter 15: The Samaritan Woman

1. Alfred Edersheim, *Sketches of Jewish Social Life in the Days of Christ* (London: Religious Tract Society, 1876), 13.

2. The complete Joseph story is found in Genesis 37–50.

3. M. G. Easton, *Illustrated Bible Dictionary and Treasury of Biblical History, Biography, Geography, Doctrine, and Literature* (New York: Harper & Brothers, 1893), 596–97.

4. Peter Colón, "The Exiles Return," *Israel My Glory*, September/October 2004, https://israelmyglory.org/article/the-exiles-return/.

5. Jack W. Hayford, ed., *Spirit-Filled Life Study Bible* (Nashville: Thomas Nelson, 1997), John 7:38.

Chapter 16: The Prodigal Son

1. Lawrence H. Schiffman, *From Text to Tradition: A History of Second Temple & Rabbinic Judaism* (Hoboken, NJ: Ktav, 1991), 106.
2. Schiffman, *From Text to Tradition*, 107.
3. Rabbi Aryeh Kaplan, "The Soul," Aish.com, May 9, 2009, https://www.aish.com/jl/sp/bas/48942091.html.
4. "Body and Soul," My Jewish Learning, accessed March 29, 2022, https://www.myjewishlearning.com/article/body-soul/.
5. Russell Resnik, *Creation to Completion: A Guide to Life's Journey from the Five Books of Moses* (Clarksville, MD: Messianic Jewish Publishers, 2006), 200.
6. "Jewish Cantor and His Family Resist Terrorism, Convert Attacking Ku Klux Klan Leader, 1991," Global Nonviolent Action Database, https://nvdatabase.swarthmore.edu/content/jewish-cantor-and-his-family-resist-terrorism-convert-attacking-ku-klux-klan-leader-1991.
7. Rabbi Michael Levy, "Shemot: Compassion Trumps Charisma When God Chooses a Leader," *New York Jewish Week*, December 19, 2013, https://jewishweek.timesofisrael.com/shemot-compassion-trumps-charisma-when-god-chooses-a-leader/.
8. Avos 1, 12, quoted in Rabbi Y. Dov Krakowski, "Disciples of Aaron," OU Torah, accessed February 10, 2022, https://outorah.org/p/27316.
9. My translation of Psalm 89:3 (which is Psalm 89:2 in most English Bible versions, as the Jewish numbering of the Psalms differs from the English numbering).
10. Stephen R. Covey, *The Seven Habits of Highly Effective People* (New York: G. K. Hall, 1997), e-book.
11. *The Preacher's Outline & Sermon Bible*, vol. 37, *Romans* (Chattanooga, TN: Leadership Ministries Worldwide, 1996), 139.
12. Robert Morris, "Set Free," Sermons.love, accessed February 14, 2022, https://sermons.love/robert-morris-sermons/free-indeed/3571-robert-morris-set-free.html.
13. Morris, "Set Free."
14. Morris, "Set Free."

Chapter 17: Cornelius and Peter

1. Craig S. Keener, *The IVP Bible Background Commentary: New Testament* (Downers Grove, IL: InterVarsity, 1993), Acts 10:1.
2. William Barclay, ed., *The Acts of the Apostles*, The Daily Study Bible Series (Philadelphia: Westminster John Knox, 1976), 79.

3. Nissan Mindel, "The Three Daily Prayers," Chabad.org, https://www.chabad.org/library/article_cdo/aid/682091/jewish/The-Three-Daily-Prayers.htm.

4. John Gill, *Gill's Exposition of the Entire Bible* (1768), s.v. "Acts 10:9," https://www.biblestudytools.com/commentaries/gills-exposition-of-the-bible/acts-10-9.html.

Chapter 18: The Power of Unity

1. Moshe Weinfeld, *Normative and Sectarian Judaism in the Second Temple Period* (London: T&T Clark, 2005), 274.

2. Gastón Espinosa, *William Seymour and the Origins of Global Pentecostalism* (Durham, NC: Duke University Press, 2014), e-book.

3. Joni Eareckson Tada, *Glorious Intruder: God's Presence in Life's Chaos* (Colorado Springs, CO: Multnomah, 1989), 82.

4. J. Robert Wright, ed., *They Still Speak: Readings for the Lesser Feasts* (New York: Church Hymnal Corporation, 1993), 66.

ABOUT THE AUTHORS

Kathie Lee Gifford is the four-time Emmy Award–winning former cohost of the fourth hour of the *TODAY* show alongside Hoda Kotb. Prior to her time at NBC News, Gifford served as the cohost of *Live with Regis and Kathie Lee* for fifteen years. In 2015 she was inducted into the Broadcast and Cable Hall of Fame, and recently she was awarded a star on the Hollywood Walk of Fame.

A playwright, producer, singer, songwriter, and actress, Gifford has starred in numerous television programs and movies in her forty-five-year career. She has written several musicals, including Broadway's *Scandalous*, which received a Tony nomination for Best Actress in 2012. In 2019 she made her directorial debut with *The God Who Sees* oratorio, shot in Israel and based on a song she cowrote with Grammy-nominated Nicole C. Mullen. Over the past year, she has written and directed three more oratorios and will be releasing the collection of four as *The Way*.

Gifford has authored five *New York Times* bestselling books, including *It's Never Too Late, The Rock, the Road, and the Rabbi, Just When I Thought I'd Dropped My Last Egg, I Can't Believe I Said That*, and the popular children's book *Party Animals*. She has also recently released *Hello, Little Dreamer* (2020) and *The Jesus I Know* (2021).

Gifford lends support to numerous children's organizations, including Childhelp, the International Justice Mission, and the Association to Benefit

Children. She received an honorary degree from Marymount University for her humanitarian work in labor relations.

Gifford is on Twitter and Instagram at @KathieLGifford.

Raised in a Jewish home in New Jersey, **Rabbi Jason Sobel** dedicated much of his life to finding truth. After years of seeking and studying, he encountered the Lord and found his true destiny as a Jewish follower of Jesus (Yeshua).

Rabbi Jason is the Founder of Fusion Global (Fusionglobal.org), a ministry whose purpose is to add high-definition to people's faith in Yeshua-Jesus by restoring the lost connection to our ancient Hebrew roots and rediscovering our forgotten inheritance in Him.

Rabbi Jason received his rabbinic ordination from the UMJC (Union of Messianic Jewish Congregations) in 2005 and has a bachelor of arts in Jewish studies and a master of arts in intercultural studies. He is the author of several books, including *Breakthrough* and *Aligning with God's Appointed Times*, as well as his most recent book, the nationally bestselling *Mysteries of the Messiah: Unveiling Divine Connections from Genesis to Today*. He also coauthored the *New York Times* bestseller *The Rock, the Road, and the Rabbi* with Kathie Lee Gifford. He is the spiritual adviser to *The Chosen* TV series, and host of *The Chosen Unveiled* on TBN. Rabbi Jason is on Twitter and Instagram at @RabbiJasonSobel.